Praise for

LENIN'S ASYLUM

Like many Peace Corps volunteers, A. A. Weiss was sent to serve in a country that did not exist when he was born. Moldova? Part of the magic of the volunteer experience is that a place you've never thought about becomes your entire world for two long years. Weiss writes beautifully, and in *Lenin's Asylum* he brings the post-Soviet society to life, with humor, keen observation, and compassion.

~ Peter Hessler, author of *River Town* and *Oracle Bones*

In spare and evocative prose, A. A. Weiss takes us to a country many of us will never visit, and in the process, shows us the simple joys and love that can be found in a place where life is neither simple nor easy. This is a generous, sometimes funny—and always loving—memoir of Peace Corps life that asks hard questions about the utility of volunteerism—and answers them with the beauty of the bonds formed between strangers across cultures.

~ Kelly Grey Carlisle, author of *We Are All Shipwrecks*

A. A. Weiss's memoir *Lenin's Asylum* throws a curveball through expectations of the post-college memoir. Weiss's book ventures into some familiar terrain–early-20s relationships, figuring out your place in the world–but geographically shifts them, and in doing so turns them unfamiliar. Throw in a deftly sketched portrait of contemporary Moldova, and you have a subtly compelling work about teaching, learning, and the process of self-discovery.

~ Tobias Carroll, author of *Transitory* and *Reel*

The best travel writers are cool-headed, reliable reporters who offer us rare glimpses into foreign lands. Through such stories, we experience the writer's transformation from outsider to insider, and witness a blossoming love affair with the people, the land, the history. Weiss is exactly such a writer. In *Lenin's Asylum*, he invites us into Moldova, the poorest country in Europe, where he paints a vivid and affectionate portrait of Riscani—from students who smoke and drink to wild rides in the back of a bread truck—and teaches us the importance of immersing oneself in another culture, reminding us that sometimes to find ourselves, we must risk getting lost. With gentle wit and self-deprecating humor, like the best travel writing, Weiss brings Moldova to life on the page. And we are all made better because of it.

~ Angela Morales, author of *The Girls In My Town*

LENIN'S ASYLUM

TWO YEARS IN MOLDOVA

A. A. WEISS

EVERYTIME PRESS

Lenin's Asylum copyright © Aaron Weiss
First published as a book June 2018 by Everytime Press

All rights reserved by the author and publisher. Except for brief excerpts used for review or scholarly purposes, no part of this book may be reproduced in any manner whatsoever without express written consent of the publisher or the author.
Any historical inaccuracies are made in error.

ISBN: 978-1-925536-50-8

Everytime Press
32 Meredith Street
Sefton Park SA 5083
Australia

Email: everytimepress@outlook.com
Website: https://www.everytimepress.com
Everytime Press catalogue:
https://www.everytimepress.com/everytime-press-catalogue

Original cover photographs (Lenin statue and Russian School in Riscani) and author photograph copyright © Aaron Weiss
Cover design copyright © Matt Potter

Also available as an eBook
ISBN: 978-1-925536-51-5

Everytime Press is a member of the
Bequem Publishing collective

http://www.bequempublishing.com/

For my brother

A note from the author

I began writing this book while still in Moldova. Everything included in these pages happened during the twenty-seven months I lived there, though the events in real life occurred in a slightly different order. My goal isn't to incriminate or shame anyone, only to reflect and learn from mistakes, so I've changed most names and some identifying characteristics. Still, for those who were there it's pretty clear who is who. My thanks and apologies. I've learned a lot.

AAW

Contents

1	Riscani
10	The Russian School
20	Chisinau
28	Malinovscoe
37	The Russian Victory Network
47	Ruins
51	Where There is No Doctor
59	Departures
62	Chismea
73	Escape from Moldova
81	Barcelona
86	The Museum of Atheism
93	A Return
97	A Victory
106	Aaron Richardovich
114	Olympiad
121	Notes from the Wedding
130	Stacking Cups
137	Corrections
143	Hirjauca
154	Ozi Buna
165	An Invasion
173	The Departed
177	Girls Leading Our World

185	Adalet
192	Three Countries in One Place
195	An Arrival
200	Teachers' Day
207	The Road to Corjeuti
213	Hram
222	Tuberculosis
228	A Gun Story
235	First Snow
241	Egypt and Jordan
247	Andrei Nikolayevich
251	Work and Travel
258	The Famous Sadie
267	COS
273	Tradition
283	Acknowledgments
285	About the Author

Riscani

I entered Riscani through an alley of vodka bars. It was just after noon and already men in tracksuits spilled into the alley holding shot glasses and sugar biscuits. I pushed past them. One vodka drinker said something to me that made others laugh. I smiled, even though I sensed an insult. Beyond the bus depot, each tree lining the town's main road was painted white at the base of its trunk. Somewhere ahead, in the Russian district, a host family awaited my arrival. Further up the street, I inspected the ruined brick skeleton of an asylum burned down by an angry mob some years back. From this spot, four bars remained in view. My hand-drawn map from a previous volunteer indicated the asylum was a major landmark; the town's monument to Lenin across the street was a second. I would later be told to avoid this area after dark.

Lenin's statue looked into the distance across the torched asylum: he wore a trench coat and clenched a crumpled hat in his right hand as though preparing to strike a child for poor attention. I turned off the street into a collection of block apartments. Children chased a brown soccer ball between courtyards. Each child paused to inspect the stranger as I passed. When I approached a young woman for directions, she stopped drawing water from a well once she saw me; I backed away with my palm over my heart because I thought she might scream.

My apartment building was all concrete, painted white and blue, five stories tall. The corridor was dark, even though it was daytime. Pale spouts of light came in from the open squares at the end of the hallway that once contained window glass.

I reached the third floor, and was breathing heavily. My heart beat faster than I would want. None of the apartment doors on this floor had numbers. I listened through one door and heard nothing. A television was on in the second apartment. I held my head close to the third door and heard the muffled voice of a teenage girl on the telephone. My pulse calmed after standing still for thirty seconds. My breathing returned to a natural rhythm. Gritty soot came off on my finger as I felt along the door frame for the bell. I held my breath. *Everything is wrong*, I thought. *I've made a mistake.*

A girl opened the door wearing only a bikini. Her top barely covered her chest and I was embarrassed about where to look. She went right past my handshake and kissed me on the cheek. This was Dariya. Over her shoulder I saw a brightly lit and clean apartment. She scurried into the next room and I kicked off my shoes to demonstrate the cultural respect I'd learned in training. I thought she'd run to put on clothes, but she returned instead with a cup of tea.

"You live here now," she said in English. "Drink this tea."

The tour of my new home began in Dariya's old room, which was now mine. Stickers of Russian pop stars covered her bureau. A pile of Dariya's clothes—pink, white, and purple—had been folded neatly and placed on the armchair.

"You have girlfriend?" she asked. "You prefer swimming or bathing?"

These were practiced questions, in English, and she didn't dwell on my answers. She nodded while smiling, as though saying—Yes, how interesting!—to everything I said.

We sat on the couch in that room, which would later turn into a bed.

"Teachers earn how much money in America?" she asked.

Dariya's parents arrived home a few moments later. She was still in her bikini, seated next to me on the couch, and I was still holding my tea saucer as a proper guest.

The father shook my hand. His palm was sweaty from working all morning. He looked at me standing next to his daughter and made an assumption. "A new boyfriend of yours?" he asked Dariya, who shook her head.

"He's the American," said the mother. "He'll be living with us."

It seemed implausible that my arrival could have been a surprise, but here we were. He looked at me and nodded. Nothing in his gaze indicated rage. In fact, the father took the news rather well, I thought, for a man who had been a soldier in the Red Army.

"He'll live here for two years," added Dariya.

Anticipating his next question, the mother said, "He'll sleep in Dariya's room."

Dariya spoke quickly in Russian to her parents, and then addressed me.

"I am happy you are here," she said. "Now I go swim in nearby lake."

I was alone with my new hosts. The mother spooned oatmeal onto two plates. Bits of meat stewed into the porridge crumbled between my teeth. The father ate without speaking. Under the table he tapped his right leg to a fast, unheard rhythm. His pounding transferred through the floor into my sock-covered feet. He muttered something quietly to the mother; I heard the word *amerikanitz*. The mother said something about the father never listening.

My hand-drawn map of Riscani indicated the school where I would teach was across the street.

Show up in a week with a tie on, I'd been told.

And good luck.

* * *

In my new room, I inspected the stickers of Russian pop stars on the dresser. Some of Dariya's shirts were still hanging in the wardrobe. I found a place for my portable heater under the window and spent twenty minutes fumbling with the metal levers that turned the couch into a bed. In my imagination, I'd prepared for monastic confinement, a room without windows, devoid of color, a cement dungeon with a candle for warmth. So this room, sparse but marked by evidence of youthful existence, felt welcoming. I pulled the lace curtain to the side and looked through the window, down over a tree. I couldn't see the school across the street because there were too many leaves, but I felt confident that I could jump to a certain thick branch and climb down should there ever be a fire or other reason for escape.

The front door opened, and two new voices began shouting to announce their arrival. Through my bedroom door, I heard shoes hitting the floor, and again the word *amerikanitz*.

"Where is he?" asked a new man, not the father, his voice not so deep.

I didn't wish to leave my room unless I was summoned, and it seemed my new host family didn't wish to disturb me unless I emerged on my own accord. My stomach gurgled from the stress of the new environment, so I chewed pink antacid tablets from my medical kit. I burped meaty oatmeal, pushed it down, and I thought I might vomit. Through the walls I heard the comings and goings of the family in the apartment, and connected the voices with their profiles in my official site paperwork: Sister Dariya, Papa Dima, Mama Katya, Brother Vova and his wife Talia. But I didn't summon the nerve to venture out until I desperately needed the bathroom.

I cracked the door of my room and darted to the toilet, trying not to run, but definitely faster than necessary to avoid a chance encounter with somebody new. I wouldn't be able to hold a new awkward conversation, hugging and kissing and such, unless I used the bathroom first. I sealed myself in without turning on the light. My breathing echoed in the small space. I ran my fingers along the wall for a light switch and only touched smooth tile. My breathing grew louder. Blood pumped through my ears. It made no difference if I opened my eyes; all I saw was black. Footsteps approached from the kitchen and someone turned the light on for me.

"The switch is on the outside," said Dariya.

"*Spaciba*," I said through the door, thank you, and held my breath until her footsteps returned to the kitchen.

During my training in Ivancea I'd only used outhouses. This apartment toilet in Riscani had a chain pull dangling from a water tank above. I pulled the chain and nothing happened. My chest tightened. A minute later, after pulling the chain another five times with no effect, I emerged and called out to Dariya. She came bounding around the corner as though I were in need of medical attention. "No work," I said in Russian, pointing inside. She had no idea what I was trying to say. "How work?" I offered. She understood after I pulled down on the chain and stuck out my bottom lip. "The chain is decorative," she said. "We don't always have water inside." Dariya took a bucket of well water from the ten-gallon drum in the hallway and poured it into the toilet. Problem solved.

Brother Vova and his wife Talia stood staring when we emerged from the toilet. Talia kissed me on the cheek to say hello and Vova shook my hand, then directed me to the adjacent washroom where we both rinsed with cold water that Talia poured over our hands into the bathtub.

"Pleased to meet you," said Talia to me, and then, giggling to her husband in Russian, "That's the only English I know."

For the rest of the night, the family gave me space as though I were a boarder in their bed-and-breakfast, and spoke to me as though I were a toddler, with small words and non-threatening body language. Mama Katya introduced dinner service with imaginary silverware brought up to the mouth. Papa Dima touched the numbers on the mounted clock by the door to indicated when they'd return from work. Later, for other concepts, they went straight to my bilingual dictionary, pointing out words like bazaar, truck and bakery as though these single images expressed sufficient motive for my understanding.

During the next day when I had to embarrass myself with language, I chose to do it with Dariya.

"How do I fix my bed?" I asked.

Dariya inspected the futon, pushed down on it with both knees, then flipped it back into place. "It is not broken," she said.

Later, I felt lucky when a thin stream of cold water dripped from the spout in the bathroom. "How long must I wait for hot water?" I pointed to the sink where I wished to shave. Dariya filled a bucket with water from the ten-gallon drum, placed it on the stove over a burner, and said, "Twenty minutes."

"And how do I cook?" I asked. I expected a tutorial of the kitchen gas valves, the location of the box of long matches.

"Potato cooking is easy," she said. And then, as though remembering an instruction from her mother, she said, "Do not worry. I make you potatoes."

And when it was time for me to emerge from the apartment and explore the town, Dariya was at my side.

* * *

Since I'd moved in, Dariya had slept on couch cushions spread over the floor in the living room. She was still sleeping after everyone else had gone to work and I'd finished the breakfast Mama Katya had left out for me. I knocked on the living room door and then said her name, stirring her.

"Is it a good idea for me to go to the bazaar alone?" I asked.

"What is your meaning?"

"Safety?" I said.

"There is no danger."

"Will I get lost? Is the road confusing?"

"You have a map," she said.

"Would you walk with me anyway?"

Again, as though remembering orders, she said, "Yes, of course."

Only two mirrors hung in the apartment, one by the front door and the other in the bathroom. Both were high-traffic areas I wished to avoid in the mornings. In my room I found the word for mirror in my dictionary and was ready to go. Dariya took longer to get ready. She took a bucket of water into the washroom and scrubbed her face. She scraped off the traces of the previous day's make-up and then made herself up all over again. She brushed her hair for ten minutes. Then she locked herself in the living room and sufficient time passed for me to think she'd forgotten about our shopping excursion. When she appeared again, she wore a flowing dress more appropriate for a formal ball than a trip to the corner market. As she laced up her high heels, I began to question myself. "Can I go outside in this?" I asked, indicating my loose white t-shirt, the type appropriate for throwing away after a day of yard work. She looked me up and down and said, "Of course." I asked why she was dressed so nicely and she answered, "Girls are different."

No one said hello to Dariya on the street, but men smiled at her and made sounds as though trying to lure a small animal closer. Her gaze remained straight, always, never distracted by the non-verbal attention. On the sidewalk I was the only one who stared at the Lenin statue. Riscani's original statue had been torn down when the Soviet Union fell, only to be replaced by the current version when the Russian population in town swelled back to the point of majority.

"Lenin," said Dariya, acting as a tour guide. "A good Russian."

At the bazaar Dariya showed me the family's bread stand where Mama Katya worked every day. We walked a circuitous path through product vendors until Dariya was satisfied everyone had seen her with the new American. We found a stall selling small mirrors and Dariya did the talking for me. "He's from the city?" asked the woman attending the stall. Dariya shook her head, but didn't answer, as though prompting the woman to begin a game. The woman asked me a question directly, but I didn't understand. "I'm sorry I don't speak well," I said in Russian.

"His accent is soft," said the woman. "He's from Poland."

Dariya shook her head, smiling.

"Germany?" said the woman. "The lowlands? The Nordic countries?"

Dariya leaned in as though about to share a secret, though she spoke loudly so that the vendors at the neighboring stalls could hear as well.

"From America," she said.

The woman smiled and nodded in the fashion of a humoring soul not willing to challenge a white lie. I'd separated a ten lei note from the other bills in my pocket so that I wouldn't flash my whole wad of cash in the presence of the many onlookers. The woman held the bill up to the sun, looking for defects, and then put it into her front apron pocket.

"He'll be here for two years," Dariya said.

The woman nodded. "Yes," she said. "Of course the American will be here in Riscani for two years." She giggled to herself as she put my mirror into a black plastic bag and tied the handles together. "Good luck to him."

The Russian School

I was born in Ohio during the Cold War.

At that time Moldova wasn't yet a country. Tucked between Romania and Ukraine, I'd never noticed it on the map during geography pop-quizzes or seen mention of it in *National Geographic* (my two childhood sources of world knowledge). Through pre-departure research I learned a recent civil war had ended, the president was a communist, and many outpost towns spoke Russian exclusively instead of the national language, Romanian. As the poorest nation in Europe, Moldova's workers had little work—one in four adults left the country to seek employment. Those who stayed used their bodies for income and sustenance, working in the fields, yes, but also trafficking themselves to those trading in sex and human organs. It lacked an international marketplace for wine—its only export—so people tended to drink up what was on hand. It had schools without adequately trained teachers and politicians without scruples. Orphanages were filled with children whose parents had either departed the country or couldn't afford to feed them.

Moldova needed a superhero, it seemed, not an English teacher.

I wasn't the first American to be stationed in Riscani. Three other English teachers had passed through before me. Their site reports didn't inspire confidence. "Kind of a ghost town," and "very Russian," one described Riscani. The mayor, a member of the communist party, was labeled "unhelpful and patronizing." The schools were "terrible environments" which suffered from "daily disorder" and "undisciplined children." Yet all the other volunteers had arrived speaking Romanian, and they'd clearly suffered for it. Each had recommended that future volunteers sent to Riscani speak Russian.

So there I was.

When I arrived at the Russian school for my first day of teaching, most people thought I was a parent dropping off a new pupil. I'd dressed in clothes purchased at the "professionals" section at the bazaar—a purple dress shirt with snapping breast pockets and a pink tie. Teachers asked if I was lost and told me where I might find my child. Sometime during the chaos of these first moments in the school, among the bodies of boys and girls and adults running to find the correct room, a small girl came up to me and complained that a boy had lit her hair on fire with a match. She showed me a collection of singed ends as proof. I understood nothing, patted her on the head and said, "Very good."

I made my way to the English classroom, met briefly with the school director—a man with a naturally angry face attempting to smile—and was then alone with a class of fifth graders.

The look of serenity on my face was completely fake. Sweat rolled behind my ear down into my collar. I loosened my tie. I opened my mouth, but nothing came out. "Does anyone speak English?" I asked. Nothing came out of their mouths. I repeated the question in Russian, and almost immediately fifteen little hands began shaking in the air to indicate fifty-fifty. We did introductions in Russian and then in English and completed forty-five minutes of basic grammar and vocabulary. I could tell these fifth graders weren't ready to write poetry. But they'd successfully introduced themselves and expressed their likes and dislikes. Nearly all had liked football and disliked mathematics. It seemed my new job wouldn't kill me.

So then I felt optimistic about my eighth and ninth grade classes. The textbook for this level asked students to express opinions about the political systems of English-speaking countries.

"Does anyone speak English?" I asked.

No one responded. I asked again in Russian and they began to giggle. All twenty of them laughed. One managed to choke out, in Russian, "Of course not."

I tried not to panic.

"Please take out a piece of paper," I said.

The students looked at each other to see if anyone understood what I'd said. A student in the front row reached into her backpack, removed her textbook, and placed it on top of her desk. She smiled at me.

Students in the back murmured. Those who had textbooks—about half the class—placed them on the desktops.

"Okay," I said. "Let's start with the textbook, then." I held the book in the air. "Textbook," I said, and the students repeated, "Textbook."

We named objects for the rest of class.

My next ninth grade class performed even worse. They didn't respond to questions, English or Russian. They stared out the windows or talked to friends at nearby desks or played games on outdated cell phones. Every child had a cell phone. One pupil recorded himself screaming monkey noises into his phone and played it back every few moments. In forty-five minutes I managed to introduce myself, nothing more, but I doubt any one of them could have told you my name later that afternoon. I hadn't exactly captivated them. Though to be fair, I couldn't remember their names either. Miroslav had been the kid making the monkey noises. The rest of the students were a confusing mix of Dashas, Mashas, Sashas and Pashas.

During the first week of lessons each boy shook my hand after entering the classroom. Each girl smiled at me before sitting down. The shock, wonder and awe—whatever my students felt about having an American teacher—didn't last long. The fifth graders, those groups attentive on the first day, now settled into the habits of the older kids, gossiping in whispers, finding interest outside the windows, claiming ignorance in all matters concerning education. Instead of answering my questions they came up with their own. What is your father's name? What can we call you? Why isn't Mr. Aaron married yet? And why are the tips of his shoes rounded? My students obsessed about my shoes. Evidently a teacher needed pointed tips to be taken seriously. I would attempt to present new material but eventually derail the lesson by committing a crime against one of a million Russian superstitions: whistling indoors, tossing a hat in the air. Twenty minutes of perfect behavior would evaporate in a second as the students argued over the practical consequences of my indiscretions.

Will Mr. Aaron die poor?

No, like this he will never get married.

But I think he will just catch the flu!

Eventually, the students' kindness and patience evaporated entirely and I was treated like any other teacher. But I could stand in front of them all day without reacting to their insults. I wouldn't understand words like *suka* (bitch) and *blin* (damn it) for a few months yet. If a child cursed I'd repeat the words loudly—"Bitch! Damn it all!"—and when the laughter subsided we'd get back to class.

Other aspects of my demeanor confused them also.

I didn't hit anyone.

If a student (almost always a boy) misbehaved in class, it wasn't because I was American. He did it because he thought school was the place a boy got away with indiscretions unthinkable at home: spitting on the floor, swearing, wrestling, and smacking girls on the butt—all were commonplace. If a student got caught, he'd get a smack upside the head from a teacher. Almost every time I approached a boy after he'd touched a girl, he'd shrivel up in preparation for taking a blow.

Several of my eighth grade boys smoked. If you smoked you had to do it outside, that was the school's only rule about smoking.

Two weeks into the job, I arrived at school and was informed by a ten-year-old pupil that there would be no classes that day. I thought he was threatening me. I advanced toward him and expected him to shrivel, but he didn't. He smiled. I turned to the brightest girl in the class who proudly announced, "Teachers' Day!"

The school's other English teacher, a young woman named Nadezhda, entered and informed me these children weren't lying. It was a holiday, Teachers' Day, a Russian tradition. We went to the gymnasium, where students recited poems, danced and sang, and student-waitresses served shots of cognac and vodka to their teachers. The entire room toasted every ten minutes. I passed time by counting how many laws this ceremony would break in America.

The next day, everyone was back at work nursing hangovers. I stayed out of the teachers' room because we were expected to finish the leftover cognac during the breaks between classes.

* * *

A month had passed since the first day of school, and my students were finding more and more ways to waste time in class. I'd ask a question, five hands would go up, and the only response I'd get would be, "*Moshna vuitia?*" And I'd scream back, "No, you can't leave! Stop asking!" and then the whole process would be repeated a few moments later.

At last, when it appeared we'd get nothing done that day, the leader of the class, a girl named Natashka, raised her hand and asked politely, in English, "Mr. Aaron, what is the Sex Bomb?"

I must have blushed. The questioner was eleven years old.

"A bad thing?" she asked.

I claimed ignorance.

"Listen," she said, taking out her cell phone and playing a song.

She wanted to know about a song. I felt less confused. I recognized the singer, Tom Jones, and I even remembered when the song had played on American radio a decade before. But how to explain the lyrics?

Natashka used a dictionary to eliminate alternative definitions of sex and bomb. But the two words together didn't make sense. While I thought about my response, two boys asked to leave and I casually waved my hand for them to get out, not wanting them to ruin the only productive thing we'd do all day.

"Well," I explained. "You know what sex means, yes, it means a lot of love. And a bomb is something that explodes. So a sex bomb is when you have so much love that you explode."

"A bad thing, I think," said Natashka.

"Yes, okay, does anyone have another song to translate?"

Every hand in the class shot up, but just then an alarm echoed through the entire school, a sound like a giant copper ladle against a metal pan. The students screamed, "Fire!"

My thoughts went directly to the two boys I'd allowed to leave class. In my mind they'd teamed up, one standing on the shoulders of the other, to pull the fire alarm.

"No one's going anywhere!" I screamed. "It's just an alarm. We're finishing class!" The students looked scared and then looked to Natashka to clarify the situation.

"Beg your pardon, Mr. Aaron. But in Moldova we don't have fire alarms, just fires."

I heard Natashka speak the words in Russian and I felt like I hadn't understood. I walked over to the door. The handle was cool on my fingertips. Through the wood I heard a commotion in the hall. I cracked the door open and saw smoke billowing down the corridor and students running in every direction. I closed the door and turned back to the class.

"Okay," I said. "Run."

The smoke was thin enough to see through. I followed the students as they ran outside into the courtyard where we found the two boys I'd excused from class. They held their palms up to me in anticipation of blame. "Not us," they said. After a minute the entire school stood collected and accounted for in the courtyard.

The school director and the vice-directors took turns yelling at the kids.

"No accident!" said the director, holding a soot-covered trash can in the air. "Firecrackers don't jump into pails by accident!"

I glared at my students from across the courtyard and they continued with their palms raised. The two boys became more agitated as I walked toward the director, alternating between flapping palms and index fingers against their lips pleading for my silence.

I returned to my spot.

"Go home," said the director. "All of you."

Plastic had burned in the trash pail and fumes had spread throughout the school.

No one ever discovered who lit the fire.

* * *

After waking up at 4 a.m. on a Saturday, I left Riscani for the first of several language training updates in Chisinau, the capital. I'd tried my hardest to slip out of the apartment without making any noise, but Katya awoke when I unlocked the front door and, from her bed behind the closed door, she yelled, "I will walk you!" I feared I'd have to wait for her to put on make-up as Dariya had, but she appeared quickly, having just tied her robe, and produced a candle and matches saved for walking at night.

Even though I knew the route to the bus station well, I couldn't deny Katya her concern. She feared for my safety because of the uncovered manholes and late-night, early-morning drunkards, policemen, dog packs, broken glass and many other things I didn't yet know to worry about. We progressed down the dark sidewalk slowly, our conversation limited to the selected naming of words I knew in Russian. "Dog," I'd say, pointing as one approached us. "Yes, dog," repeated Katya as she stomped the ground to scare the mutt away. She barely reached up to my shoulders in height, but her presence comforted me as she walked a step ahead, cupping our small light from the wind. We passed Lenin and then I became aware of the ghost town the other volunteers had described. The only other person passing through at this cold early hour was a policeman on his way from his car to the station. He smoked and didn't say hello when we passed.

"This isn't a village," said Katya. "Don't say hello to people you don't know."

The sun still hadn't broken through when we reached the bus station. A minibus sat with its lights illuminated and its engine running, a sign in the front window: Chisinau. The driver smoked a cigarette through his open window. Katya stuck her head inside before she let me step up, yelled a little bit and made the driver promise he'd see me to the capital. He didn't promise anything until I heard the word *amerikanitz* from Katya. "*Da, da,*" said the driver, yes, yes, and this satisfied her.

"*Udachee*," said Katya to me before leaving, good luck, and I pretended to know what it meant. It seemed a comfort, so I thanked her. "Hello," I said to the driver, and regretted it, feeling childish. He nodded sleepily.

The baseline smells of the bus were stale sweat and slaughtered animals. I could also smell the vodka my fellow passengers had consumed the previous night. I sat in the back. The sounds of the bus were Russian murmurs, talk of the coming cold, and accordion music. Every bus driver owned a cassette tape of electric accordion music. The audio systems of these antiquated machines only had one volume—just high enough to keep the driver awake.

We took to the road and I said to myself, "Can't we go faster?" Then we hit a pothole and someone screamed, "Watch the road, Vasia!"

The sun rose twenty minutes after we started driving. Now I could better see the other passengers: on this morning, on this bus made for twenty, there was a group of ten young people in tracksuits, larger women with bandanas and grandchildren on their hips, and a few skinny older gentlemen who wore cloth caps fashionable a hundred years ago. Some were traveling to the capital for work. I don't know what the others were going for. It cost 150 lei round-trip from Riscani to the capital—about fifteen dollars—and this wasn't a sum that people tossed around lightly.

Cracks in the road forced the driver to swerve into the opposite lane, oncoming traffic be damned, and conversely for opposite drivers to wander into our path. In the back of the bus, alone, I was tossed up and down. Soon I learned my lesson and traded physical comfort for bad smells. I found a place closer to the front next to a man about my age in a tracksuit who smelled of alcohol. My movement woke the woman across the aisle and, before returning to sleep, she looked at my face and then at my shoes.

Soon, in the future, after a few trips on the same road, I would wake up from a brief nap en route and know exactly where I was, the names of each village, how far from Riscani we'd traveled, how far until we'd reach Chisinau. What changed on each trip was my state of mind upon awakening, of feeling a physical relief grow with each kilometer separating me from Riscani, or, as on this first trip, the growing tension of reconnecting with the world in the modern capital city, learning just how well the world outside had continued to function despite my absence.

Chisinau

Entering from the north, my first sight of the capital was a billowing smokestack next to a billboard that read, "Chisinau is a beautiful place!" This city contained over half of all people living in Moldova.

The Peace Corps headquarters was fortified like an embassy and the staff had contingency plans for repelling mob attacks. The compound was just under four hours from Riscani and only six hours from the farthest placed volunteer. In other Peace Corps countries, a typical commute from site to headquarters might be ten hours. Puddle-jumper plane flights aren't unheard of when a volunteer must get to the capital. So I was lucky to get off with merely a bumpy, swerving bus ride.

As I passed through the metal detectors at the front gate, I heard shouts and laughter coming from the lounge upstairs. When I entered, the whole floor buzzed with activity like a newspaper office an hour before the big deadline. The *Armed Forces Channel* was tuned to a baseball game. All the wall-sockets were taken with charging laptops. Several people were circling around the library, necks bent inspecting book spines. The whiteboard outside the bathroom was filled with a dozen names of people waiting in line for a shower. I didn't recognize any of these folks. They were all volunteers from previously arrived groups whose names I hadn't committed to memory.

The sweat on my neck and behind my knees felt abnormally cool in the air-conditioning. Deodorant overtook my sense of smell whenever someone walked past me.

The one face I recognized was Jesse, my friend from training. We shook hands as if we were reconnecting with other Moldovans. Our conversation about coming into Chisinau, a touch melodramatic, contained several prison metaphors concerning parole.

"Not to complain," said Jesse. "But my village is more mud than land, my host family speaks a weird dialect of Ukrainian, and my students are a combination of aggression and stupidity."

"But you're not going to quit, right?" I asked. "You'll make it two years?"

Jesse's face scrunched. He balled his fists.

"Not unless I get the plague," he said. "They'll have to strap me down on a helicopter and evacuate me. And even then I'll fight it."

Before Jesse and I went for more language training, I got to the head of the line for the internet and sent off an email to some friends and extended family:

Dear Friends,

I've joined the Peace Corps. Sorry I didn't get around to telling everyone before I left. Moldova (between Ukraine and Romania) has been wonderful to me. The food is abundant, at the moment it's got pleasant weather, and by Eastern European standards I am a highly skilled dancer. I've just finished my training in a small village called Ivancea, where I lived on a farm with a host family and their livestock. I've attached a picture of myself with Ivancea's mayor (ex-KGB). As you might imagine from the photo, people here think I am dangerously thin. I'm force-fed pork cutlets daily, but otherwise life is good. A typical day so far includes eating, sleeping, getting through class, and studying Russian. Life in my new site, Riscani, is going well. There's a statue of Lenin in the main square (no joke). I'll tell you more when the good and bad points have evened out in my head—that way you'll get an accurate picture. Hope to talk with you all soon,

Aaron

Once Jesse and I met with the Russian instructor, we understood how far we'd progressed after immersed living. We'd both arrived in Moldova knowing nothing about Russian—no phrases and certainly not the alphabet—and now, three months later, we conversed freely with Russian speakers in places like markets and bus stations. I still didn't understand everything at school, but the instructor assured me that vocabulary would arrive with patience. We wouldn't starve, we wouldn't get lost, and we could scream a class of twenty children into submission.

"You are now quite advanced," said the instructor as though it were a surprise to her as well. "So now your lesson will continue in the city."

I raised my hand, and turned my notebook around for the instructor to inspect.

"Could you first help me translate?" I asked, pointing with my pen to a list of phrases in English.

The instructor took my notebook and smiled.

"Why do you wish to know these phrases?"

"For classroom order," I said. "And survival."

The teacher laughed and began writing on the chalkboard.

> *Ne ligeetya menya!* (Don't lie to me!)
> *Ne trogay ye-yo!* (Don't touch her!)
> *Zakroy rot!* (Shut up!)

* * *

Our language instructor gave us directions to a landmark in the center of town, and we soon realized the directions had been intentionally complicated so that we'd have to ask questions of locals. Away from headquarters, we passed a yellow, onion-top church and were then sucked into the central bazaar, an outdoor black hole of discount merchandise. Anyone dealing any type of transaction came at us with booming Slavic accents, as if their words need only enter our physical space to stun us and take control of our wallets. I considered buying cheese, batteries, soap packets, tin cups for drinking, but managed to pass through without losing money.

Vendors conversed with their friends in shouts from stall to stall. Flip-flops, light machinery, dried fish, bulk tea, clothing, duplicates of keys, endless buckets of salted cheese, olives, rice, cucumbers, tomatoes, liters of wine in reused soda bottles. These vendors were the types who'd ridden with me on the bus in the morning—old babushkas selling whatever they had too much of at home. Grandchildren ran wild in the corridors of the bazaar, dashing in between, behind, and under the vendor stalls with their rubber toy guns.

It seemed everyone in the capital spoke only Russian. Romanian might have been spoken at home among family members, but Russian was the language of money, spoken openly at shops and on the streets. And though I understood the majority of volunteers sent to Moldova would learn Romanian in order to serve the poorest communities, I didn't envy them. Unlike other colleagues, Jesse and I would never complain about policemen and bazaar women refusing (or unable) to speak Romanian, checks from all restaurants presented in the Cyrillic alphabet, and host families only speaking an angry-sounding foreign language to them at home, expecting them to respond to the sharp sounds as though they were dogs.

The din of commerce activity decreased once we left the maze of the bazaar. We hadn't yet asked directions, still waiting for someone who appeared within our age range to approach. A girl walked fast and picked up speed as we addressed her, perhaps to shorten our opportunity to harass her. But she stopped shortly after passing us, having responded to the softness and insecurity in our accents. She pointed toward a busy intersection a block away and seemed disappointed that we ended our conversation by wishing her health and happiness. I think she wanted to tell us her name. At the intersection a woman selling popcorn perked up when she heard our accents and pointed across the street to a sidewalk art sale. At the art bazaar a man selling Russian stacking dolls said we were on the right track and asked where we were from, and recommended dolls to match any personality. He thought our accents sounded Polish. A block farther we stopped another girl and she pointed across the street to our destination.

McDonald's.

For an hour we sat drinking beer in the courtyard, stacking the empty plastic cups in a tower. A waiter appeared to explain that empty cups left on a tabletop brought bad luck.

"*Spaciba*," I said.

"Yes," said the waiter. "And how much money do restaurant servers make in America?"

Jesse invented a number, and the waiter went away nodding his head.

Our mission accomplished, our language skills validated, we strolled through the nearby public park and flower market on a slow walk to the hotel where we'd stay that night, the Zarea, a tourist hotel with basic rooms and a communal toilet in the corridor.

The woman at reception didn't wish to help us until she heard us speak Russian. Her features softened, as though tired. "I know American volunteers," she said. "I don't know why you can't all speak a cultured language." She complimented our fumbling attempts to designate a proper check out time. *"Shashliva vam,"* she said before finally giving us the key, happiness to both of you.

We shared the elevator with a young blond woman who didn't smile. I kept looking her way, preparing to smile politely in case she made eye contact. As I looked at the floor, I focused on the fishnet stockings that disappeared into her high black boots. She pushed up on her toes and flexed her calves, again and again, rhythmically, ready to pounce once the door opened. Jesse, attempting nonchalance, held his breath. As she exited, I thought we'd been rude, remembered the conversation with the woman at the desk, and said, *"Shashliva."*

The girl didn't look back or react in any way, but once the elevator closed we could hear laughter through the walls and then below as we ascended.

* * *

The next day, on the minibus designed for twenty people, I was the twenty-fifth passenger to climb aboard. I stood in the aisle between two elderly women wearing wool sweaters. After another five passengers pushed their way on board, the driver squeezed into his seat. The engine turned over and the temperature shot up ten degrees. Only one of my hands was free to grab the luggage rack above for support. The minibus labored its way out of the parking lot. As we hit bumps, everyone standing bumped into each other. The pressure from the women flanking me held me in place; I could have lifted both feet off the ground and still remained upright.

After an hour, several passengers got off at their villages and I was able to sit down and massage my legs. I caught the stare of a young woman wearing red in the back row. I smiled at her and she smiled back.

She moved forward and sat across the aisle from me. "You speak English," she said. "I know from your accent."

I hadn't said a word.

"Yes," I said.

"From America?"

I nodded.

"And I think you must be Mr. Aaron, the new teacher in Riscani."

Her name was Aliona and she was also from Riscani, and also an English teacher. She worked at the Russian School's rival, the Moldovan Lyceum across town.

"You must know Cate," Aliona said. I said I didn't. "She is also from America and worked in Riscani. She was my teacher ten years ago…"—she struggled for the next words—"from Peace Corps."

I recalled the site reports from Riscani's previous volunteers. I wondered if Cate had been the one who called Riscani a "ghost town," or perhaps the one who called the mayor "unhelpful and patronizing."

"I don't know anyone from before," I said.

Aliona nodded and asked where I was from. She didn't know Maine; she'd heard of Boston, but didn't know where it was. "Above New York," I said. Aliona perked up, "A very nice city, I think."

She faced forward and we didn't speak again until we neared Riscani. The man behind me who'd been sleeping awoke and asked me how far until Riscani. I answered in Russian, "We just passed Balti." He thanked me and returned to sleep. Aliona was laughing. "Your Russian sounds strange. Cate spoke Romanian."

"Yes," I said in Russian. "I learn a little more each day."

She nodded to indicate she understood me, but continued to speak in English.

"And the Russians?" Aliona asked. "They treat you well?"

"Very well."

She smiled. I sensed her doubt. "Then you should have no problems in Riscani. If the Russians are your friends, no one is left to make trouble."

At the Riscani bus depot Aliona said she hoped to see me again soon. She spoke Romanian with the man who met her, and the space between them and the chaste nature of the kiss they shared on the cheek made me think they were siblings. In passing, I listened for a variation of the word *amerikanitz*, but didn't hear that or anything else I recognized.

Malinovscoe

As I scratched around the keyhole with my key, unable to find it in the dark stairwell, the door opened and light flooded the hallway. I squinted. Katya stood half concealed behind the door, and flailed her hand to indicate I should enter quickly.

"You've come back," she said.

"Yes," I said. "Of course."

She repeated my words with a giggle, "*Kaneshna—of course*," and I wondered if there was a reason I shouldn't have returned.

"And how was the weather in Chisinau?" She walked to the kitchen doorway and watched as I took off my shoes, nodding when I put them in the correct place under the bench where people wouldn't trip over them. "Strong winds? Rain? Could you see the sun?" I think she would have asked similar questions of astronauts returning from Mars. Overcast would have been a good description of Chisinau, hazy and gray, but I didn't know those words.

"Normal," I said.

Katya said something unintelligible and I nodded (*Yes, I absolutely understand*) before I walked back to collapse in my room.

After a week in Riscani, I'd stopped folding my bed up every morning back into a couch. And a week after that Katya had stopped going into my room every morning and putting it up herself. I'd changed the position of the bed so that my head was by the window. This way I could read with natural light and see anyone who came and went in the apartment through the frosted glass of my bedroom door. The colors of the room were no longer brown and pink—just different shades of brown. Gone were the poster cards of Russian pop singers and piles of t-shirts and jeans covered with glitter. My desk held my electric kettle and a large steel filter for boiling water. The space heater was nestled in between the desk and the sofa chair where I read at night when I wasn't in bed. In the armoire, my own clothes were solid-colored and durable. The bulky winter coat I'd bought at L.L.Bean remained on its hanger waiting for use. And in the armoire shelf space Dariya had used for her make-up, I now kept my medical kit, laptop computer, foldable clothes, boxes of tea, teaching supplies, winter boots, toothpaste to last two years, some hats, a tin mug, and the small library of books I'd taken from headquarters. Back in high school I'd written reports on several books I'd never read: *A Day in the Life of Ivan Denisovitch* and *Crime and Punishment* among others. In my life, I'd never completed a book by a Russian author. Now, I had the chance to redeem myself. My library contained Solzhenitsyn, Dostoyevsky, Tolstoy, and Pasternak—but at this moment of return from Chisinau I found myself reading a novel by Clive Cussler about the descendants of Hitler plotting to take over the world from their headquarters in Antarctica. I'd start in on the Russian essentials in translation once I finished with *Atlantis Found*.

    Twenty minutes of reading had passed when my stomach began to growl. I needed protein or vitamins—something essential. Through the frosted window in my bedroom door, I watched movement in all directions. Dariya walked back and forth between her bureau and the mirror in the washroom. Katya opened and closed every drawer and cabinet in the apartment in search of some missing object. Missing also were the sounds of pots and pans clanking, dishware sliding across the tabletop, and a tin ladle touching the bottom of a ceramic bowl as it poured soup. I'd grown accustomed to the different smells associated with the frying of cutlets, boiling of noodles, and the innumerable ways to cook a potato. Now, I smelled nothing.

The doorbell rang and soon after I heard Vova yelling. The family was late for something and he didn't even want to come inside; he just wanted to leave. I heard his wife Talia's voice also; once Vova stopped yelling, Talia said that Dariya looked pretty in her dress.

Katya came to fetch me. "Aaron!" she said. "We go!"

I froze.

She had spoken with such clear authority, but responding to a simple phrase still wasn't so simple as hearing the words and acting. In one Russian word—"*we go*"— Katya conveyed: "*We are going by motorized ground conveyance in one direction with only a 50% chance of returning home in the same manner.*"

My hesitation confused her.

Katya turned and fast-talked to Dariya who came back to my room to translate in English: "We go!" Her dress was red; I lost focus and she had to repeat herself. After she found eye contact in my vacant face and repeated herself I finally understood that we'd be traveling out to the village to visit granny. It was to be a dual celebration of Dariya's eighteenth birthday (already a week past) and the birthday of the village in which Katya's mother lived.

Dariya entered my room and clapped. "Get moving, Aaron, we go!"

Katya had applied make-up and, for the first time in my presence, was wearing a dress. I was still in the stale clothes I'd worn on the bus and I didn't care to be an underdressed fool everyone stared at during the party. Not until Vova poked his head through the front door did I feel like including myself. He screamed, "Let's go, now or never." He wore boots under plastic athletic pants and a brown sweater with a darker-brown stain spilled over the front. The stain still looked wet and I suddenly felt comfortable.

We descended to the street as a family, and piled into the bread truck waiting below. Vova was the deliveryman for the family bakery. His truck was a Ford wagon from the 1980s with two seats up front and the back hollowed out to transport baguettes and pastry trays. Katya sat up front. Vova jimmied the back doors open with a screwdriver and then I was inside, sitting on a towel with my legs crossed in a triangle. I leaned forward and helped Talia into the car and she commented to Dariya, "I didn't know he was a gentleman."

I don't think there's a word for *gentleman* in Russian, because Talia just said *gentleman*.

"Careful," said Dariya. "He speaks Russian now."

Talia squealed slightly and covered her mouth with her palm. "I didn't know!"

Vova drove like the bus drivers, swerving around other cars, swearing after crashing into potholes, using either side of the road as he pleased. Every bump over cracked pavement sent a jolt of pain through my cramped knees. As we drove through the dark, Talia distracted me from the possibility of death by speaking as though I were a toddler.

"School," she said a few decibels louder than necessary. "Good?"

Dariya giggled.

"What?" asked Talia.

"He's not slow," said Dariya. "Talk normally."

"School not bad," I said to Talia. "Fire there was."

Everyone in the car nodded. They all knew. I'd expected the concept of a fire at the school to earn more respect. From the front seat Katya said, "Bad kids do bad things."

"Thanks, Mom," said Dariya.

"You know how it is there," Katya said. "But you're a good one."

* * *

Granny lived in a village called Malinovscoe.

"Really," said Katya. "This is the most beautiful place in the world."

The dirt roads felt bumpy and soft at the same time. The back door opened to darkness after Vova freed us with his screwdriver. Out of the van, I stepped into mud.

My memories of what happened next are borrowed.

I met Granny. She was unimpressed by the concept of a foreigner, which is not to say rude; she was too old to indulge in world wonder, she said. She treated me well as she would have treated any stranger in her home.

On the table were plates of meats and cheeses, a bottle of sunflower oil Granny had mistaken for wine when setting the table, and a second bottle of something called *garilka*. I smelled this last bottle, and at Granny's prompting I took a shot. She pushed a biscuit into my hand while I coughed.

Evidently, I spoke to Granny for the next hour, taking a shot of *garilka* every few moments, much to the amusement of Katya and Dariya. Granny exclusively wore wool and I imagined it would be hot sitting next to her on a bus.

After we left, Dariya asked me what I'd talked about with Granny.

"Life," I said. Everyone in the car laughed.

"She doesn't speak any of the languages you speak," said Katya. "Granny only speaks Ukrainian."

We arrived home to find Dima eating alone in the kitchen. He'd worked all night at the bakery instead of going to Malinovscoe. Everyone said goodnight to me and I stumbled back to my room. After I closed my door, I heard my name shouted and thought I'd imagined an emotional echo. Again someone voiced my name—"Mr. Aaron"—this time quieter but closer. A second later Dima was at my door, knocking and opening at the same time. "A hundred grams," he said. "*Choo-choots*." He measured the amount in the air with his thumb and index finger. He wanted a drink and didn't wish to drink alone.

On the small kitchen table, Katya had laid out leftovers from the dinner in Malinovscoe. Rice in cabbage leaves, salami slices, chicken legs, potato salad with ham and peas. A bottle of vodka with two glasses. Two chairs around the card table.

We took the first shot after toasting health.

Dima bit into a slice of bread and said, "I heard you spoke with Granny." I knew it was a joke because he smiled. He never smiled. He smiled now unnaturally by flexing the muscles in his cheeks.

"About life," I said.

His smile turned briefly into a giggle.

"I can't speak with Granny either."

He paused to bite a stuffed pepper.

"Gagauzian," he said, his mouth full. "It's a language in the south. Growing up I didn't speak Russian until I got to school."

While he spoke he kept a hand on the bottle, ready to pour. I listened to his words while watching his hand, nodding as a proof of my understanding.

"I belong to one of Earth's smallest ethnic groups, the Gagauzians—Christian Turks who were expelled from Turkey and followed the Black Sea coast up to Southern Moldova. So the language, yes, Gagauzian is similar to ancient Turkish. I'm pretty sure I can speak Turkish."

Dima was down to his undershirt and shoveled the food into his mouth—not without manners, but with the mannerisms and muscle movements a man would use to shovel soil from one place to another. I thought, *This man is a worker.* Gray and white hairs over his ears betrayed age, but the number itself could have been anywhere from forty to sixty. I wouldn't know his exact age until his birthday a month later, in December, the night before I left for Spain.

"Why are you here?" Dima asked after placing his fork down. "I still don't understand." He poured two more shots. "Dariya talks to you and she doesn't understand either. Nobody in town understands. They ask Katya and me and we've got nothing to say."

Although I remained silent, Dima saw I was thinking. He tried to help me along. "You don't get paid. There are better jobs in America. Here you can't speak your own language. Living with us you can't be alone; no one can start a family like this. So tell me, please, what is here for you? People ask. Everyone knows you are happy, yet no one understands why!"

How to explain?

Americans aspire to travel. Families happen later. Languages are valuable skills to place on a résumé.

"I'm in Moldova instead of in the Army," I said. "In two years, I'll get a good job because I was in Moldova."

Dima poured two more shots but didn't push mine forward. He nodded as though my statement had confirmed his long-held suspicion that nowadays Americans weren't forced to fight.

"How much money will you earn after returning home from Moldova? How much every month will you make as a teacher? How much does a driver make, every month, and how much for a baker?"

He finally pushed my shot forward. We picked them up, gulped them down, and then scooped the last bits of rice and mayonnaise off the plate with bread.

"I was in the Army," he said. He held his empty glass up to the light and shook the final clinging drops of vodka onto the floor, as mandated by a Russian custom I'd never before seen in action. "I prefer wine," he said. "In the Red Army they gave us a glass of wine with our food. I didn't like it as much in Germany. There it was beer with the meals, which I didn't care for."

"The Army sent my dad to Germany also," I said. "On the other side, of course."

Dima nodded. "Is that so?"

The subject of Germany ended. Dima stood and he shook my hand. I went back to my room and as I began taking off my clothes, Dima again knocked on the door. He wasn't ready to end the conversation, it seemed, before he cleared his mind.

"Where I grew up it wasn't a good thing to know English," he said. "At first we learned Russian so that we could speak in school and then, later, we learned French. People didn't learn English in the Soviet Union."

He stopped speaking for a moment as he looked over the contents of my table. He walked over and picked up my copy of *Atlantis Found*, passed his fingers over the raised letters of the author's name. His lips moved like he was sounding out the words in English. He placed it back on the table.

"Do you like your profession?" Dima asked. "You like teaching?"

I'd never thought of teaching as my profession. Dima was a baker; baking allowed his family to survive. Teaching was the way for me to justify living abroad, what the Peace Corps had given me to fill my days.

"I do," I said.

"Well," he said. "I'm happy you're a simple guy. I wanted to say that."

I, too, wanted to say that Dima was a simple guy, but felt that repeating his words would weaken his compliment. He shook my hand and closed my door. Through the wall I heard him tell Katya, "I'm glad he's a simple guy."

The Russian Victory Network

At first I found nothing special about the teachers' room. In the cabinet in the corner the class journals stood as a reminder I needed to write my grades in the school register before the parent-teacher conferences. The school director had spoken to me sternly about recording my grades, but he'd spoken in Russian and I hadn't felt shamed enough to compute them instantly as he wished. Then I saw the television set. It looked new and the electrical cord was plugged into the wall. I didn't want to get my hopes up. I stood and approached it slowly as though it were an animal that might kick. Warmth radiated from smooth plastic into my palm when I touched it; someone had been watching TV recently. I touched the power button tentatively as though it would surely shock me. Nothing happened. I gave up and returned to my seat. A minute later, after I'd cursed myself for thinking the TV would work, the picture and sound blinked on. I was then watching the Russian national team play water polo some time in the past. They were still called the Soviets. And they were winning—finishing off a water polo massacre, in fact, up by a dozen goals. I'd stumbled onto the RVN: The Russian Victory Network. I invented this name after watching endless replays of Russian athletes dominating world sports. In the coming weeks I learned to expect the near-impossible comeback in cross-country skiing and never to bet against a Russian getting pummeled in a German boxing hall.

Nadezhda, the school's other English teacher, entered the lounge with an elderly woman whose hair was dyed an unnatural orange. The woman was a Romanian language teacher. Nadezhda and the woman nodded to me as they entered and sat on the opposite side of the room to safely speak about me in whispers. They looked in my direction frequently, and turned their heads away rapidly when I turned to look at them.

The pair of language teachers hardly seemed interested in sport.

"You like sport?" Nadezhda bellowed across the room.

I said that I did and Nadezhda poked the ribs of the Romanian teacher (a poke, perhaps, for the fire-haired woman having doubted Nadezhda's ability with English). Nadezhda was only twenty-four years old—young for the faculty at this lyceum—and rarely spoke to me in English without having prepared her statements in advance.

"What do you think of Alabama?" Nadezhda asked next. "The state in America."

I didn't know what to say. She obviously hadn't misspoken.

"Why?"

Nadezhda took a paper from her breast pocket and reversed the folds. She presented me the sheet, on which I read a series of minimum-wage job listings in Montgomery, Alabama. My first thought went to the former president of Mexico, Vicente Fox; he'd once gotten in trouble for saying his Mexicans were only offered jobs in America even the blacks weren't willing to touch. Now I read over a list of jobs for Moldovans in Alabama—jobs nobody else on Earth would take.

"The people are friendly," I said.

She asked about the work and shook her head when I described the duties of motel chambermaids and theme park custodians.

"Just an idea," she said. "Work and travel. Like you."

Nadezhda translated everything I'd said to the Romanian teacher, who shook her head while saying *nyet, nyet, nyet*. The woman told Nadezhda she should trust me; I'd voluntarily come to Moldova and wouldn't lie about bad jobs.

Nadezhda smiled, though I could tell she was disappointed. Then her expression changed to authentic joy. "Do you remember your first day?" she asked. "A girl came to you saying a boy had burnt her hair with a match." Nadezhda covered her mouth before laughter overcame her. She stifled her giggles with her hand and said, "You patted her head and said, 'Well done.'" She quickly translated for the Romanian teacher and the two began cackling. "People have been laughing about you ever since."

The pair left after wishing me health and happiness.

Shortly after, I ended my day with eighth graders. The girl who normally kept order through intimidation was absent, skipping class, and I knew there was going to be a problem; Miroslav was sitting in the front row. He was the boy who enjoyed playing recorded monkey noises on his cell phone to distract me. He wasn't sitting close in order to learn.

"What do you want, Miroslav?"

"To learn."

"Give me your cell phone."

"No."

"You're in Nastia's space."

"She's not here."

"She'll hit you when she hears of this."

"Not a problem, Mr. Aaron."

So we began the lesson with a focused Miroslav front and center. I remember thinking he seemed mature. Ten minutes later he stood to leave. He went around shaking the hands of each boy. The girls received hugs. I told him to sit.

"No, I have to leave now."

"Do you have a note?"

He smiled and walked out the door.

"He's leaving," said one of the boys.

"I see that."

"To Russia. He's leaving school to find work. You won't see him again."

I looked at one of the girls I trusted and she nodded to indicate it was true. I ran into the hall and caught up with Miroslav.

"I didn't understand," I said. "I'm sorry."

The boy shook my hand as an adult would have. He was fourteen. From one day to the next he'd decided to switch off his childhood emotions—and he'd done it. Now he was going to find work outside Moscow. The thirty-hour bus ride departed in a short while.

"I wish health and happiness to you," said Miroslav. "And much luck with these very bad students."

A lump in my throat prevented me from saying anything. The corners of my eyes watered.

Afterword the students remaining in class were silent and respectful. I wanted a girl to cry so that I could support her.

"Where might he go?" I asked the class.

"Who?"

"Miroslav."

"Moscow," said one boy. "He said Moscow."

"But that doesn't mean anything," said a girl. "Wherever there's construction."

We never talked further about Miroslav.

The bell rang to change periods, and the pupils moved along. My hands shook as I stuffed my notebooks into my backpack. I, apparently, was the only one in need of counseling because of Miroslav's departure.

Not wishing to leave the school, I returned to the teachers' room and watched a hockey match, the Reds versus a blue team, the match without score for the first five minutes until the blue goalie let in a soft dribbler, and then the floodgates opened.

Nadezhda entered the room breathing heavily as though she'd just stopped running.

"I have a request you won't like," she said.

"Of course," I said.

"Tomorrow you have only one lesson. I will be absent and want you to teach my lessons. Only two more classes for you to teach."

"Of course," I said.

She smiled. "That was easy."

At home I ate a plate of potatoes in pepper sauce and took a nap that lasted into the night. Dima woke me to play cards in the living room so that Dariya could do her homework on my desk. Katya was napping in the other bedroom. There was more space in the apartment now because Vova and Talia had since moved out, paying for a small apartment of their own with the money I gave to the family each month. Dima and I played *durak* until I lost five consecutive rounds. We'd pause after each round to listen through the walls to Dariya singing while she completed her class work. Her voice was beautiful. She sang English songs—Toni Braxton, mostly—and didn't like that I understood the words.

"Her old hobby," said Dima. "But not anymore."

When Dariya reappeared, I said in English, "You have a beautiful voice." She blushed instantly and Dima demanded to know what I'd said to make her turn that color.

I ate more potatoes, and once back in my room I read briefly and played hearts on my laptop. I fell back asleep and the next morning, back in my classroom, it felt as though I'd never left the school. In class we worked without distractions, reviewing the grammar and vocabulary that would be on our next test. The eighth graders didn't seem distraught over the loss of Miroslav—going to work in Russia was nothing to lament.

My lesson completed, I went to find Nadezhda's classroom.

At first glance the classroom I found was empty. In the corner a girl sat hunched over two pads of paper, transferring the day's homework into her friend's notebook. It was Dariya.

"What are you doing?" I asked in English. Her head shot up as though she'd been caught at something dangerous. Her shoulders dropped and her face softened once she recognized me. And then after thinking about the situation her face hardened as though she was about to attack a weaker being.

"What are *you* doing here?" she said, in Russian, with a smile.

Her attire was different than what I'd seen her wearing at breakfast. She'd ditched an all-covering sweater in favor of a t-shirt with a low neckline, and had applied lipstick.

Another pupil entered, walked past me without saying a word, and after inspecting the notebooks asked Dariya why the homework wasn't finished.

"Nadezhda Ivanovna will be here any second," complained the girl, clearly one of Dariya's friends.

"She's absent today," I interrupted. "You're very lucky."

The girl looked at me with her eyebrows scrunched together. "Oh," she said. "I didn't think you spoke Russian." She pumped her fist in the air upon realizing I'd be the substitute.

The bell rang and no one else entered.

"We'll wait a few moments for stragglers," I said.

Dariya couldn't pronounce the word to ask what it meant. *Straaglaaire.*

"A late-arriving pupil."

"Only us," said Dariya. "There's one other boy but he rarely comes."

"This doesn't make sense," I said.

Dariya shrugged her shoulders. "He's Ukrainian. A very strange boy."

"No, not him. Why are there only three pupils in your class?"

"The others take French," explained Dariya's friend. "The other nine."

So then I realized the graduating class that year would consist of twelve pupils. And only to clarify, to make sure I understood everything, I asked, "Dariya. How many students started with you in the first grade?"

"Two hundred," she said.

I thought of Miroslav leaving school the previous day. Dariya and this girl had said goodbye to classmates in this manner their whole lives, counting down slowly from two hundred to twelve.

We didn't speak more about the size of their class. For them it wasn't an interesting topic. Dariya's friend, another Aliona, had heard much about me that she wished to confirm. Why wasn't I married? Why did I not like discotheques? Why wouldn't I like to accompany her that very night to the discotheque to see if I liked it with her?

The bell startled us. It seemed we'd just started to talk freely. We'd spoken Russian the entire period and never opened the textbook. Dariya's friend called me an excellent teacher.

The tenth grade entered next. A mix of ten boys and girls—boys sitting with boys, girls with girls—had been assigned to ask me questions about America. Nadezhda had left me a note to record the names of those with no work.

Only the girls raised their hands. This was the first time I'd officially met this class, but they seemed to know me quite well.

Why you are not married? Where you will find your wife? In Moldova or America? How much you are paid in Moldova, and who pays you? How much you get in America? And how much do we get as sweepers? As trash men? As bus drivers? How much money each month? And what is this we hear about your resistance to discotheques? You, Mr. Aaron, make no sense as a person.

"That last one's not a question," I said.

"Then tell us," said one of the boys in frustration, at last bored with his own inactivity in class. "What do you do?" His name was Sasha.

"I read," I said.

The children expressed their shared boredom with a collective sigh. They wanted to know an exciting American.

"I also play basketball."

The room became silent. I'd only intended to indicate my enjoyment for sport, specifically basketball. But I'd accidentally touched on one of their preconceived notions of American culture—the street basketball player in a gang who used drugs and carried wads of money.

"You play basketball!" said Sasha.

"Basketball is dirty," said a girl.

"You're dirty!" said Sasha. The girl advanced at the boy quickly and nearly connected her slap, only to swat the air as he ducked away. *Nice move*, I thought. *That boy's an athlete.*

"Calm," I said. "Don't hit."

"But seriously," said Sasha. "We play basketball in Riscani. It is something we do. You play basketball also?"

"I do."

"On a team?"

"Back in high school."

"With black men?"

"Sometimes."

"But yes? Black men players?"

"Yes, I've played with African-American teammates and opponents."

"In Africa or America? I am confused."

"African-*Americans*," I said. "In America."

The classroom gasped.

"Did they ever hurt you?"

"No, no, no."

The room was quiet for a moment. A girl in the front row then turned to address the rest of the class.

"Mr. Aaron is a *BADASS*."

* * *

My day finished, I walked home slowly, dragging leaves into piles and kicking them up. A collection of young pupils following behind laughed at me. They were smoking. "Don't smoke," I said over my shoulder, and they laughed more. The boy Sasha caught up just as I was crossing the street.

"Mr. Aaron," he said. "In Riscani, we also play basketball."

"I know," I said. "You told me in class."

"You come, then?"

"Absolutely. I'll come in the future. Let me know when."

"OK, OK, OK," said Sasha, and ran off toward the center of town.

At home, lunch was borscht. I rolled the idea of basketball around in my head while I waited for the soup to cool. Up to that point in Moldova I hadn't been exercising; I rarely got out of the apartment, let alone went for a jog. I wasn't in bad shape, however; my weight was down ten pounds since I'd arrived. In a typical Moldovan day I consumed half of what I would eat in America. The portions were small and there weren't snacks between meals. It seemed realistic that I might get some muscle onto my body if

I exercised a bit instead of sitting at home and reading. I wasn't the best basketball player, but I wouldn't embarrass myself.

So I decided to play basketball. I'd run after school to get in shape, give Katya extra money to put more protein in my diet, and after a couple of weeks I'd go down to the gym and show the Russians how the game was meant to be played.

In the kitchen I stretched my arms above and behind my head to gauge my flexibility; whatever mobility I had possessed in high school was still with me. I'd show them behind the back passes, between the legs, no look—and if the rims were anything lower than regulation, I might even get close to dunking.

The doorbell rang. I was fully into my daydream and nearly finished with my soup.

"Aaron," said Katya. "For you."

I saw Sasha's face in my mind—he was the last person I'd spoken to. I looked around the corner and it was indeed Sasha at the door. In my mind he'd been dressed as he had been at school. Now he stood in the hallway wearing basketball shorts, a gym bag slung over his shoulder. "You have good shoes?" he asked. "I give you shorts and t-shirt. No problem."

"Now?! We're playing now!"

"Yes. I tell everyone," said Sasha. "Everyone in town knows you're coming. Mischa and Stefan. The priest's son. All very good players. All are ready to play against the American."

Ruins

Throughout northern Moldova crumbling remains of buildings dotted the highways and roads leading from town to town. No one could afford to finish the construction work or remove the bricks that were already in place. In Riscani, there were two such examples of Soviet Ruins on the main street: the burned-out asylum, and an uncompleted factory next to the police station. All that remained of these two buildings were the foundations, bits of the walls, and staircases that led up into thin air. Children played war games in these spaces and stray dogs slept in mounds.

I mention this aspect of the Moldovan landscape—the Soviet Ruins—because the Riscani Sport Complex, where Sasha took me to play basketball, had somehow survived this architectural death sentence.

As we approached in the dark, the building rose like a castle. The only light came through a broken window in the second-floor gymnasium. From outside, I heard equal parts Russian and Romanian shouting. I followed Sasha's white sneakers through the dark lobby. I couldn't see the rest of him. He said hello to someone older in the dark and didn't stop to introduce me. Basketballs thudded into the floorboards overhead like cannon fire.

At the end of the corridor was the locker room. All conversation died when I entered. Everyone looked at me—some smiled, some sneered while flexing their arm muscles—and my initial instincts told me I'd have to fight them all. Although I'd never met them, the names were familiar: Vova, Mischa, Alex, another Vova, Anton. Sasha let all but one make their introductions to me. When they'd all finished Sasha pointed to the tallest boy and said, "Mr. Aaron, this is Stefan." Stefan wore real basketball shoes and a yellow Kobe Bryant jersey—number 8. The other boys had canvas shoes appropriate for gardening. "He's the priest's son," said Sasha. And by this I was meant to understand the boy came from wealth and was entitled to things such as a scooter, three meals a day, and the ability to dunk a basketball. But I understood none of these entitlements and assumed Stefan would have to leave early for night mass.

As I changed, the boys took turns asking me questions about black men, my sneakers, discotheques and Dariya. Everyone knew Dariya. The boy Mischa made a joke about her chest and became offended when I didn't laugh. "We'll see just how well Americans play basketball," he said.

The group of basketball players reversed back through the corridor and ascended a dark stairwell. I followed Sasha's white shoes again until I lost them in the complete darkness and followed the wall upward with my hand. At last a light appeared around a final corner of the spiral staircase and opened into the gymnasium. "This looks dangerous!" I blurted out. Wooden boards were loose and out of place on the court. A soaked-through towel lay at mid-court to collect water leaking from the ceiling. As we entered to warm up, the young men from the locker room moved en masse around the court as though playing a new, more violent form of rugby. The physicality extended to punching in close quarters and tripping in open spaces. I was certain, even from a distance, that I saw blood on the ball.

Sasha pulled me onto the court. He found me a ball (a bit smaller than American regulation) and I dribbled around to get a feel for the floorboards. The ball failed to bounce in some areas as though caught in syrup. In other areas it bounced sideways. The court lines were European and unfamiliar. I launched up a shot from the 3-pt line and made it in. Everyone had been watching me and now began to clap.

Teams formed quickly. Mischa claimed the priest's son, Stefan, and three other athletes. As the other captain, Sasha picked me along with three of his skinny friends from the Russian lyceum.

We hadn't discussed positions, but Sasha seemed to be the point guard. He threw up a shot that clanked off the rim. Another of my skinny teammates went for the rebound and was punched in the face. An argument ensued over whether this poor kid on the ground was acting. Then his nose began to trickle blood and the other team conceded a foul. From the baseline Sasha threw me the ball at the top of the key. I wanted to pass, but all nine of the other players were under the rim, looking up at the net, waiting for the rebound. I stepped back behind the 3-pt line and made the shot.

My teammates clapped.

Now back on defense, I guarded Mischa. Stefan yelled from under the basket for a pass. He was a foot taller than the boy guarding him and could have dunked from a standstill. Instead, Mischa tried to pass the ball to himself through my legs. The ball bounced off my shin. I pounced on it and I passed it forward to Sasha, who, I now realized, had never come down court to play defense.

5-0.

After that basket I turned to see an old man screaming. On a bench in the corner sat an unshaven man in a wool sweater and brown pants. This was Ivan Vasilyavich: former Soviet basketball player, current Riscani basketball coach.

"Everything I just watched," he said. "Was a disgrace!"

He yelled at Mischa for not passing; he yelled at Stefan for not taking the ball from Mischa; he yelled at the tall boy for not playing tough and at the short boy for not playing tall. He didn't object to my play.

He shook my hand.

"Do I know your father?" he asked. "What is your family name?"

"He's the American," said Sasha.

Ivan Vasilyavich laughed suddenly and then coughed for a full minute. Players on the court took this time to practice dribbling through their legs. When Ivan Vasilyavich finished coughing, he split the boys into two groups and had me watch from the sideline as the boys ran through practice drills. The Russian coach watched my reactions to the good and bad of his players on the court. Then Ivan Vasilyavich came to me after the boys had finished and conducted a brief interrogation.

"Drink preference: Moldovan wine or Russian vodka?" he asked. "Woman preference: Moldovan or Russian?"

The game restarted with our original teams.

Ivan Vasilyavich yelled more and only gave encouragement when another player performed well against me.

I played well though timidly so as to escape without wounds or enemies. Everyone insisted on shaking my hand before I left at 9 p.m., well before the game would end. I excused myself by saying I had school in the morning.

"You sound like a teacher," said Ivan Vasilyavich. He had never thought to question why I was in Moldova.

"It is so," I said. "The Russian school."

Ivan Vasilyavich's eyes rounded. He advanced very close and spoke into my face. His breath was stale vodka. He kept his voice low so that no one else could hear. His tone was one of warning. I didn't understand a single word; he spoke half Russian, half nonsense. He wouldn't let my hand go. I bowed my head repeatedly as to indicate I understood that his words would save my life.

As Ivan Vasilyavich let go of my hand he whispered, "To your health, then."

Where There is No Doctor

The next morning, every part of my body ached. The pain of using my leg muscles for the first time in ages felt familiar, but I couldn't remember a time I felt so drained after exercising. My twisted ankle would surely feel better once I took Advil and stretched. But the pain in my fingers concerned me. I struggled to stir the sugar into my tea.

"Old man," said Dariya at the breakfast table. She touched a bruise on my shoulder that must have come from an aggressive rebound.

I ate my potatoes and worried about vitamin deficiency.

After changing into my clothes, before heading over to teach, I took out the resource manual the Peace Corps nurse had given each volunteer at training: a glossy illustrated textbook called, *Where There is No Doctor*. The text offered equal amounts of amusing, practical, and nightmare-inducing information. It warned never to blame local witchcraft practitioners; you never should have trusted them in the first place. (An illustration labeled "NO" shows an incriminating finger pointing at a wrinkled woman with a hooked nose.) From this book I learned how to make a toothbrush from a twig, and also a bone splint from several twigs. The book, in fact, assumed universal twig availability. The scariest thing to do with a twig: retract a parasitic tape worm from your abdomen by tying one end to the twig and twisting a little each day; the idea being to pull the worm from your body a centimeter a day, for as many days as it took (i.e. weeks).

According to the book, today my symptoms indicated scurvy.

* * *

In class that day interruptions marred my lessons. The school's other teachers, many I'd never spoken to before, walked into the classroom to invite me to their parent-teacher conferences. Each teacher in the school (except me) was assigned a homeroom, which would host the conferences. Word about the American teacher had passed through town and parents only wished to speak with me. Anything the Riscani teachers said about their students was considered speculation. My opinion carried weight. If Nadezhda called her students miscreants, it was her own fault; parents would say she didn't know how to manage a classroom. But anything the foreign expert said was fact.

I sat down and presented the lessons from my desk. The students were unnerved that I didn't walk my normal circuit around the classroom to see if they were cheating or using their cell phones. Today, they wanted to prove they weren't cheating—if only for the day. Most asked what I would say to their parents. Students who hadn't spoken a word all semester asked for extra credit assignments. One offered me a bottle of vodka if I pretended not to know who he was.

These were the best hours of teaching I would ever experience: kids trying to earn a last minute reprieve. No one played *durak* when my back was turned to the board. Girls weren't smacked on the behind. There wasn't a single request for a cigarette break. Everyone had a book. All the hands were raised.

Life was peaceful until the final bell rang and the parents arrived.

I first made my way to the conference for the fifth graders. Their homeroom teacher, Lyudmila Petrovna, had been kind to me in the past and I felt obliged to help her. Muddled screaming from many classrooms floated through the corridor. When I cracked the door open to peer in, the voices stopped and everyone looked at me. Lyudmila Petrovna welcomed me inside, enunciating my name clearly, MEE-STAIR AH-RON.

Ten women and several small children occupied the classroom. Many of the women were too large to stay on the little classroom chairs without a struggle. In the back, I recognized Andrei, a student from one of the older grades who said *Good Morning* whenever he saw me—morning, afternoon or night. After eight years of English classes it was the only phrase he seemed to know. We shook hands and he cleared his coat from the seat next to him for me to sit.

I'd interrupted one of the school's Romanian Language teachers, the woman who I'd last seen in the lounge when Nadezhda asked me about life in Alabama. After everyone stopped looking at me, she continued her diatribe about poor performance, poor behavior, and poor future prospects for the students. Holding aloft a supposed "essay" scribbled over a piece of notebook paper, she wondered aloud, "How will this student write home to his mother when he's in the army?" She produced a list of grievances and singled out every student she felt needed a reprimand. Only she didn't say, "reprimand"; she recommended mild beatings. The parents cut her off by promising the beatings and then all turned around to look at me.

Lyudmila Petrovna asked if I could say a few words.

I'd prepared a stern lecture about the importance of homework and intellectual discipline. Pupils shouldn't cheat. I wanted to explain why students needed books every day and couldn't share pencils while taking notes. And though I didn't wish to lecture anyone on proper parenting skills, I thought I might touch on the need to curb the smoking, drinking, and sexual assault in the school zone.

But I abandoned this prepared lecture. I feared anything negative I shared would lead to beatings.

So instead, using my best Russian, I painted a less dire picture. "Moldova is different than America," I began. "My pupils are struggling, but that is to be expected. I don't teach like a Russian. I expect different things and it will take the pupils time to understand these things. They play with each other too much, true, but they understand me more each day and I think soon they will speak English."

All the faces in the audience smiled at me and I felt pleased with myself. The parents would be patient with their young learners. They would communicate that students should be patient with me, do everything I say, and stop sexually assaulting their classmates. I honestly thought we'd all come to this amicable conclusion.

Lyudmila Petrovna looked at the floor while she considered what to say next.

On several occasions she'd rescued me when my classes got out of control. Her room was just down the hall and when she heard more than five kids screaming at once she'd rush into the room and threaten to kill anyone who didn't shut up and respect me. The little ones feared her. And now she wanted the little ones to fear their parents.

"Any behavior problems?" asked Lyudmila Petrovna.

"Oh, certainly," I said.

"We demand names!" shouted the parents in unison. And when I failed to list the offenders they shouted family names for me to inform on.

"Crimiac? Does he listen?"

"Osipov? Did he start that fire?"

I placed my palms in the air. I surrendered.

"Okay," shouted Lyudmila Petrovna. "One at a time."

We spent the next ten minutes going down the class roster. I named names. Little Sasha didn't do his homework.

Maxim didn't stay in his seat. Anya habitually cheated. And so on.

The parents promised immediate improvement. I feared for these children.

But I no longer feared repercussions from their parents. These weren't parents. As Lyudmila Petrovna called on each raised hand, she introduced the woman and her role in the student's life. Before me were a handful of grandmothers, aunts, distant cousins, neighbors—but few actual parents. Things became clearer for me: many of those who acted up in my class had parents elsewhere in the world, working jobs in Russia or still farther away. Grandmothers looked after grandchildren. Neighbors stepped in. Older siblings took larger roles. I had assumed Andrei was sitting in the audience with his mother, but in fact he was there to represent his younger brother, Maxim. When their mother next called home he would give his report of little Maxim's poor behavior and she would scold him over the phone from Italy.

Everyone thanked me before I left. One of the grandmothers asked when I would marry. Seeing this as an opening for questions, others shouted out the suspicions they wished confirmed. How much could I be making per month in America? How well did I speak German? What type of spying had I accomplished in the past? Was the Peace Corps a consequence associated with the American penal system, and if so what had I done?

* * *

After the conferences I went to the lake. It was cold out and I could see my breath in front of me, but the absence of wind allowed me to remain outside comfortably. From the bar on the lake I bought a liter of Ukrainian beer in a plastic bottle and sipped it on a bench near the waterline. I thought about the conferences and the missing parents and before I knew it the beer was gone. I stood and threw twigs into the water. The beer made my fingertips buzz inside my gloves and soon I felt calm enough to leave. I put a handful of twigs in my pocket in case I needed them for medical purposes later.

On the way home, I passed the sport complex and heard the familiar shouting coming through the broken windows on the second floor. Above all the other voices, I heard Ivan Vasilyavich shouting basketball commands. I didn't have the right shoes or pants to play, but I decided to go inside anyway. It would've been rude to pass by without shaking any hands.

* * *

By the next morning, my body felt better. My joints no longer ached. The only symptom remaining was a sore throat whenever I swallowed. I'd probably breathed in too much cold air by the lake. In any case, I still needed vitamins. After my potato breakfast, I went to the bazaar to buy an orange.

People now recognized me on the street: the American, the Russian school's new teacher, the basketball player, the one who paid for trips to Chisinau on the weekends. Most felt comfortable approaching me to engage in conversations. Other passersby snickered and covered their mouths while they whispered about me to their companions.

When I spoke to strangers, I rarely got a speedy response. I would have to wait while they worked out the possibilities of my origins. Many guessed I was Polish. Some thought I might be German, though with only a basic education. Katya said my accent in Russian sounded familiar but soft, as though it belonged to someone from simpler times. I'd need more presence if I desired an audience; I'd need to project a force that anyone receiving my words would experience as we engaged in conversation, the unspoken subtext of all speech to establish my physical presence, the possibility of instant domination.

Buying an orange proved a difficult chore.

My use of language had become rather specific. At school and at home I'd grown accustomed to being understood. I knew well how to boss kids around a classroom and how to ask for less sugar in my tea. Through practice with my many linguistic imperfections, the kids and Katya frequently knew what I wanted before I could open my mouth. In training, I'd been warned that strangers wouldn't understand me because of my accent. Ethnic Russians in this part of the world weren't accustomed to hearing foreigners speak their language.

At the first stall with fruit I said *oringe* instead of *orange*, with the result being total incomprehension. The next two women laughed off my request and asked where I was born. A fourth woman complimented my Russian. "You have a beautiful voice," she said. "You should read poetry." She handed me an apple. "Yours for free, Mr. Aaron," she said. "Please continue to take care of Andrei." I didn't know who she meant. There were seven Andreis spread across my class rosters. "Of course," I said, and I bit into the apple and smiled. It was brown on the inside and inedible.

In the alley of vodka bars I tried to buy orange juice. All I could find was orange *drink*. The woman yelled that I was wasting her time; I'd asked for juice and then refused it. I thought it over and decided to pick this battle. "*Drink* and *juice* are different," I explained. She yelled and I yelled back. Nobody in a crowd of a hundred turned to look. She said the equivalent of "take it or leave it," and I left. Before exiting the bazaar I bought a hot dog. In Riscani, hot dogs off the street were topped with dill, carrots, cabbage and mayonnaise. I convinced myself the vegetables on top were rich in vitamins.

I went for a walk instead of going home.

An hour later, my throat began to scratch whenever I swallowed. Before returning home, I backtracked to the bazaar and bought orange drink from a different vendor, pointing with my finger instead of speaking.

Departures

After my experience buying an orange in the bazaar, I desired formal training in the Russian style of argumentation. One afternoon at home, Dariya came to me for help with her English homework. It had become common practice for her to simultaneously knock on my door and enter at the same time with her notebook in hand. She would sit at my desk. I would place a bookmark into the passage she'd interrupted, close my book and listen. We worked well together. Before she left, I politely informed her that she would be my new Russian teacher.

"I am a student," she said. "Not a teacher."

"We'll meet twice a week," I said. "Maybe three times."

"Not possible."

"I'll pay you fifty lei an hour."

She hesitated. Teachers at the Russian school made 100 lei per day.

"I must ask Mama and Papa."

"You'll do it!" screamed Dima from the living room. He'd muted the television and overheard the entire conversation through the walls. Dariya swore to herself in Russian and asked what I'd like to learn. "How to pronounce long words," I said. "I must also learn to argue at the bazaar. And all the curse words."

"No, no, no," said Dariya.

"I must understand what my students say about me in class," I said.

Dariya laughed. "Okay, we'll make this work."

* * *

By mid-December I'd lived in Moldova six months. I'd never been away from America that long—and still, six months represented less than a quarter of the time I'd committed to being away.

Since arriving in Riscani, several brief friendships had already ended.

An elderly gentleman from Oregon decided to quit after realizing the modern Peace Corps didn't live up to his bohemian lifestyle.

A twenty-something woman from Colorado felt she'd mistakenly abandoned the love of her life.

A woman who found a lump in her breast was flown back to D.C. for a medical evaluation. It turned out benign, but she wasn't allowed to return when her gall bladder unexpectedly ruptured while she was waiting for transport back to Moldova.

Closer to me than these, a young married couple from Oklahoma had decided against returning to Moldova after visiting the wife's sick grandmother in America. They'd lived and taught an hour away from me in a village called Mihaileni. Their village was within the limits of the Riscani province, and false rumors quickly spread from village to village in the manner of a fact-twisting gossip tree. Word arrived that all Americans in Riscani province were to be ordered home by the United States government. I received a dozen phone calls asking when I would be leaving. Katya and Dariya took turns answering the phone and explaining the truth.

Even if the majority of the volunteers were content, everyone I knew was ready for a break. Headquarters addressed this by giving each volunteer a monthly stipend of U.S. dollars for "vacation" expenses. If a volunteer left his vacation money alone (as I had) he could afford a plane ticket for the New Year's holiday. Moldova might have been isolated from the world economically, politically and socially, but many inviting locations were a stone's throw away.

Jesse decided to spend his Christmas in Turkey. Others were off to Hungary, Romania, and the Balkans. Some even decided to pay for a quick trip back to the States. The decision was taken out of my hands; I'd become involved with an American woman, another volunteer, who wanted to visit Spain. If given the choice, I'd have gone with Jesse to Istanbul, but I couldn't complain. This woman was good to me, made me feel less isolated, and I'd never seen Barcelona.

In Riscani a combination of cold weather and a twisted ankle from playing basketball kept me off the streets. I slept and ate. I read and watched movies on my laptop. As a bookmark for *Doctor Zhivago*, I used the plane ticket I'd purchased a month earlier.

Dima openly questioned if I'd return from Spain.

"I wouldn't," he insisted. "Not if I were you."

"And who is Callie?" asked Katya.

I mixed up my words in Russian and mistakenly said *pillow* instead of *girlfriend*.

"She's my pillow," I said confidently, hoping to impress them with my vocabulary.

Katya started laughing, and then Dima and Dariya. I'd inadvertently stumbled onto an old Russian joke about a lonely man with a pillow instead of a girlfriend. Dariya looked a lot like her father when she became purple in the face. Dima calmed and told me the joke. I wanted to laugh, but it wasn't that funny. It seemed they were laughing at something else, some recorded family history with pillows and girlfriends, something I'd never understand unless I'd been there to see it the first time.

Chismea

At one point in *Doctor Zhivago,* the protagonist hides in an abandoned house in the Russian countryside. It is winter. He leaves to get supplies in town and is kidnapped into medical service by a band of soldiers.

This scene haunted me for many nights: abduction; the doctor conscious that the life he knows is ending, another forced upon him.

On the night before I left for Spain, Dariya knocked and entered my room with her teaching notebook. She'd settled in comfortably as my language instructor. That night we continued our discussion of motion verbs: the differences between going one way to a destination or there and back; of general "wander-going" without destination; of moving between locations by foot or by motorized conveyance; of which word to use when any type of "hovering" was involved. Russian contained enough variations of the word "go" to fill the lessons of several days.

Dariya rummaged through the contents of my desk while she waited for me to conjugate the verb, "to go one way by ground conveyance." She scanned several Peace Corps documents for passages she understood. Discouraged, she flipped over the novel I was reading. Her lips fluttered as she sounded out the letters of the title. Her eyes grew wide. She slapped at my shoulder to stop my writing and said, "I've read this!"

"What have you read?" screamed Dima from the living room. He entered quickly.

Dariya showed him the book. He nodded his head. "I approve of Pasternak."

He took the chair from Dariya (she moved to the bed) and asked me what other Russian writers I knew. We listed names for the next few moments. Dima wanted to know which authors the typical American would know.

Dostoyevsky. Tolstoy.

"Of course," said Dima. "The basis of modern intelligence."

Pasternak. Gogol. Chekov.

"Brilliant men," said Dima. "Poets."

Nabokov.

"I hear he is good," said Dima.

Solzhenitsyn.

Dima shook his head. "No. We never read him."

The family possessed a collection of antique books that they kept behind glass next to the fine china. But I'd never seen them read, even when the television was broken.

"Okay," said Dima. "Let's have a little drink."

In order to get out of Riscani the next morning I needed to be on the early bus before sunrise. "No, no, no," I said.

"We'll toast Pasternak," Dima said.

"I soon go for Spain," I countered. I'd messed up the motion verb and turned to Dariya to apologize.

"Then we must drink now, before you leave Moldova." Dima pretended a tear, dragging a fingertip down his cheek. "Goodbye, Moldova!"

"I've already told you I'll return. I'll promise, if you like."

"No, Aaron. You must drink. Today is my birthday."

I turned to Dariya. She looked defensive, as though I'd asked her an uncomfortable favor. "Someone has to drink with him," she said.

I turned to Dima, "Of course we drink, Papa."

He nodded. "You're a simple man."

He turned forty-nine that night. During my Russian lesson with Dariya, Katya had been working in the kitchen to prepare potato salad, cutlets, buttered noodles and dessert breads. We drank successive shots of champagne, wine, cognac, *garilka*, and then two final shots of vodka. After each shot, Dima reminded me to eat, picking up my fork and scraping food toward me. A man was only an alcoholic if he refused food. I remember feeling extremely warm and happy. The last fragment of conversation I remember concerned Jack London. Dima knew all sorts of things about Jack London.

* * *

My alarm clock went off at 3 a.m. I slammed the clock silent. I swallowed a handful of ibuprofen and fell back asleep.

Sunlight woke me sometime later. My headache was tolerable. I still tasted a mixture of alcohol under my tongue. I was fully clothed. But I was happy. I remembered Dima hugging me before I went to sleep and felt pleased that I'd settled comfortably into my new Russian life. I wasn't merely an observer, not any longer.

I was aware, vaguely, that I'd forgotten something.

When I opened my eyes, I saw my travel pack leaning against the door. I swore at myself in Russian—*chort*—and decided I didn't need to change clothes. I needed to hurry. I was late for a commitment from my other life; I was late for Callie.

* * *

I'd first met Callie six months earlier in Philadelphia.

Our group was sheltered at the *Holiday Inn* for three nights before we departed for Moldova. She was nervous and hardly spoke to anyone until we all went out for drinks on our last night. By coincidence, we sat together in a booth. She downed a shot of Jägermeister and, while sipping on a beer, told me she probably wouldn't get on the plane. She already wanted to quit.

Callie talked about how much smoke her lungs could tolerate, and how she would never apologize for enjoying herself at a Kid Rock concert. After another shot of Jägermeister, we went to the back of the bar and she revealed part of her tattoo of a colored tree that covered her entire back. I only saw the top. The roots disappeared below into her jeans.

"You wanna see the roots?" she said.

A day later, in the airport waiting area, I wasn't nervous about the flight, about leaving my family, about fulfilling a voluntary two-year exile; I was terrified my illustrated woman would quit before starting and that I'd never see the full tattoo.

In the end she got on the plane.

Once in Moldova, our group was kept apart for a month. I was paired with Jesse in our training village, and I didn't see Callie again until the embassy threw a July 4th party at a campground outside Chisinau. Peace Corps volunteers and marines stood in circles around kegs of Moldovan beer. Frisbees flew in all directions. Fanning hands kept flies away from platters of barbecued meats and cheeses. There was dancing and close contact with Callie, and after a few drinks, we found some privacy and I finally saw the tattoo.

After three months of teaching, all my students knew why I went to Chisinau on the weekends. Callie's tiny village, Chismea, was only a half-hour drive from the capital and she was always relaxing in the volunteer lounge at headquarters. I didn't mind the seven hour round-trip from Riscani to see her. A typical day together involved a walk around the city, a restaurant, drinks, and finally a hotel room. On one of these good days, we bought plane tickets to Barcelona.

Katya and Dariya assumed anyone calling for me was Callie. Dariya would pick up the phone, hear words she didn't understand, and scream, "Callie's on the phone!" Sometimes it would be other friends, once or twice my Mother calling from Maine, but usually it was Callie looking to vent some steam.

"This village!" she complained. "Thieves and scoundrels!"

As the season grew colder, Callie grew more irritated by everything around her. Chismea was all mud, and no one respected her at school. The host family wasn't feeding her and she suspected that the family's daughter stole from her. And the nights were too cold. And the outhouse was too far away. And one of these days she'd fall down the hill leading to school and have to teach in muddy clothes.

But, to her credit, she refused to quit. Moldova wouldn't beat her. We'd refresh ourselves in Barcelona and then everything would be fine.

* * *

After deciding to stay in the clothes I'd slept in, I grabbed my pack and went for the door. I stopped. Katya had left breakfast for me on the table and I felt guilty about leaving. I scooped some noodles and cheese into my mouth and downed the cold tea. In the living room Dima was still passed out; too drunk to operate the folding couch, he'd made a pallet out of cushions instead.

I knew Callie was waiting for me in her village.

My hangover returned in the airless bus to the capital. A large old lady in wool sandwiched me against the window. My left side overheated against her girth while my right side froze against the cold glass. Snow had yet to collect in the fields. The cold weather had only added frost over the brown landscape. The roads were frozen over with ice, and yet Vasia didn't change his style of rapid transport.

Half of me screamed, "Slower before we die!"

The other half complained, "Faster, faster!"

Once in Chisinau, I raced to the next bus. The transport to Chismea was empty, but once on board I saw that dozens of plastic bags occupied the seats. The bus wouldn't leave for a half-hour. As people slowly populated the bus, I realized I would have to stand. If I wanted to sit I'd have needed to come an hour earlier, break into the locked bus (as others clearly had) and reserve a seat with my backpack.

I'd learned to judge the time I'd spend in a bus by how much the ticket cost. An hour equaled twenty lei. But the ticket to Chismea cost me ten lei and two hours on my feet. The driver stopped for commuters every hundred yards. We drove south through vineyards and dirt fields. Snow had fallen in this part of the country. I saw out the window in the moments when the driver braked for animals and the entire mass of standing passengers shifted forward in unison. Whenever the door opened to take in another body, a burst of wind would pass through the cabin and freeze the sweat on my neck.

I didn't know it at the time, but everyone on the bus was spying on me. All the passengers were from Callie's village.

After living in her village for a week, Callie had received numerous offers of marriage—from intoxicated men, mostly, but also from women trying to match their sons. She'd taken to lying; she put a ring on her finger and claimed she was already engaged. When pressed into giving more details, she'd give them my name.

On the bus, I heard my name spoken in whispers and thought I was hallucinating. The bus contained Callie's students, friends of her host family, the women who sold her cookies at the corner store, the men who followed her in the streets. A pack of drunken men in the back of the bus were sizing me up. I knew they were talking about me when an old lady interrupted their conversation to say I looked clean even though I hadn't shaved.

We arrived.

I stepped off the bus and breathed in the cold air.

Chismea was situated on a descending steppe. The thin snow cover hadn't eliminated the brown hue of mud from the fields.

Over half the men in this village had emigrated elsewhere. Most had gone to Moscow, but others had gone the other way into Romania. It was a dying village, with very little to keep a person happy.

I saw Callie from a distance, and felt like a child about to be punished. I came up and kissed her on the cheek. She didn't react at first. Then it seemed she didn't wish to cause trouble, so she just said hello.

"Barcelona," I said, shaking her shoulders. She smiled.

We walked uphill. Every house looked the same: square houses with white, green and blue painted trim. I looked ahead and then behind, downhill, back uphill, and now had a better understanding of why Callie complained all the time. Mud everywhere. No places to walk except to the store or to the fields or back to the bus stop.

She didn't speak. When the ground leveled and I caught my breath I explained about Dima's birthday and my hangover.

"Who's Dima?" she asked.

"My father. My host father."

She nodded. "I've got Advil in the med kit."

We reached her homestead. It could have been a frontier cabin erected a year before or centuries past; fresh paint hid the rot. Callie reached her hand into the gate and unlatched the peg from the inside. I had to use the outhouse before going inside, but Callie wouldn't take me there. It was too far away. She pointed. The courtyard was deserted; the animals that had left all the visible droppings were caged for the winter. I smelled pigs and heard chickens. I stepped on something and recoiled, but was relieved to discover the animal shit had frozen solid. After passing through a maze of empty barrels, cages, unused and rusting tools, I made it to the outhouse. Cold had warped the door and it wouldn't close. I peed from the safe distance of the threshold, not wanting to enter and absorb the smell into my clothes. Brown liquid splashed back out of the hole. I'd never seen that happen before—an outhouse completely full.

Inside the house, I shivered. I walked through the door in socks and said hello to a girl sitting at the kitchen table.

"Good afternoon," I said in Romanian. She didn't return the greeting. She pointed toward Callie's room.

Callie's space had a bit more color than the rest of the house, mainly decorated with colorful cookie wrappers and boxes of tea, candy bars from Moldovan and American convenience stores.

"What's with that girl?" I asked.

"She doesn't like speaking Russian."

"I spoke Romanian."

Callie shrugged. She undid the belt to her jeans and got into pajamas. I'd lost track of time, but it was still afternoon.

"You were right about the outhouse," I said. "Every word you said is true."

"I don't use it anymore." She pointed to a plastic bucket in the corner covered by a tin saucepan lid.

She took a book from her windowsill and began to read. I recognized every one of the books from the library at headquarters. Not wanting to end all chance at conversation,

I asked if the girl at the table was the one she'd talked about, the host sister who stole from her.

"That's one of them," she said. "They both steal."

I found her med kit and took Benadryl instead of Advil so that I'd fall asleep.

"Don't take them all," said Callie, peering around the book cover. "I'll need some for later."

* * *

Callie woke me gently by rubbing the hair on the back of my neck. She was next to me on the bed and she smiled. I'd been asleep long enough for the sun to set and it felt like another day. I thought it might be morning and time to leave for Spain.

"Dinner," she said. "We should eat with them."

Something was cooking in the house but I didn't recognize the smells. I heard frying and thought *cutlets*. Something had been boiled, but it wasn't potatoes. A knife knocked against the countertop after passing through meat. This was a different type of butcher sound, not repetitive salami slicing, nor the breaking of pork bones, but a soft deliberate cut with little resistance. The familiar clatter of ceramic mugs scraping across the table calmed me; at least there would be tea. But whatever we'd be eating, it wasn't anything Katya had ever fed me.

The host sister who stole and didn't like talking Russian sat in the same place I'd seen her before. The host mother stood with her back to me, finishing up over the stove. She turned and placed a platter of fish on the table. At first all I saw was a collection of eyeballs. The host mother was slimmer than most women her age. *She wouldn't take up much space on a bus*, I thought.

"How beautiful," remarked the woman in Romanian.

I thought she was talking about the fish heads.

"She's talking about you," said Callie.

"Oh," I said, thinking of the right Romanian word to use. "*Multsumesc*—Thank you."

Callie picked at her fish while the host family interrogated me. How was my job? How much money could I be making in America? When did I plan on marriage? When did I plan on leaving Moldova? The mother spoke Russian when she wanted specific information. After discussing Callie's beauty, we talked about a wedding. At first I thought she meant the imaginary wedding Callie had invented to ward off village drunks. I worked hard to keep a straight face. The mother asked a serious question and, by reflex, I answered, "Yes. Yes, of course." I hadn't understood the question, but I knew that was the answer the woman wanted.

Callie sniffed the air loudly, a disgruntled giggle.

"What?"

"You just agreed to come back for the wedding."

"Whose?"

"The other sister. The other thief."

I continued smiling at the host mother. "When?" I asked Callie.

"February."

"Oh," I said.

The mother excused herself to make phone calls. She had to increase the guest list of her daughter's wedding by one. Another American was coming.

"You're in the shit now," said Callie.

The sister also excused herself. Callie and I sat alone. "I wish we could leave now," she said. I lifted up the body of the fish with my fork, inspected the slime coating the underbelly, let it fall back to the plate. "It's from the village lake," she said. "Don't eat it."

"I'll go to bed hungry," I said.

Callie gave me a candy bar when we got back to her room. I ate the chocolate and she ate a few Benadryl.

Escape from Moldova

The bus to the capital stood on the road, windows frosted. This time there was space on the bus to sit. Callie sat close to me, hugging my arm to keep warm. Men and women greeted her as they entered the bus. These were the relatives of her students or the friends of her family or just people who knew her name. She couldn't always tell people apart. Two of her students entered and lowered their eyes to the ground after seeing us with our arms intertwined. They found seats near the back and giggled

 A man who'd been standing outside chain-smoking threw down his final cigarette butt and came aboard to collect ten lei from each passenger. The cheap-smelling tobacco on his breath was something to distract me from the cold. I felt a sense of relief after the driver started up the bus, and a sense of accomplishment once we rolled beyond the village limits. Callie couldn't relax until we were off the bus and away from the people who knew her.

 The bus to Romania was smaller than I'd anticipated. It was a half-bus and appeared sickly next to the other diesel buses going elsewhere in Moldova. The engine turned over on the fourth try and black smoke poured out the exhaust pipe. I wouldn't have trusted this bus to get me back to Riscani, let alone out of the country.

 Our flight was scheduled to leave in fourteen hours, in the morning after an all-night ride.

 We found our seats toward the back and Callie asked me to sit against the window. She wanted to use me as a pillow. The other passengers filling the bus didn't appear to be embarking on the same type of international excursion we were. Most were women with oversized wool sweaters; women dressed for normal working days, not for the extended discomfort of a night sleeping on a bus. These women carried gym bags with them into the cabin after already having deposited large rolling suitcases into the back compartment. Callie and I assumed these women were moving to Romania and carried everything they owned.

The bus filled to capacity, all the seats occupied, and then the driver squeezed his way to the back and put wood boards between the aisle seats so that village women getting off before the border could sit.

A large woman sat next to Callie and elbowed her ribs to get more space. "Bitch," said Callie under her breath.

The radio played electric accordion lullabies.

Sometime later a recognizable sound woke me: the crackle of masking tape stretched and torn from the roll. I tensed because the sound had no place on a bus. I imagined we'd broken down and the driver was trying to fix the problem with tape. Then we hit a bump and I knew we were still moving. I opened my eyes. The numbers on the bus had thinned out. Villagers had departed. The remaining girls and women stood up from their seats to get more room for movement in the aisle.

"Turn on the lights!" a woman yelled to the driver. "We can't see what we're doing!"

The driver complied. The cabin filled with light and I had to squint.

Callie pushed toward me as far over as she could to avoid the flying elbows of the woman next to her. This woman had taken off her skirt and was taping packs of cigarettes around her stocking-covered thighs. She had managed to strap over a hundred packs to her body. She wasn't alone. Nearly everyone but us, it seemed, took turns with a passing roll of tape to strap cigarettes around their calves, waists, and under their breasts. Every time someone brushed against her, Callie pushed into me, poking my ribs with her finger tips to share her discomfort.

After the skirts and oversized sweaters were pulled back on, the small heads of these women smugglers no longer matched the engorged, lumpy shapes of their bodies.

"Hope they all get caught," said Callie.

I imagined they wouldn't. These women appeared to know what they were doing. Romania would pass into the European Union on New Year's Day. They would make a killing on these marked-up cigarettes.

We reached the first border crossing an hour later. A woman in a modified army uniform took our passports. Another border controller poked through the back luggage compartment and found nothing suspicious. The officer returned the stamped passports and waved us through. The whole process took twenty minutes.

Goodbye, Moldova.

We could see the Romanian station ahead, just beyond the no man's land.

Three guards stood side by side in the road with their arms up, preventing the bus from going any farther. The fattened-up smugglers swore in panicky voices.

"Calm," said the driver.

One of the controllers came aboard and took the passports. The heat left the bus after he'd opened and closed the front door. We sat thirty minutes, waiting, before the frame of the bus shook when border agents opened the back compartment.

A controller came back onboard. "Everyone off the bus!"

The Romanian guards escorted all the passengers into a glass building where they could inspect the bags away from the cold. They offered to take the warm outer coats off the smuggling women, who of course refused. "We'll be here awhile," insisted the guards. "We're really quite fine," said a woman. I was already starting to sweat. Callie and I took off our coats and draped them over the bags. Evidently the guards didn't suspect Callie and me of smuggling. All could see we hadn't taped anything to our bodies. For me this was entertainment; I couldn't wait for the guards to open up the suitcases. Would there be more cigarettes? Harder drugs? Kidneys wrapped in ice? Callie was less amused. She looked at her watch every few seconds and started pacing. We were already behind schedule and hadn't even yet suffered my predicted bus breakdown.

A man approached me and said hello in English. "Vasili," he said, extending his hand. I didn't know why a border controller would want to get friendly. But then I realized this man merely wanted to distance himself from the group of smugglers. He was a passenger from a bus that I'd overlooked.

Callie was pissed that Vasili didn't offer to shake her hand. She wouldn't have wanted to touch this strange Vasili under normal circumstances, but had grown sensitive about this oft-repeated social slight.

The border guards finally matched each smuggler with her luggage and began the formal searches. "This is not good," said Vasili. I nearly told him to shush; he was ruining the surprise with talk. "Not good," he mumbled.

As if resigned to her fate, the first woman stopped the controller from opening her suitcase while it was upright, not wanting the contents to spill onto the floor. She struggled to shift and control the weight, but finally got the suitcase onto its back on the floor. "Okay," she said.

It's a body, I thought.

The guard bent down and grabbed a bottle from the suitcase. It was a plastic two-liter filled with red wine. From my vantage point I saw more bottles neatly arranged. There were perhaps twenty in the suitcase.

Vasili turned to me. "You can't do that," he said.

The delay was now beginning to irritate me also.

"You can only carry two bottles of wine and two cartons of cigarettes into Romania," explained Vasili. "Sad," he continued. "They were trying for one last trip before they'll need a visa for the E.U."

Each smuggler waited her turn. The process of opening all the bags took an hour. The guards catalogued everything, slowly, item by item. And then, when it seemed our part in the ordeal was over, the guards then said, "And what about cigarettes?" And they instructed the women to take off their coats. So then we had to wait another hour. I went outside to find a bathroom. Callie didn't mind that I left her. By this point she enjoyed watching the smugglers getting processed.

A guard wandering the complex with a machine gun pointed to a toilet some distance down the road. Vasili followed me.

"You're English, yes?" Vasili asked.

"American."

"Excellent. What kind of accent do I have? If I went to America it would sound like American?"

He sounded like Dracula.

"More British, I think. Your accent is thick and English."

Vasili grinned.

We entered the bathroom at the guard complex, and before I could get to the urinal, a new guard with a machine gun came inside yelling. He screamed in Romanian for us to leave, I think, because the bathroom was only for guards. Instinctively, I said, "Sorry," in Russian, and then the guard pointed his weapon. The guards on the Romanian border did not like to hear Russian. Vasili exchanged words with the guard in Romanian, got new directions, and then we were both walking back, toward the glass house and then past, into the darkness. We ended up pissing in the no man's land between the two countries. "The nasty guard told us to go here," said Vasili. "Is that the right word, *nasty*?"

I was trying to piss and wanted Vasili to stop talking. "For what?"

"For the Romanians."

"For these ones, yes. Perfect word."

As we returned up the road, the guard with the machine gun stopped us. "You can't walk across the border without permission," said the guard. Vasili started yelling at him in a loud voice until another guard took notice, came down the road to inspect us and eventually vouched for us to pass.

Back inside the glass house, Callie asked where I'd been. "Almost got deported back to Moldova." She didn't ask me to elaborate. She was moments away from full panic mode. The guards and the smugglers were at a standstill. The guards hadn't found guns, only cigarettes and wine, and weren't going to arrest anyone. But they weren't letting the women pass through freely; the women could either leave the goods behind and pass into Romania, or hold onto them and wait for the next bus heading back to Moldova—in ten hours. The women had been debating for twenty minutes. The driver finally threw his hands in the air and said, "Decide in ten seconds."

He waved all the non-smugglers (seven total including Vasili, Callie and me) back onto the bus. He started the engine, looked back to the glass house, didn't see anyone step outside, put the bus into drive and took off toward Bucharest. We'd lost three hours.

The crossing from Moldova into Romania was a passage into a different world. Functioning streetlights illuminated both sides of the road. A thin blanket of snow covered the road. Far ahead, yellow house lights dotted the mountainous landscape.

The driver had lost most of his passengers, but had kept all their money. He couldn't have been happier. Now it seemed he was trying to set a land-speed record from the border to Bucharest. The bus weaved through mountain slots without slowing. The streetlights lost their novelty; the lamps in the valley below showed how far down we would fall.

The breakdown came twenty minutes later. The bus pulled to a stop at the bottom of a hill, far away from civilization. Snow fell and heat left the bus cabin. The driver didn't explain anything, and no one asked any questions. Everyone knew that buses broke down. Once the engine cooled, the driver got out and beat it with a hammer. He came back inside for a wrench and tightened something and then hit the engine again with the hammer. He tried the key in the ignition and then went to beat the engine with his hammer; he repeated this several times. Whatever he was doing, the revving grew louder and stronger after each beating. Finally, the engine turned over. Callie woke up. "We broke down," I said. She asked how long we'd been sitting. The breakdown had lasted a half hour. "Hope we make it," she said, and went back to sleep. We were now on pace to be in Bucharest at seven in the morning. Our flight was to leave at half-past seven.

Vasili came back to sit with me as the bus entered Bucharest. He'd been a cool customer back at the border crossing, very much in his element when swearing at the nasty guard. Now he was nervously sweating. He asked questions to me, hoping to confirm what he already knew. Drinks are free on the plane? They'll give me food? The flight assistant will speak the safety instructions in a few languages? I'll understand the safety instructions?

He took the passport from his breast pocket and had me inspect his visa. "Yes," I reassured him. "Everything looks in order."

"I've never flown," he said.

Bucharest seemed to be a city quite spread apart. I never saw a center. The route to the airport led through trees and past car dealerships, gas stations that charged by the liter.

"I've never been outside of Moldova," Vasili confessed.

I finally asked where he was going. He'd been waiting for me to ask since we'd met.

"To Norway," he said. "To practice my English." Vasili handed me a paper with expressions in English that he wished to say to the director of his work and travel program. *Thank you for this opportunity...*

None of it made sense to me. The words on the paper, yes, I suppose, but a Moldovan going to Norway for English improvement, certainly not.

The bus finally arrived at the airport. I wished Vasili health and happiness. It was five before seven. The driver smiled broadly when I thanked him. "We made good time," he said, and wished me health and happiness.

"We did it," said Callie, like she'd accomplished something by leaving Moldova. She'd expected an unseen hand to pull her back at the last moment: the bus to run off the road; smugglers to implicate her; border guards to arrest her; time to run out and the airport to deny her right to leave and find happiness.

She kissed my neck.

Barcelona

Once on the ground in Spain, I compared everything with Riscani: the smells, the cuts of dresses, the lack of trash on the roads. No comparisons with America came to my mind.

Our hotel was in the red light district. The women lining the streets were from different Latin American countries and they spoke with their pimps in slang that Spaniards wouldn't understand. Callie held on to my arm tightly so that no woman would talk to me. For prostitutes, I thought they dressed rather modestly. My own students—the Mashas and Dashas and Natashas—would have felt quite comfortable in the dress code of these back streets. My fifth graders would have complimented these women in sweet, chirpy voices. "How pretty," they'd say, stroking the fabric of a micro-skirt.

That first night we didn't leave the hotel room. When we walked out the next morning in search of coffee, the red light district still had the same characters, now dressed for conversations over breakfast. Pimps sat next to their prostitutes at coffee shops and flirted and made fun of each other like family members.

The next five days are blurred together in my memory: passing by statue performers that moved when you tossed a coin; waiting in line at the Picasso museum; mixing Russian words into my once-fluid Spanish; translating a film into Callie's ear at a movie theater; listening each night to the chatter of street walkers in the alley; drinking coffee each morning at Dunkin' Donuts.

What I remember clearly are the last two days in Barcelona—Callie growing more and more despondent when

Moldova entered our conversations. She overlooked monuments, refused to go on long walks, drank cups of coffee in single gulps, asked me to stop translating the film into her ear at the theater, preferring to stare vacantly at the screen. We didn't kiss on New Year's.

In retrospect, I could have been more supportive.

On the last morning, she wouldn't get out of bed, so I yanked off the covers. She went stiff when I tried to move her legs, so I took away her pillow. It had been our joke that Callie wouldn't leave Spain; I'd laughed at the notion, even though she hadn't. Now I took her seriously. "Come on," I said. "The plane leaves soon." She finally got up after I started collecting her belongings and stuffing them into her pack.

"You're doing it wrong," she said.

At the airport, she compared her emotional state to the time she was terrified at JFK Airport in New York, just before we left for Moldova.

"It's different now," I said. "There's no uncertainty."

"No uncertainty that I'll be miserable."

I shook my head. I was angry because I was looking forward to going home and she wasn't; because she didn't see Moldova as the adventure I did; because she'd shut herself off; because she tried to share her pissy emotions with me, certain I'd understand. Moldova was hard enough with my own emotions; I was going to last two years and she wasn't. I didn't want her pulling me down. I could function and live happily with that specific, personalized guilt; I'd already chosen to.

"Maybe I'm not cut out for this," said Callie rhetorically, opening the door for me to erase my indifference and comfort her.

"Probably not," I said.

Color and emotion returned to her face. "Motherfucker."

"If you're unhappy then quit. Nothing's keeping you in Moldova."

"I won't have a job. I don't want to live with my parents."

"Then stop complaining. Move or quit or shut the hell up. No one cares."

"Motherfucker."

"Your problems aren't special."

I left her to walk around the airport. Rarely do I have the self-awareness to know when I'm being an asshole. But I was pleased to have yelled at her. She might quit now and then be happy.

I returned to Callie with this simile: "It's like when you feel better after puking," I explained. "Don't hold it all in…"

"Shut the fuck up," she barked.

When the time came, we both got on the plane.

At the airport in Bucharest, a girl cradling a lamb approached Callie and asked her to pet the animal for good luck. After, the girl demanded a dollar. Callie refused. I looked around for people selling contraband cigarettes. Callie hailed the first taxi she saw and we both got in, leaving the girl and her lamb.

We decided on taking a train back to Moldova instead of a bus, and after that we didn't speak. On the ride back, the train paused at each station but never took on other passengers. Apparently, no one else was traveling to Moldova.

* * *

The trip seemed longer than the fourteen hours it took to reach Chisinau: stopping every few dozen kilometers in the hope of finding passengers at empty stations; switching tracks at the border to accommodate the irregular fit of the Soviet railroads; passing through the countryside at dawn; and, for a time, running parallel to a road on which a minibus carried morning commuters, the bus keeping pace with the train until slowing for pot holes and eventually falling behind out of view.

Callie and I stepped from the train into the frozen city and went separate ways without saying goodbye.

The minibus home reached Riscani well after dark. The bus driver I'd come to know on a first name basis, Vasia, offered to drop me closer to my apartment, but I knew it was out of his way and told him I felt like walking. Another man I recognized from the sports complex stopped his Lada to pick me up, but I waved him on. It wasn't cold and I wanted to stretch my legs before settling in. The bars were empty and dark. The policemen on their stoop nodded to me as they smoked, never pausing their conversations. Walking by, I could see the profile of Lenin's statue through the purple darkness.

As I approached the apartment block, walking uphill, I braced myself for the energy rush of Dima pouring a shot and Katya forcing food onto me. But as I walked up the stairs and rounded the last unlit corner, I saw no light trickling through the crack under the door. I fumbled with my key in the dark. After a moment of scraping the key against the lock a light turned on, the lock turned from the inside, and Dariya poked her head out the door. "Hi, Aaron," she said. She'd been sleeping. As I took my shoes off she walked into the kitchen and turned on the burner to heat some leftover kasha. "Where is everyone?" I asked. Dariya covered a small yawn with her hand. She looked different because she wasn't wearing make-up, her eyes smaller. "Still working," she said. "Christmas is busy time." She poured me tea and plopped two pickled tomatoes onto the pile of kasha. "Goodnight," she said. "Glad you returned."

Alone now in the kitchen, the tension in my mind washed away. The tomatoes broke apart when I stirred them into the kasha, turning the mixture a brownish-pink. I blew steam away from the tea. I finished my food and went to sleep relaxed and very happy.

The Museum of Atheism

Orthodox Christmas came in January. Dima and Katya lay prostrate on the unfolded divan, still wearing the Barcelona sweatshirts I'd given them three days before. Dariya wore her new sweatshirt also—red and yellow like Spain's flag with the number 7 thrown across the back. She read quietly in the chair after Dima had complained the TV volume was too much to handle. Both Dima and Katya had worked twenty-hour days for the past week in preparation for the strains Christmas brought to the baking world; Christmas Day itself was for bakers to relax.

I woke and joined them in the living room, slipping into the chair next to Dariya. I wore the bright red Soviet propaganda t-shirt the family had given me: *CCCP—Always Forward!* Everyone wished me a Merry Christmas; I spit the Russian words back at them and all seemed pleased. And then, suddenly, everyone in the room (except me) discussed my religion; I wasn't orthodox, they knew, so therefore a Baptist or a Catholic, like John F. Kennedy. I explained, as best I could, that my father's family descended from Hungarian Jews and my mother's from French Catholics. Dima and Katya repeated old stories of hard working Jews that had lived in Riscani years ago before emigrating to Israel; they talked of President John F. Kennedy, a man they seemed to associate with religion even more than the Pope.

"But can Aaron go with me?" asked Dariya.

"It should be fine," said Dima. "Just don't let him touch anything."

"Go where?" I asked.

"Yes, don't let him touch anything," agreed Katya. "And take his hat off at the right time."

"Go where?" I repeated.

"To Church," said Dariya. "Go put on better clothes."

* * *

What had changed in Riscani since the fall of the Soviet Union? A history text would mention the collapse of the farming collective, the breakdown of local government that led to widespread corruption, perhaps the cutting of the trade pathways that provided markets for the locally manufactured goods—cheese, wine and perfumes. In Moldova, I observed the effects of Soviet collapse every day, but only understood the fragments of disrupted life as they affected my new family. Dima spoke frequently over vodka shots of longer workdays and fewer vacations; a decade had passed since he'd relaxed by the sea in Odessa. Katya complained about the value of the family's bread decreasing slowly every year; soon the people would expect bakers to give it away for free. And Dariya worried, with reason, that her education was far inferior to the quality of the common village schools her parents had passed through decades earlier.

But gloom did not permeate everything; the collapse had destroyed the compulsion to worship the state. Riscani now had a proper church—a gray, sloping, Orthodox Church—situated on the path leading to the bar on the lake. This church had been constructed before WWII. It had survived that conflict, only to be stripped of its icons, murals, priest, and renamed "The Museum of Atheism" during its time in the hands of the Soviet Union. Now the church had taken back its name.

To this church, Dariya took me to worship.

* * *

Dariya took off her Spain football sweatshirt and put on a wool sweater that hid her breasts. She borrowed a flat-soled pair of Katya's shoes and wrapped a red shawl around her hair. Dima and Katya inspected her from their positions in bed, giving her tips as she dressed on how to look pious. They argued briefly about make-up, resulting in Dariya agreeing to forgo eyeliner.

Snow had fallen the previous night, but none had collected. The cold had now set in and most predicted it would last until June. The only people on the back streets of Riscani all walked in the same direction, toward the lake; all kept their hands in their pockets and elbows pressed against their sides, chins tucked to protect the eyes from the wind, frozen breath clouds exiting downward. I'd kept my vision on the heels of a man in front of me, and when he continued past the church, Dariya took my arm to correct my path and guide me toward the church gates. She gave two lei to a Roma boy with his hands cupped at the entrance. A line extended out the door, and I realized then that I'd be standing the entire time during this ceremony.

Before we entered the church Dariya turned to me and said, "Take off your hat."

"I know," I said.

Dariya brushed her hand over a wandering patch of my hair and patted down the rest. I hadn't fully appreciated Dariya's love for the Orthodox Church until this moment in the crowded antechamber. Dariya, the youngest in the family, the baby without Soviet memories, was the only one to publicly express her faith. She carried laminated saint cards in her purse, and she passed her hands over her chest to form a cross whenever we encountered shrines while walking, afterward kissing her thumb.

Inside, the space resembled an old school house suitable for twenty children. The warmth of the interior came from the parishioners. Fifty people stood together on a collection of thin carpets over wooden floorboards. There were no chairs. Dariya stood with me for the first half hour, splitting her attention equally between the priest and me, and then worked her way through the clustered, big-boned, wool-draped worshippers to the front, where other members of the choir had collected.

A moment later, an altar boy walked through the congregation using both hands to carry a large candle. The priest followed him, swinging a brass cauldron that puffed smoke. A second altar boy trailed behind the priest with another candle. The crowd parted to accommodate the priest, as they hadn't for Dariya. They turned in place as flowers following the sun, never letting him see their backs. He spoke his chants in a booming voice in a language I didn't recognize; it seemed ancient, a mix of Russian and Latin. Women held hands up as he passed as though to feel the cloth of his white gown, though no one actually touched him. As he passed by, we briefly made eye contact, and in that moment I was certain he knew who I was; his eyes changed to express recognition, surprised and friendly. He continued his round, never interrupting his chant.

I unzipped my coat and found a place where I could stand away from the overwhelming heat. I shifted my weight from leg to leg. The language of the priest's chanting doubled back on itself and became a repetition. Women and men took turns kissing portraits of the saints framed in gold on the wall.

Three hours passed. The priest made several passes. Worshippers had come and gone, but most had stayed the duration as I had.

At the end, when the chanting stopped, everyone formed a line and took turns kissing a large silver cross the priest extended from his hand. I observed from the back as the priest blessed Dariya and she kissed the cross.

The ceremony ended.

All the saints on the walls had been kissed, but people remained because the priest had not yet removed his tall, white hat. He waved from his pulpit; someone had forgotten something. He waved to a person at the back door. I turned and saw several worshippers frozen in place, pointing among themselves, not sure which person he was trying to reach. Finally, he sent the second altar boy to the back. The boy pointed to each parishioner, passing from one to another, waiting for the priest to nod his head. The priest finally waved the boy back and whispered something into his ear; then the boy came directly to me.

"American," he said. "The priest wants to bless you."

I looked to the priest and pointed to my chest.

"Yes," he mouthed. "*You.*"

Everyone watched as I approached. The priest put his hand over his heart and bowed once I arrived; I mimicked him. He smiled. He knew the words he wished to speak, but didn't wish to waste them on deaf ears. He pulled the altar boy by the sleeve and asked him to translate. The boy protested, "You know I don't speak English well, Papa." Dariya rescued this boy by saying, "Speak to him. He understands Russian." The priest smiled again. Sweat beaded on his forehead from the physical exertion of his service. In a voice heavily accented with Romanian, the priest thanked me for worshiping, for respecting other traditions, for taking advantage of the brotherhood of Christianity.

A murmur filled the room behind me: "*Katólik*," they said. "The American is *katolícheski.*" Then the churchgoers stood without making noise, perhaps not even breathing, as the priest talked with the American.

"I've wanted to tell you for quite some time," he began. "I really like your beard."

This was a joke; people laughed.

"Your son is a strong athlete," I said. "He seems a hard worker."

He smiled broadly and grabbed my shoulder. He said something completely unintelligible, but in quite a flattering tone. After an awkward silence it seemed he wanted a response, so in polite, formal Russian I said, "Right back at you."

He scrunched his eyebrows together. Someone in the background stifled a giggle.

"Do you know what I just said?" he asked.

I admitted that I did not.

"I just blessed you," he said. "You can't bless me back."

No longer able to contain their laughter, a pair of women ran out of the church, surely to inform the world.

"May health and happiness pursue you," said the priest. "Traveling is good. One learns that God's children fight over similarities, not differences." I looked at the silver cross in his right hand, held against his breast. He followed my eyes and then extended the cross. I kissed it at the bottom, where other lips hadn't left marks, and the priest smiled. He snapped his fingers and the altar boy gave me a bag with Christmas candies, biscuits and a small orange. The priest placed his hand over his heart and bowed a final time. I felt a hand take my elbow; Dariya motioned for me to follow her to the door.

"I'll see you tomorrow," she said. "I will stay with the choir and sing until dawn."

We'd arrived just before eleven and now it was just past two in the afternoon.

"It's a tradition," she explained in English.

The priest waved goodbye from his pulpit, and I instinctively, stupidly, flashed him a peace sign. He mimicked me, and he and many others laughed.

Outside blood returned to my legs with every step. The wind had relaxed enough for me to raise my chin and look forward. Instead of returning home directly, I walked to the lake. The Roma boy who'd begged two lei from Dariya stood far down on the sloping dam near the artificial shoreline, spitting sunflower seeds into the water. The wind picked up. I buried my head down into my coat and returned home.

As I entered, Dima spoke in a loud voice to Katya. They were both in the kitchen. He wanted me to hear but pretended I wasn't there.

"Did you hear the joke about the priest and the American?" he asked Katya. She started laughing and pressed a dishrag against her mouth.

"*Bless you, my son*, says the priest."

Katya's forehead turned purple.

"*No father*, interrupts the American. *Bless you!*"

Dima pounded the table with his flat palm as he erupted with laughter. Katya removed the dishrag from her mouth and joined him at full volume.

How could they have known so quickly?

I entered the kitchen smiling and accepted a plate of jam pastries. We paused in thought, shots of vodka elevated in our hands, as we struggled to think of something new we'd never before toasted. After a moment we settled, like always, on health and happiness.

A Return

A cold front descended over Riscani. I wore a wool hat at night and I slept in my sleeping bag under the normal winter blankets. Unwilling to splash my face with cold water in the mornings, I stopped shaving completely; a neatly trimmed goatee turned into a full beard. Stories of cold-related school cancellations passed from volunteer to volunteer, but Riscani continued on as normal. I returned to work on the Monday after Orthodox Christmas.

The cold had also brought a communal flu to Riscani. The day before I returned to school, a Sunday, Katya came home early from the bazaar; everyone was sick, no one was in the market to buy, and after a few hours no one was there to sell either. Dima had only left bed that morning to call and tell Vova he wasn't coming to the bakery.

On school morning, I woke to find my breakfast already on the table; Katya had prepared noodles and cheese the night before so that she wouldn't have to wake up. She'd stayed up late at night with a headache brought on by the cold. Dima was too weak to work and only wanted cups of tea, no food. Dariya was coughing through the walls and wouldn't go to school the entire week. I, too, had a cough. My throat hurt, but I'd managed to keep my energy by eating all the food Katya gave me. Instant coffee and pickled tomatoes must have also helped me—such large quantities of daily intake would have had a negative effect otherwise.

Light snow had fallen during the night. I slipped when crossing the street and walking up the driveway to the school. The windows of the lyceum were empty. No round faces filled the frosted square panes, no tiny hands tapped the glass to get my attention. I kicked the snow from the tread of my boots on the doorstep of the school. A bucket of water was there to clean the boots properly, but it was clean water, not yet polluted, and that seemed to me permission not to use it.

My classroom was locked, and when I found the cleaning lady who kept the keys she shook her head. "I was given the news," she said. "Mr. Aaron will not be back after winter recess."

"No. I am here."

"On good authority—reliable news that you had gone to work in Spain."

"No."

"Well," she said, opening my door. "Life can be difficult. I'm sorry Spain didn't work out."

I thanked the woman and assured her I'd be in Riscani for the next year and a half. "Don't be negative," she said. "Better work will find you, I'm sure of it. You're a nice man. If Spain didn't work, you should try Italy. I have a neighbor in Italy. People find work in Italy, you'll see."

"Thank you."

"Yes, your Russian is getting much better," she said. "I understand you now."

Nobody showed up for my first class of ninth grade students. I read *A Day in the Life of Ivan Denisovich*. I finished the book within the hour, sharing the bittersweet smile readers have made for years as Ivan recounts his many blessings before he falls asleep.

Two pupils appeared for the second period fifth grade class. They burst into the room in full winter-wear and screamed with disappointment once realizing their English teacher had come in to work. These two had been forced to attend school by relatives who didn't want to watch them for the day. "Can we draw?" they pleaded.

"You may draw," I said.

They cheered.

"Just be quiet," I said.

"No problem, Mr. Aaron. But what should we draw?"

"Anything."

"Tell us something! We must know what to draw!"

"The world."

"Something smaller!"

"Moldova."

"More interesting!"

"Jean-Claude Van Damme."

"Yeeeeeeeeeeeeeeeeeeeeesssssssssssssssssssss!!!!!!!!!!!!!"

The boys calmed into artistic concentration once I ripped two pages from my lesson plan notebook and gave them each a pen. They'd come to school without any materials.

The two boys, Oleg and Pavel, remained occupied by fights and punches and other scenes from dubbed karate movies they'd seen on Russian TV. Artistic inspiration abandoned them after they'd recreated the climactic scene from *Bloodsport* with black-pen stick figures; they'd used my red correcting pen for the blood spots.

The bell rang, but the boys refused to leave. A single pupil appeared for my final eighth grade class. She stopped in place a step after entering the room. "Oh," she said. "You returned."

"I did."

She nodded and said again, "You returned." She crooked her neck to inspect the boys' drawings before walking to the back row and taking her normal seat. A minute later, before the second bell rang to start class, she asked if she could go home.

"No problem," I said in English.

"I don't know what that means," she said. "Talk Russian."

"He said no problem," said Oleg and Pavel, still drawing.

The girl's cheeks turned red. She'd sat in the back of my class for the entire first semester without talking; she'd skipped class nearly every day, but had decided to come to this one, thinking I'd be away. She swore at the boys to mind their business, then thanked me and left.

Twenty minutes later, a teacher barged into the classroom—the Romanian language teacher with hair dyed like fire. She screamed at the boys because they'd skipped her class to stay with me. They picked up the pens when she came in and pretended to keep drawing, never making eye contact.

"No problem," I said in Russian. "Take them now."

"No," she said. "I'm cold. Keep them while I go home." And then she left before I could say anything.

"Cow," said one of the boys—I didn't see which one.

"Go home," I said. "Or go play in the snow."

A Victory

A little more snow collected each night. In between the apartment block and the school, I walked on the snow-covered grass as other pedestrians did, avoiding the slick road surfaces. My class rosters slowly returned to normal. Each day more kids appeared at their desks wrapped in jackets and scarves and wool hats. Most took off a single glove in order to write, but others kept both on, refusing to attempt more than listening.

Ana and Nastia of the eighth grade asked politely how my trip had gone, but they had no interest in learning about my experiences or Spanish culture; they wanted to know how the stylish women of Spain dressed. I recalled the Latin American prostitutes that lined the road leading home each night.

"Very similar to Moldovan women," I said.

All the girls in the class smiled.

Once the fifth grade returned to full strength, we continued with our lessons. Oleg and Pavel disappeared in the back of the classroom; they now drew pictures every day from memories of American movies. As the others completed group work, I walked over to inspect their artwork.

"Write some words," I suggested. "Say something on the paper in English."

"We don't speak English."

"That's how you learn. Start with single words."

Oleg continued drawing blood splotches as though he hadn't heard me. Pavel stared at me blankly.

"What words do you know?" I asked Pavel. He cocked his head to the side and looked at the ceiling. "Shit," he finally said. "Fucker."

"Do you know what that means?"

Pavel demonstrated his knowledge by pretending to defecate in his hand, then throwing the imaginary shit; he didn't know how to play-act *fucker*, and wanted me to tell him what it meant.

"No, no, no," I said.

"So it's bad?"

"Listen to undubbed movies on TV more carefully next time. You'll learn something."

"Tell me what *fucker* means!"

"Wait for it on TV."

Pavel pestered me and screamed until a classmate, Dasha, came to the back waving her punching hand. After chasing him through the room, she finally caught him and knocked him on the head until he agreed to stop bothering me.

"Pavel is asshole, Mr. Aaron," said Dasha in English.

"Where did you learn that word?" I asked. Dasha sensed she was close to trouble and tensed. "In the dictionary," she said. "Is it a bad word?"

"Yes."

"Well, not in Russian."

"So, Dasha, it's okay if I call you a *zalupa*?"

The class exploded with laughter.

"Mr. Aaron!" screamed Dasha. "That's a bad word! Tell me immediately who told you that word!"

(Dariya had begrudgingly taught me the word during a lesson in my room. It translated roughly into English as *dickhead*.)

"No," I said. "You'll punch them."

"Yes, I will."

"Enough punching," I said. "And enough swearing."

"You watch it!" said Dasha, smiling as she punched her left palm with her little fist. "I'm the enforcer here."

"How old are you, again?" I asked.

She mumbled in Russian.

"In English!" I said.

"I ten years."

I awarded Dasha with a daily grade of 9 out of 10. "Good use of English today," I told her. "You lost a point for intimidation." She punched her palm, threatening me in jest, until the bell rang.

*　*　*

After my lesson with the swearing fifth graders, I needed to kill an hour until my final class started. I was walking toward the teachers' room to watch the Russian Victory Network when a familiar sound caught my attention; a hollow ping echoed through the corridors. Groups of older students huddled together, collectively focused on two boys yelling at each other. At first I thought it was a fight. The crowd parted for me—I got pats on the back from older boys who felt like they knew me, even though I didn't know them—and I emerged in the center of the crowd to find a table tennis match in progress. The table had been pushed into the hallway. Sasha, the boy who'd taken me to play basketball, was challenging a boy with an unlit cigarette dangling from his lips. They paused the match to greet me.

"You know sport?" asked Sasha, pointing to the table with his paddle.

I nodded.

"Then I play you next."

An excited "oooooooooh" went through the crowd. The boy with the dangling cigarette handed me his paddle and said to Sasha, "Play him now." He stood to the side, wanting to watch me hit a couple of strokes before he went outside to smoke with his friends, unlit cigarettes tucked behind their ears like pencils. Sasha lobbed the ball over gently, as he would begin a match with a toddler. I snatched it from the air with my hand and tossed it back to him. "Serve it for real," I said. A few boys laughed. "Don't make Sasha angry, Mr. Aaron," said a boy. Evidently Sasha was the best player at the school. He served it with spin and I smashed it back in his face. Twenty boys screamed, "AAAAGGH!" with top outside voices. Sasha smiled. "I think we should play for real." I nodded. The other boys made a production of putting their cigarettes back into the pack. The bell rang for the next class. "Don't you all have somewhere to be?" I asked. "We're not going anywhere," said Sasha.

I took off my coat. Sasha stretched. Our cold breath hung in the air.

"Your serve, Sasha. I insist."

Sasha was indeed talented. He knew how to put spin on the ball. His quick reaction time was admirable. He made adjustments, got me off balance. We played closely, exchanging points back and forth. We'd nearly finished the match when a booming voice yelled, "What the hell is this!" I couldn't see the man who was screaming—he was shorter than the boys—until they parted for him.

Sergei Stepanovich had the greatest seniority of any teacher in the school, which meant he'd been around for everything I knew about the Cold War. From his home in Riscani, he'd experienced the Cuban Missile Crisis, Khrushchev pounding his shoe on the UN podium, the Olympic Basketball game, the Miracle on Ice, the Berlin Wall—all the way through Glasnost and Perestroika. He slurred his speech as though he were always drunk, especially when yelling. He taught either physics or physical education, I never confirmed which. All I knew for sure was that he'd been in the Red Army; every time we spoke, both of us with cognac breath, he mentioned Afghanistan.

The boys, including Sasha, were skipping his class in favor of this table tennis contest. "What the hell is this!" he repeated, continuing to scream at the boys while he came over to shake my hand.

"I challenged Mr. Aaron," said Sasha. "And I couldn't leave until we finished." Sergei Stepanovich nodded his approval to Sasha. "And the rest of you? The break isn't long enough for you to smoke?"

"Mr. Aaron is good," said a boy.

Sergei Stepanovich's cheeks regained color. Strain left his face. He asked the score and then nodded. "Give me the paddle, Sashka." Sasha reluctantly surrendered his paddle. "We play match," Sergei Stepanovich said to me, holding the ball in the air between two fingers so that it wouldn't surprise me.

"Warm up first," I said.

"No need. I played in Army." He pointed to the table with his paddle. "More playing than fighting." He laughed.

Sergei Stepanovich didn't offer to let me serve.

Although the corridors were frigid, we both perspired. Two white, slicked-down streaks above his ears were all that remained of hair on Sergei Stepanovich's head; sweat held them in place. He needed a rag to mop his brow, but only had the wool sleeve of his sweater. He jerked his arms and breathed deeply and coughed cigarette-stained phlegm and I thought he might lose consciousness at any moment. Finally, I beat him. The score wasn't close.

While Sergei Stepanovich shook my hand in defeat, he grabbed my arm with his free hand to hold me in place and said, "This is serious, boys. Go and fetch Andrei Vasilyavich."

Two boys sprinted down the corridor in search of the technology teacher. The rest murmured, "*Patron, Patron, Patron.*"

"Get ready," Sasha told me. "*Patron* is serious about table tennis."

"Is Andrei Vasilyavich better than you?" I asked.

Sasha hesitated. "*Patron* is the best player in Riscani."

In the distance, somewhere inside the school, small children screamed. The whole school must have heard them. The din grew louder and soon paired with the shuffling footsteps of a crowd. A group of little children led by a full-grown giant emerged at the end of the corridor.

Andrei Vasilyavich, the *Patron*, shook Sergei Stepanovich's hand and leaned close for the old man to whisper into his ear. "Play with care," said Sergei Stepanovich. "The American knows how to win." Andrei Vasilyavich nodded silently. He walked around the table to shake my hand. "So nice to find another man who plays tennis," he said. "Shall we?"

I nodded.

In this moment I considered the Russian Victory Network. A month ago I'd watched a Soviet woman destroy her Baltic completion in table tennis. A brass band played when she won. Dozens of pupils circled us now in the corridor. Andrei Vasilyavich would feel pride when he beat me.

Sergei Stepanovich yelled at the older boys for passing money; the old man grew especially angry because the first bets had gone against Andrei Vasilyavich. "Save your money for cigarettes, you hooligans!"

Andrei Vasilyavich kept his coat on. We volleyed for several seconds without spectacular play on either side, until finally Andrei Vasilyavich smacked one into the corner, beyond my reach, and the crowd began cheering.

"*Maladits*, Andrei," said Sergei Stepanovich. "Well done."

I unbuttoned my collar, and then took off the over shirt entirely. A chill swept over me and then went away. My breath was still visible, but I was also sweating.

"Look!" said Sasha. "Look at his shirt!" A spontaneous chant erupted in Russian. The small children from Andrei Vasilyavich's class joined in, and in time so did Sergei Stepanovich. Everyone knew the words to the chant. Under my over shirt I'd worn the Soviet propaganda t-shirt my host family had gifted me for Orthodox Christmas. It was a red shirt with a picture of a sickle and hammer and the letters CCCP.

Andrei Vasilyavich took off his coat. He took off his tie as well and then rolled up his sleeves. He was the type of overweight man without wrinkles, who'd been large all his life and knew how to move his body. He'd have been a lineman if he played football in America. "My serve," he said.

Sergei Stepanovich no longer cared that the students passed money. He pulled a lit cigarette from a boy's mouth and told him to take it outside. "I'm not missing this," said the boy. Sergei Stepanovich took a drag off the cigarette and passed it back to the boy.

I had my hands full. Andrei Vasilyavich, the *Patron*, was trying to intimidate me with his size; he threw his stomach at the table with extreme speed, only to love-tap the ball over the net once I'd backed up. "Americans don't learn to play correctly, I think," said Andrei Vasilyavich. "They are not students of the game. Not serious students, at least."

I nodded.

"Do you know what your shirt means?" he asked me.

I nodded.

"Tell me, then."

"It's an antique. The colors are pretty."

He laughed and then tried to force his next serve down my throat. My spin serve completely unnerved him; the ball hit off one side of the table and then moved directly into his stomach; it went straight up into the air and out of play if he got the paddle onto it at all. When he backed up to defend my overhead smash, I'd softly tap the ball over the net. "Nice," he said, standing by the window ten feet away.

Sergei Stepanovich offered his colleague advice. "Who are you talking to, Old Man?" said Andrei Vasilyavich. "Certainly not me."

The little children laughed. The older pupils were now silent, as the stress of losing cigarette money dawned on them. Sasha encouraged me in a quiet voice, not wanting Andrei Vasilyavich to know he'd bet against him.

We were close to the end. We'd played for a half an hour without declaring a winner. Sergei Stepanovich had kept the score.

"Match point," said Sergei Stepanovich.

"Finally," said Andrei Vasilyavich.

Sergei smiled. "Mr. Aaron only needs one more point."

Andrei Vasilyavich stared daggers across the table. He waved his hand for me to hurry up with my serve. I bounced the ball over softly, without spin, and—attempting to kill me, I think—Andrei Vasilyavich missed his spike and smashed the ball into the net.

The match was over. I stood up, correcting my posture, but didn't put the paddle down, sensing I might need something in my hand to defend myself. The *Patron* came around the table and shook my hand.

Children cheered. Money changed hands. Boys went outside to smoke before the final class of the day. Sergei Stepanovich and Andrei Vasilyavich motioned for me to join the smokers outside also. Andrei Vasilyavich patted me on the back. "*Maladits*," he said, offering me a cigarette. "You play very nicely." I thanked him and declined his cigarette. We stood outside in the cold until the bell rang. As the pupils departed, some older boys began chanting:

"USA...USA...UUUUUU...SSSSSSSSS...AAAAAAA!!!"

Sergei Stepanovich and Andrei Vasilyavich both shook my hand before I went back inside, and then saluted me as if all present were soldiers.

Aaron Richardovich

I arrived late to my last class of ninth graders. The room was empty and cold. All the students had gone home.

Instead of going home directly, I walked toward the bar on the lake. But the wind was too fierce. I stopped into a small shop halfway, across from the town hall. The door caught the wind and I had to fight to close it. The lady behind the counter said, "By God, close the damn door." I nodded to her instead of voicing any apology. The woman didn't sell the type of Ukrainian beer I wanted. Her eyesight was bad, otherwise she would have known who I was and offered me something expensive. I walked around the small space, her weak gaze following my every move. I grabbed a bag of potato chips, couldn't tell what flavor they were, and replaced them on the shelf. "What, by God, do you want?" the woman said.

"I want vodka."

"Of course," said the woman.

"You're very kind," I said. "I don't speak very well. You're kind to understand me."

"Oh," gasped the woman. "You're not from here! The American? And you speak so well! Yes, well done! *Maladits!*"

"Thank you." I bowed my head slightly and pointed at the rows of alcohol behind her. I purchased a ten-lei bottle of vodka.

Now all smiles, the lady gave me a plastic baggie filled with biscuits so that I wouldn't drink on an empty stomach. I thanked her a second time and she said I was the nicest man to ever come by her shop for vodka. "Return soon," she said.

"I've got all the vodka you need." And she didn't complain when the cold rushed in as I opened the door to leave.

My idea then was to wait for Dima; he'd return from work after dark, we'd eat noodles and sip vodka while playing cards.

Unspent energy from the table tennis competition pulsed through me. I was happy and would have walked every street in the city twice if it weren't so cold. The roads and pathways through loose soil were slick with ice and I couldn't walk as quickly as I wished. Once home, I found the apartment empty. I made tea in my electric kettle and read a novel—the same thing I did every day in the winter until someone came home. The small library of books I'd taken from headquarters contained travel books, story collections and poetry, but my reading felt unproductive unless I was consuming great, thick novels. If I were to be trapped inside the apartment for the duration of winter, then at least by spring I'd have conquered writers like Tolstoy and Dostoyevsky.

The boredom of another afternoon trapped inside the apartment by winter dulled the excitable memories of the table tennis victory. But then I untied the bag of biscuits from the shopkeeper and ate them with my tea. Soon, I felt immense happiness. Thank God for these biscuits! For adding a wrinkle, a variety however small, into this monotony. I decided to make these biscuits part of my routine until spring; I'd indulge any happiness to keep the winter from bringing my spirits down.

I began reading an English translation of *Anna Karenina* at nightfall on the day of my table tennis victory and wouldn't finish the novel for another three months.

* * *

By the time Dima and Katya returned from the bakery, I was ready to begin toasting. After finishing my tea—sitting in my room, cold and bored, reading about cold and bored Tolstoy characters who talked philosophically about existential cold and boredom—it had taken much willpower to keep from opening the vodka bottle.

Dima's greeting indicated his mood. If it had been a good day, he would kick his shoes off and walk directly into my room to see how the students had treated me that day; if he'd overworked himself, he'd grumble a brief hello to me and walk into the living room to see if Dariya had finished her homework and kick her off the couch so that he could crash in front of the TV and watch Moscow news.

The door opened and heavy feet entered. Two pairs of boots hit the floor. Katya said, "Oh what a day," and Dima didn't say anything. I emerged from my room to greet them and they both waved to me. "Quite a day," said Dima. I'd never seen him wearier. His eyes were puffy and sunken. His movements to extricate himself from the wrappings of wool and cotton were labored and slow. Finally, he was down to his undershirt. He sat on the bench by the door to take off his socks. Katya went into the kitchen and lit the stove. "Come, Aaron," said Dima. He motioned toward the living room. I held the vodka bottle behind my back. We each settled into a chair. "We'll eat later," Dima said through the walls into the kitchen. "Come rest, Katya."

"It's already on the plate," she said.

Dima nodded to me and motioned toward the kitchen as though to say, "Quite a woman we've got here."

We stood, and then entered the kitchen and took our seats next to Katya. Each plate on the card table had a pepper filled with rice and little bits of pork. Katya asked if we wanted tea or coffee. "If it's okay," I interrupted, placing the vodka bottle on the table. "Oopah!" said Dima. Katya said she'd take *choo-choots*, indicating what that meant by measuring a small distance in the air between her thumb and index finger.

Katya washed out three shot glasses in the bucket of water by the sink. Water wasn't running from the faucet that day. She placed the three glasses on the table and insisted I be the one to pour. We drank, and then we all cringed and smiled at the same time. It was stronger than normal vodka, closer to consumable paint thinner than tasty alcohol. Katya flicked her middle finger against her neck and laughed. Then Dima did the same, flicking under his jaw in the same motion. They both laughed.

"What does that mean?" I asked.

"This," said Katya, flicking her neck to demonstrate, "means DRUNK."

We all laughed as I poured another shot. Katya protested and complained and still drank the shot. She emptied the few remaining drops from her glass into the sink. "No more," she said. "I feel a headache."

We ate the peppers and then retired to the living room to watch the Moscow news. Katya fell asleep instantly on the couch.

Dima and I sat back in the sofa chairs and would have fallen asleep had the news not reported about Americans in Afghanistan. "You don't like wars," said Dima, more as a statement than a question. "You're in Moldova instead of in the army."

I nodded.

"I was lucky to avoid Afghanistan. As are you, Aaron. They sent me to Germany instead."

"I remember you saying that."

"And I remember you said something about your father."

"He was in Germany instead of Vietnam. They sent him to Germany instead."

"And what did your father do for the American Army in Germany?"

I struggled to say anything and Dima assumed I didn't know the right words in Russian. "Was he a mechanic or a driver?" prompted Dima. "Did he work with radios or maps?"

"He's not allowed to say what he did," I said. "He's never told me. But I think he listened to Germans over the radio. Or maybe listened over telephones."

"That's like me!" said Dima, erupting from his vodka-induced calm.

"You worked with radios?"

"The secrecy. No one is allowed to know what I did. I signed privacy statements. My work must always remain a secret."

"Same with my dad.'"

"Big coincidence," said Dima.

I remembered back to the first time I'd tried to tell Dima about my father in Germany, back when I hadn't spoken Russian well and Dima hadn't believed what I was saying.

"What is your father's name?" asked Dima.

"Richard."

Dima struggled to repeat the unfamiliar name. *Reee-chard.*

"Then your name is *Aaron Richardovich*," he said.

I shook my head. "My second name is Anthony—my name is Aaron Anthony."

"No," said Dima. "Here your name is Aaron Richardovich."

We settled into watching the news. The other stories provoked no further conversations. When I stood to return to my room, Dima stood as well. He shook my hand and wished me a good night in addition to health and happiness. At that moment Dariya returned home, well after curfew. She stood in the doorway as though waiting for permission to enter.

Dima was too happy to yell. He told her to close the door before all the cold came inside. He went to the kitchen to pour everyone a shot. "I don't drink," she protested as she unzipped her knee-high boots. "You know this, Papa." In a whisper she asked if Dima had gotten me drunk. I shrugged my shoulders. I flicked the side of my neck with my middle finger and Dariya laughed. Dima returned and we all toasted to health and happiness.

* * *

The next morning didn't feel very cold and I couldn't see my breath when I walked outside. The energy from the table tennis victory returned to me once I entered the school, and I felt tremendous American pride. In my classroom, I looked at the book pages for the day's lessons and decided to save them for another time. Instead, I would teach the *Star Spangled Banner*. If the students asked why they must learn America's National Anthem, I'd invent a holiday: America Day or American Excellence Day. Using chalk, I copied down the anthem lyrics by memory. They weren't perfect—a few words clearly invented—but they still matched the melody. I pinned a small American flag into the wood above the chalkboard.

The ninth grade students arrived and demanded to relax during the class period. Nobody wanted to work. The cold outside took away energy. "Fine," I said. "We'll sing instead." The girls in the class cheered and the boys put their heads down to begin sleeping. The girls scribbled the words on the board into their notebooks. My classroom was rarely as silent as it was in that moment. After the girls finished writing, Ana and Nastia demanded that I sing.

I nodded my head and stood. I coughed to clear my throat, and then the song came out naturally, as though it had been waiting to escape. The boys woke up. I sang loudly, but not very well. A girl clapped at a pause because she'd thought I'd finished. It surprised me that I knew all the lyrics. While singing, I'd instinctively corrected the mistakes I'd written on the board (fight, not night; glare, not flair).

All the kids clapped. I corrected the errors on the board and then asked for volunteers. I wanted singers.

"I know that song," said a boy, Edgar, from the back row. I was extremely surprised; not that he recognized the song, but that he'd spoken out in English. This boy had sat in the back all year and slept more often than worked. "It is America song," said Edgar. "From sports."

"Would you sing it for the class?" I asked.

Edgar hesitated and I offered him a perfect test grade. He counter-offered to sing from his seat for the grade, and I agreed to a quiz grade. After he stood I flinched. The way he stretched his shoulders back and arched his body, I could tell he was going to make some noise. I closed the door and waited for the boy to start screaming. Instead, he folded his hands over his breast bone and began singing deeply, in the manner of the choir I'd seen at the church at Christmas. He was slightly built, and struggled to imitate a man with a deeper voice. But he didn't sing the *Star Spangled Banner*. His words praised the motherland—Russia. "*Ro-si-ya! Ro-si-ya!*" he sang. "*Ro-si-ya! Ro-si-ya!*" and on and on.

A couple of the boys half-heartedly joined Edgar. Then all the girls joined in and the classroom felt like a pep-rally in Red Square.

At this moment of patriotism, Nadezhda entered the classroom, clearly drawn by the noise. The students stopped singing and stood when she entered. She sat them down with a wave of her hand. "What is this?" she asked me.

"He didn't know the anthem," said Ana.

"He taught us his America song," added Nastia. "And we taught him ours."

Nadezhda looked at the words I'd placed on the board and nodded her approval. "*Atlichna!*" she said. "Fantastic!"

Nadezhda turned her back on the students as if it were only she and I in the room, and asked if I had plans for the weekend, specifically Saturday from eight to noon.

"Regretfully, yes," I lied. "I'm expected in the capital."

A boy giggled, thinking I'd made a sex joke.

Nadezhda stared daggers at the boy, and then regretfully informed me that my presence was required in a professional capacity in Riscani at the Inter-lyceum Olympiad. Before hearing my response, she wished me a pleasant day with health and happiness.

Olympiad

On Saturday morning, the phone rang at the time Nadezhda was supposed to pick me up. Dariya answered and reported that Nadezhda didn't wish to talk to me, only to pass along the message that the Olympiad was postponed until the next morning.

"Thanks a lot," I said out loud. Dariya dutifully translated into Russian and passed along Nadezhda's well wishes in return. Neither Dariya nor Nadezhda understood sarcasm, and I made a mental note to teach it to my students in the spring.

So the following morning, Nadezhda met me outside the apartment block and led me to the Moldovan Lyceum. We walked uphill, through an unfamiliar section of town. As we approached the rival school Nadezhda told me, "Do not feel intimidation. Hold our ground. Make the Russian School a winner."

I had no idea what her ramblings meant, but students had informed me of the Olympiad's importance. Each year every school in the country competed in contests of Language Arts, Science and Mathematics to determine Moldova's top scholars. Teachers of winning pupils were also rewarded. The Russian School of Riscani, known regionally for subpar students, perennially lost to the rival Moldovan Lyceum up the hill. But this year the odds were in the Russians' favor, as I—Mr. Aaron, the town's foreign expert—would be the guest Olympiad judge.

Today's contest was in ecology, a subject of which I knew nothing. Regardless, the presentations would be in English and I was therefore the authority. The entire event transpired over a hectic two-hour period.

We arrived at the Moldovan Lyceum, a castle with narrow windows that had once been the residence of the town's founder. A legend stated the fortress had withstood an assault by raiding Turks. Once inside, I was introduced to the Moldovan half of the judging panel: a biology teacher from the Moldovan Lyceum and a Romanian language teacher from Mihaileni, one of the competing lyceums from a village within the district. Nadezhda and I were the other two panel members. The two Moldovan teachers knew Nadezhda and hated her. I did not know where this animosity came from, but I witnessed it in the side-whisper conversations and the politely sterile manner in which they greeted her by her full name, Nadezhda Ivanovna.

The competition began; presentations would precede a multiple-choice test.

The Moldovan team presented first, speaking about the need to use conservationist principles when building houses. I thought the presentation very fair. The two girls presenting were polite when they addressed the panel, spoke clearly, and despite repeating each sentence for effect, made some decent points about man's impact on nature.

The Russian team went next, speaking about the need to clean apartments regularly unless one wanted to kill his family with the poisons that the human body produced every day and shed into the environment. I left the presentation unconvinced of the scientific rigor of the team's investigations, but they'd presented with loud voices and had clearly convinced Nadezhda of their superior ecological intellect. She poked me in the ribs and nodded as though to say, *winners*.

The village team from Mihaileni went last, presenting about the need to protect well water. Their presentation was exceptionally well researched; however, I felt they'd relied too heavily on the bilingual dictionary. I audibly groaned when a young girl used the phrases "excrement cocktail" and "repeated, daily consumption" in the same sentence. Nadezhda—an English teacher herself—found no objection in that usage. And though I'd expected as much, I then knew for certain that the other Moldovan panelists did not speak English, and were merely grading these presentations on the volume and emotional conviction of the speakers.

The judging panel stepped outside during the multiple-choice test. The biology teacher from the Moldovan Lyceum tried to speak to me in Romanian so that Nadezhda wouldn't understand the conversation. "He only speaks Russian," said Nadezhda. "He speaks only modern languages."

The biology teacher absorbed that insult and quietly told me in a weak Russian voice that a neighbor she respected greatly had immigrated to the state called *Mareland*. She asked about the climate and the people and wanted to know, ballpark figure, how much this neighbor was making per month as a street sweeper in Baltimore.

The classroom door swung open and the moderator waved for us to come back inside.

"Time to grade the exams," said Nadezhda. "I think victory for the Russian school."

We sat at the tables where the pupils had deposited their completed exams. The village teacher was given her team's papers to grade, the Moldovan biology teacher was given her team's exam, and I was given the task of correcting the Russian team's papers. "This is not correct," said Nadezhda. "I will grade the tests of the Russian school." She took the papers from me.

The moderator, a secretary from the mayor's office, shook her head.

"It's my decision," she said, taking the stack of papers from Nadezhda and giving them back to me. "Now let the foreign expert alone to do his work."

I'd heard the moderator speak Romanian with the other judges and knew she wasn't Russian. Nadezhda didn't trust her.

"Okay," said Nadezhda. "I'll just sit in the corner."

"There's a good bench outside in the corridor," said the moderator.

Nadezhda smiled, and as she walked outside she whispered into my ear, "Let's try to help our team win." She slipped a blue pen into my pocket that I could use to fix any incorrect answer.

I grasped the red correcting pen and went to work. The moderator read off the answers and I marked the errors the Russian team had committed. They'd answered thirty of fifty questions correctly.

The biology teacher from the Moldovan Lyceum looked over at my stack of papers, which I angled so that she could get a better view.

"Oh, thank you," she said. "You're polite."

After viewing the Russian school's score, the woman then smiled and said to the moderator, "I think we can invite Nadezhda Ivanovna to rejoin us now. I want her to see this."

Both the village and Moldovan lyceum teams had outscored the Russians. Easily. Combined with the presentation marks, the Moldovans were victorious for the tenth year in a row, followed by the village team. The Russian School had finished a distant, embarrassing third place.

"How did it go?" asked Nadezhda, reentering the room. She looked at the scores written in chalk on the board; she covered her mouth and I thought she might vomit from humiliation. The biology teacher approached her and said, "No worries, Nadezhda Ivanovna. My kids were very good this year. Too intelligent to lose in district competition. I think they will score well nationally."

As the village panelist shook my hand, saying she was pleased to meet me, the moderator from the mayor's office leafed through the exams and said, "Everyone please wait."

Color still hadn't returned to Nadezhda's face. Her lips were purple.

"I do not agree with these results," said the moderator. The biology teacher swore in Romanian. The village teacher looked amused. Nadezhda took her first breath in several moments.

"Look here," said the moderator, placing the papers side by side on a desk. "I see two different shades of blue ink on this test." She was pointing at the test belonging to the Moldovan team. "And here also." She pointed to the test of the village team.

Everyone then looked at my test, which had no false markings.

"I must review these test grades myself," said the moderator. She held up three blue pens, as though anticipating the panelists' objections. "I know which marks are true. I distributed these three pens and watched the pupils write. I know which answers are true and which have been manipulated. You must all leave now," said the moderator. "I will announce the winner when I have finished."

We all waited in the hallway. Nadezhda smiled. The biology teacher began sweating and fanned herself with a paper. The village teacher shrugged her shoulders. The moderator emerged a few moments later and announced:

"Mihaileni has been deducted twenty points for test manipulation and has finished with seventy-two points. The Moldovan Lyceum of Riscani has been deducted twenty points for test manipulation and has finished with seventy-five points."

The biology teacher looked at me as though I'd punched her in the face.

"The Russian School of Riscani," finished the moderator, "has won the Ecology Olympiad with seventy-six points. Congratulations to the Russians."

The biology teacher screamed, "And what of their deductions!"

"None," said the moderator, pointing to me. "He didn't cheat."

Nadezhda ran from the castle cheering. Once outside, she wouldn't let me return home. "No," she said. "I demand that we celebrate with wine." I remember little else from that day. At her home she fed me pickles and pitchers of wine. I returned to consciousness the next morning at 3 a.m., fully clothed in my own bed. I thought hard and couldn't remember how I'd returned home. I vaguely recalled sipping wine in Nadezhda's living room while she scribbled notes onto a notepad. She was updating her résumé to include the Russian School's win in the Ecology Olympiad.

* * *

Nadezhda took the week off from school to celebrate the Olympiad victory, leaving her classes to me. So I inherited some of the older pupils. I tried to speak with them in English as much as I could, but inevitably the class would break into arm wrestling competitions, translations of pop songs stored on cell phones, and card games of *durak*. Each day I learned different ways to curse in Russian.

I pinned up the little American flag over the chalkboard and taught them the pledge of allegiance. "This is what Americans do every day," I told them.

"Before or after fucking?" asked a boy in English. Only one other girl in the class laughed. She translated and then everyone else laughed.

The week developed more slowly than most. The cold kept me in bed, inside my sleeping bag, longer in the mornings. I stayed at the school twice as long because of Nadezhda's absence. My stomach had turned sour on Monday, after I'd woken up with a wine hangover, and still hadn't cleared by Friday.

On Friday afternoon, alone in the apartment, I collapsed into bed for a nap. The phone rang and I didn't get up to answer. It died. Ten minutes later it rang a second time. Again, I let it die. It rang a third time minutes later, and it became a test of will not to answer it. It died after twenty rings. Ten minutes later, the phone rang again. I jumped out of bed, stormed over to the phone and screamed into the receiver in Russian, "What! What is your business!" A weak voice in Romanian asked for Aaron. It was Callie. We hadn't spoken since Barcelona.

"You forgot," she said.

"Forgot what?"

"The wedding. You promised to come and now they're asking for you. You remember? Of course you do. It's tomorrow. See you then."

She hung up.

Notes from the Wedding

1:00 p.m. – Arrive at the wedding house in Chismea. Uncountable number of people holding hands, dancing in circles on the frozen lawn. Bride in her dress emerges to applause. Callie remarks, "She doesn't normally look that pretty."

2:00 p.m. – Drink cognac shot with a man who'd been in Ireland for three years cutting marble. My Romanian is weak, so he's the only one I can talk to. Has a Romanian/Irish accent when speaking English. Claims the reception will last twelve hours.

3:00 p.m. – Callie explains her hostility. The groom still has a girlfriend in Ireland. Everyone knows.

6:00 p.m. – A friend of the bride pins a flower to my shirt, marking me with honor. Claim my seat in the reception hall—each table holds an entire fish, a platter of assorted salami, a bottle of vodka, another of cognac, and a pitcher of red wine.

6:01 p.m. – Begin drinking at our table with shots of vodka. We're at the "young" table. Other tables classified for "generic veteran," "women in wool sweaters," and "athletic pants okay."

6:30 p.m. – Swept into extended circle dance. Kick feet in wrong direction at wrong times.

7:00 p.m. – Chastised for taking a shot of vodka and not immediately consuming the forkful of fish held in front of my face.

7:50 p.m. – Extended relatives take turns shouting into a microphone, sharing memories of the bride and groom as children.

8:15 p.m. – Bride and groom placed on a chair and smothered with blankets. No explanation given.

8:30 p.m. – More circle dancing.

10:00 p.m. – Money announcements. Each member of the reception party is handed the microphone to announce the money they are gifting the newlyweds. Mayor of Chismea presents a thousand Euros. Callie scolds the groom in English. Her voice goes to a dark place, with deep Carolina tones, and even I can't understand everything she says. Before surrendering the microphone, Callie announces, "This is his third engagement, you know!" I clap.

12:00 a.m. – Enjoy renewed vigor in the ongoing circle dance as a new day begins.

12:45 a.m. – Callie sips from the drinks left by others on the table when they go to dance. She says something unintelligible to me. Her tone indicates strategy. I nod.

1:00 a.m. – Walk outside to get air with the groom and his friend with the Irish accent. The two speak in Romanian to each other. They smoke. I nod at everything as though I understand. When we reenter, someone takes a picture of the groom hugging me.

1:15 a.m. – A moment of silence for bride's father, who passed away in her childhood, killed by a drunk driver. Callie puts her head down on the table and is immediately shaken awake by the three closest people.

3:30 a.m. – Subdued circle dancing continues. The newlyweds are commanded to see how long they can sustain a kiss.

4:00 a.m. – Coffee served by the liter.

5:30 a.m. – Groom hugs me. The bride kisses my cheek. Callie is elsewhere.

6:30 a.m. – Home? Not home? Village. Drunk. A woman is crying in another room. Where am I? And how am I responsible?

* * *

I awoke in Callie's bed an hour after the last bus to Riscani left Chisinau. We'd slept long and hard and the sun was now descending; I'd need great luck to get back to Riscani in time for class the next morning. "I'll walk you to the bus," Callie offered. I told her to stay in bed. Everyone else in the house was still sleeping, so I exited without saying goodbye. I wouldn't see Callie again for a couple of months, shortly before she left the country.

Night had fallen in Chisinau by the time I arrived at the north autogara. The Riscani buses were gone; my only option was to get onto a bus to Balti and try to find transport to Riscani from there.

Two hours later, I stood outside in the cold at the abandoned Balti bus station. Panic didn't reach me until I'd spent an hour stamping my feet to keep warm. I didn't have enough money for a taxi or a room. Riscani felt more than an hour away. I carried only two hundred lei. I envisioned buying a liter of vodka and bribing my way into the graces of local drunks who'd started a fire. I imagined walking the city all night to keep warm until the first Riscani-bound bus pulled into the station at four in the morning; I'd be in Riscani by five, get home, drink tea, eat biscuits, and still get to class on time.

After two hours a bus finally arrived, going farther northward, but away from Riscani, to a town near the Ukrainian border called Lipcani. The driver offered to take me on the highway and drop me where the roads to Riscani and Lipcani diverged.

Only a handful of passengers were on the bus.

At the crossroads, I stepped off the warm bus back into the cold. But I wasn't alone. Another man stumbled off and walked toward me. "What do you think?" he asked me. "Shall we walk to Riscani or drive?"

By the way he walked, I could tell he was drunk. I wouldn't let him stand close enough for me to smell the vodka on his breath. Riscani was 5km to the west. The road was straight, I'd walked it before, but it was too cold now. In the fall, this route home had taken me over an hour. It was now 10 p.m. and the temperature well below zero.

"We shall walk," said the drunk man. "Follow me."

I questioned if driving were an option.

"You have money? We need fifty lei."

I nodded.

"Follow me."

I walked ten steps behind him as he approached the closed gas station some distance up the road. Over his shoulder, the man talked back to me. He could tell I was foreign and wondered if I spoke German. When we reached the station he began knocking on the windows and shouting, "Wake yourself! Wake yourself immediately!" A dog in close proximity began barking, and then suddenly a German Shepherd appeared and began tearing at the drunk man's pant leg. The man freed himself by kicking the dog in the head. A security guard grabbed the dog away by the collar. "Get away, drunks!" screamed the guard.

The drunk man looked down to his foot and casually remarked, "Oh, I'm bleeding." He turned to the guard and said, "May we use your telephone now?"

The drunk man went inside the dark gas station and reappeared a moment later. "Let's walk toward town," he said. "The taxi will cost less if we meet along the road."

During the walk the drunk man, Igor, asked questions about my shoes.

"Is it more comfortable to be rounded?"

Headlights appeared on the road. The driver was hesitant to allow Igor in his cab, but let us both in when I showed him the money we intended to pay. Igor seemed shocked that I lived so close to him—he lived next to the Russian school, across the street from my block—even though we'd covered that fact three times in conversation while walking.

Once home, the driver took my money and sped away.

I thanked Igor for helping me get home. He insisted that we go to a bar he knew close by.

"On the lake?" I asked.

"Yes!"

"Another time," I said, and I walked away.

Igor called after me, standing in place, calling out the name I'd given him—"Anton! Come drink!"—until I rounded the corner. I imagine he then forgot about me.

* * *

While I had been celebrating at the wedding in Chismea, all hell had broken loose in Riscani.

I'd missed the English Language Olympiad on Saturday morning. No one could agree on final scores, and old ladies with a combined thousand years of teaching experience nearly ended up in a brawl.

Acute disharmony surrounded the scoring of the tenth grade Olympians. In the end, as always, the main dispute was between the Russians and Moldovans of Riscani. The Russians had triumphed by a single point, and no one believed this to be possible. Others were certain Nadezhda had cheated. She explained herself by claiming that the American's presence at the school, as a foreign expert, had greatly increased the speaking and writing abilities of the entire school. No one could tell with certainty how greatly she was lying.

First thing Monday morning, I entered my classroom and knew something was peculiar; the fifth graders were in their seats, not shouting over cell phone music or wrestling each other to the floor. The school director sat in my desk chair. Nadezhda stood behind him.

"You've been summoned by the mayor," said the school director. "But first you must look over these writing samples." Several students' essay papers were spread over my desk.

"Here," said Nadezhda, pointing to the peculiar weave of a girl's script. "You must remember this style. We must not let them take our victory."

The boy from basketball, Sasha, entered the room and smiled when he saw me, swung his arm around to give me a handshake and a hug at the same time. "Sashka!" shouted Nadezhda. The boy stiffened up. "No foolishness. Take Mr. Aaron directly to the mayor."

"My classes..." I said.

"Will be monitored by Nadezhda Ivanovna," said the school director.

Nadezhda smiled at me. "You mustn't change the scores," she said.

Sasha and I left the room. "No foolishness, Sashka!" growled the school director as we walked away. "This is serious!"

* * *

So the mayor had called for me to clean up the mess of the English Olympiad.

I looked forward to meeting this mayor, the one other volunteers had described as, "condescending, combative and extremely communist." When Sasha and I arrived at the mayor's office, a woman began yelling immediately, too quickly for me to fully comprehend. But I understood the gist—we were told to go away; no one had been sent for; the mayor was not aware of any "foreign expert," and perhaps we should go bother the education minister.

In another office at the town hall, we found the woman who'd called for me, an assistant of the Riscani District education minister who'd been assigned to sort out the mess. The woman thanked Sasha and then told him to go away, preferably back to school.

Also in the room was the head of the Moldovan Lyceum's foreign language department, who'd formally submitted this current protest. This woman was overtly kind to me, shaking my hand, though clearly skeptical of my intentions, assuming her rival, Nadezhda, had corrupted me. The minister's assistant asked that I evaluate five essays, and that I explain my conclusions. The names and the initial scores had been removed from the essays.

The two women watched me work.

Although I'd ignored Nadezhda's handwriting samples, it took only moments to determine the authors of the first two papers. The essay prompt concerned explaining why family was a divine gift. I assumed the first essay belonged to a Moldovan contestant: the script was a flowery cursive, and the argument included the phrase, "Family is the flower of happiness that erupts in the springtime of life." That statement actually appeared three times: as the author's thesis, as the body of the essay's evidence, and also as the conclusion.

The second essay clearly belonged to a Russian contestant. The letters were blocky and evenly spaced and, though I was not positive, I assumed the thesis statement belonged to Lenin, "Family is machine with many parts... allowing life to occur."

I gave matching scores to these two essays. The Moldovan essay had repeated too much content in order to bolster the word count, and the Russian essay deviated from the theme. In truth, they were equal.

The next two essays belonged to village contestants. Neither demonstrated a command of the English language. One included Romanian words, and the other seemed to misunderstand the theme completely. I graded them accordingly, below the first two essays.

The final essay made me smile. The author identified herself as a girl from a small village, who took care of her younger brother. She avoided defining family through philosophy, and instead spoke intimately of her own mother and father working abroad. She spoke of family in terms of responsibility and pressure, of negativity, but also as a source of hope and support. She was the only contestant to recognize that the word "divine" referred to God, and that things coming from God aren't simple.

Simple mistakes in grammar and usage aside, in my eyes this final essay had won the Olympiad.

"Are you certain?" said the education minister's assistant.

The Moldovan teacher frowned at me. I defended myself by explaining why the first two had tied, and by praising the insight of the final girl's essay.

"Although the essay does not utilize a traditional syntax," I explained, "the author has demonstrated an advanced mastery of style including the type of simile and metaphor only discernible to a foreign expert."

The two women conferenced without me, speaking in Romanian softly, not realizing that I understood, more or less, what they spoke of through hand gestures and tone.

In the end, the original scores stood. The minister's assistant had given the Moldovan teacher a choice, which was really no choice at all: lose by the old scores, or lose by the new ones. The first option, losing to the Russians, was an embarrassment. The second option, being displaced by a village lyceum, would be shameful.

The minister's assistant switched back to Russian and thanked me for my service, as did the Moldovan teacher. Before excusing myself, I extended to shake their hands. The minister's assistant smiled in embarrassment and finally relented in the spirit of silly foreign exchange.

Stacking Cups

A day came when the ice on the streets melted. One morning, I woke up sweating in my sleeping bag. The next night I slept only with a sheet to cover me. My walks in town stretched farther through new neighborhoods before ending back at the lake, where I could comfortably hold a beer bottle without gloves. And then, one evening, *Anna Karenina* ran out of pages, seemingly ending itself; I felt empty and considered starting the novel again.

At school, the students grew more despondent with each sunny day. Many arrived in class with drooping eyelids and dirty fingernails. Now, in the springtime, the work at home—in the gardens, in the fields—far outweighed their school obligations.

And then, one day, I arrived at school and my classroom smelled like a bar.

The ninth graders had decided to mark the last day of winter by leaving their books at home, instead bringing 2-liter soda bottles filled with wine. Evidently, they'd planned in advance, as each student brought a different type of wine, ranging from white varietals through the rouge mixes into dark reds. Another pupil brought plastic cups and another came with a bottle of vodka because his family didn't make wine. Edgar calmly informed me that it was a holiday—the official last day of winter—and therefore we wouldn't be conducting a normal class.

"We can sing some more," he offered. "But only if you insist."

"This is very wrong," I said as Edgar poured me a cup of red wine.

Ana and Nastia, seated as normal in their front row seats, assured me it was not. "This is not America," said Edgar. "This is different tradition."

Edgar waited for me to drink. He'd filled a plastic bottle that morning with wine from his family's cellar; his mother wanted to know the American's opinion of her wine. It tasted like juice with vinegar and I told Edgar to tell his mother that it pleased me greatly. The students clapped.

It wasn't yet noon. Even the tiny girls drank, and then drank refills.

The hour passed quickly and the kids winked at me before leaving. I still had another class to teach, so I planned on watching the Russian Victory Network during my break over the next hour. The school director found me immediately once I exited the classroom. I felt trapped but not in trouble, as the man had transformed from ogre to delicate angel after the victorious Olympiad season. He loved his foreign expert.

"I think you may go home," he told me. "Your sixth graders—another teacher has already sent these pupils home."

"Oh," I said, briefly allowing the school director to catch a glimpse of my wine-tinged teeth.

"Were the ninth graders drinking wine in your class?" he asked.

"Is that bad?" I asked.

"Well...I think..." He hesitated, trying to think of stern words to convey a message he himself cared little about. "Not *very* good," he said finally, and then he shrugged his shoulders and departed after wishing me a pleasant afternoon.

* * *

After nine months, Chisinau had lost its charm as a weekend refuge.

In the past, when I felt burned out on teaching in Riscani, I longed for the city-life of the capital. But now, once there, in the busy urban center during the first days of spring, I longed for the beauty of the countryside emerging from its winter cover.

My friend Jesse, the other Russian-speaking volunteer, also experienced this conundrum. We'd go somewhere this weekend, be tourists in Moldova, perhaps in the south, where there was a river with tube rafting, or in the east, where there was a monastery carved into a cliff side. That was the plan. But first we'd have a beer at McDonald's.

Paul and Colin were already there, two other volunteers from our group who were stacking empty plastic cups on the table. They were two deep apiece, and when Jesse and I sat down to join them they seemed enthused, given more life, to be able to retell their horror stories.

In his village, Zgurita, stalkers followed Colin home from school, swearing at him in Russian, whenever he assigned low grades. In the town Telenesti, Paul had grown dejected after a student presented him with a floppy disc and asked, "Please can you give me the internet? I wish to take it home." The girl had cried and called Mr. Paul mean when he couldn't do as she wished.

"My host sister steals," said Paul. "So now I'm moving."

Colin nodded, deferring as though Paul were winning some type of terrible contest among us.

For an hour we sat drinking beer in the courtyard, stacking the empty plastic cups in a tower. Colin was the only member of his family from Virginia who wished to travel.

Paul had deferred law school at the University of Cincinnati to join the Peace Corps.

A waiter appeared to remind us that empty cups left on a tabletop brought bad luck. We thanked him. Paul and Colin asked us to translate what the waiter had said. I'd forgotten they only spoke Romanian.

"Oh," said Colin. "Of course!"

"The waiter kept pointing at the tower," Paul explained. "We didn't know what the hell he was saying."

"So we kept nodding *yes* and getting more beer," said Colin.

After another beer, Paul was the first to stand up. "Got to go," he said. "Have to move a couch." Somehow Colin understood this statement; Jesse and I clearly hadn't. "Long story short," said Paul. "I had to move out of my host family. So I found an empty room across town. I bought a couch so I'll have something to sleep on."

Now Paul made sense.

"Need help?" I asked.

Paul shrugged his shoulders. "If you're not doing anything else."

"Let me see," said Jesse, holding his hands in the air and flipping through an imaginary appointment book. "Looks like my schedule's clear." Jesse laughed at his own joke until he couldn't breathe.

* * *

Two hours later, all four of us arrived in Telenesti, Paul's site in Moldova.

"God," said Colin as he stepped off the bus. "This place is a shithole."

It hadn't rained for days and still mud puddles dotted the dirt roads; there wasn't any dry sand or grass to walk on. As we marched away from the bus stop, toward the town center, skinny dogs snarled when we got too close. People fought over the price of kindling in the bazaar. *Twigs*, I thought. All the people we passed spoke about us in low Russian whispers.

Paul wanted to know what a collection of men smoking on the corner had said to us in passing. They'd called us gay—and Paul said, "Thought so."

On the main street of Telenesti we found the furniture store closed, Paul's couch locked inside. "Of course," said Paul. "I hate Russians."

Paul banged on the window, and soon a man came to the front, unlocked the door and screamed, "What, what!"

"My couch," said Paul pointing into the store. "You told me to come today."

"Take it," said the man. "And never bang my door again."

When Jesse and I thanked him in Russian, the owner of the furniture store offered the assistance of his cousin's horse cart to carry the couch.

"Civilized people don't carry furniture through town," he said.

We thanked him, again, and carried the couch out the front door.

"It's not cultured!" the shopkeeper shouted from the open door. "Use the horse!"

The separate actions of the hundred Telenesti residents within view immediately ceased. Paul and Colin carried from the front, Jesse and I from the back. Cars honked when they inched past us. Horse carts trotted by. Children pointed. The guys smoking on the corner called us homosexuals.

We paused on a hill to collect our breath and admire the cement bones of an abandoned building far off in the distance. It struck me as modern art. Twenty years earlier, the Soviets had invested several million dollars in the construction of a school to serve the needs of the entire region. But they'd run out of money to pay the workers, who abandoned the project mid-way.

"We're close," said Paul. "Just down this hill."

At first I thought he was moving into his own house. We hefted the couch down a driveway covered by a canopy of grapevines. The house was large, one story, but sprawling. Paul directed us to the back, around a white Lada parked at the end of the driveway.

Out back, a large tool shed with two doors like a garage separated the property from the next plot of land, the grass on either side of the dividing line a different shade of brown. A mud-caked dog tethered to the house by a chain sprang to life, barking, and we swung the couch around in a long arc to avoid it.

"Home sweet home," said Paul, nodding his head to the right side of the shed.

An open sewage ditch separated us from Paul's apartment across the yard. We lifted and pulled the couch over the ditch without touching any part of the slow moving water trickling through. "I want to cry," said Jesse. A ramp for wheelbarrows led up into the shed. The doors of the apartment swung open wide, and we got the couch inside without a problem. Inside, Paul's single room was empty except for a duffel bag of clothes and a decorative rug Paul had taken off the wall and spread over the floor.

"No," said Colin. "I could live here."

I'd expected the inside to smell like a tool shed, with traces of fertilizer or gasoline, but a pleasant incense from burned candles filled the space instead.

"Bathroom's out back if anyone needs it," said Paul. "Flush toilet."

I pictured the sewage ditch outside snaking its way downhill.

Paul picked up the corner of the rug and dragged it to the wall. "I won't be sleeping on this anymore." We hung the rug up, Jesse and Colin holding the corners against the wall while I handed nails to Paul, and afterward we all left, carefully stepping over the sewage ditch, back to the bus depot. But before separating we all agreed to avoid Chisinau the next weekend and instead meet in Jesse's village.

"They speak Romanian there?" asked Colin.

"No, no," said Jesse. "But there's a good bar. They've never cared how many cups I've stacked."

Corrections

After school each day, I walked, enjoying the sun. Everyone else in Riscani had the same idea. I couldn't make it ten steps down the sidewalk without a parent or a student (or someone who thought I looked strange) stopping to ask where I was going and for what purpose. My business was theirs.

Near the bazaar I came upon my host brother Vova chewing on a handful of sunflowers seeds. "Where are you going?" he asked.

"Nowhere. Just walking."

"Very good," he said, pouring half of his seeds into my cupped hands. "Enjoy the walk." He went off toward the apartment blocks. As I continued walking, people no longer interrupted me. The inquisitive stares of other pedestrians darted from my eyes to my shoes to the seeds in my clenched fist. "Enjoy the walk," said those who knew me. For the first time in Moldova strangers passed me without looking sideways. Was this another Russian custom I'd stumbled upon? A superstition? Would interrupting a man ambling through town with a handful of seeds disrupt his future? Would I be harming his? I never found out. But the tone of my sidewalk conversations changed after adopting this new habit of spitting half-chewed seed husks at my feet as I walked. *Where are you going? Where have you been?* No more of that. I was neither coming nor going; I was in Riscani. "Enjoy the walk, Mr. Aaron," became what I most often heard. And, after a few encounters, I conditioned myself to reply, "And you, also," and not think of it further.

* * *

It was Thursday. The kids who came to school that morning didn't come prepared to work. We'd adjusted for daylight savings the previous Sunday, and everyone's body clocks were still off. The sun rose early and was the strongest it had been all year. The kids wanted to sleep or play card games or listen to music on cell phones. The eighth graders were especially problematic.

A boy named Andrei decided he didn't feel like sitting. He stood in front by the board and drew chalk outlines of naked classmates. "This is Mariya," he said, trying to get a rise from a girl in the back of the room.

"You're a moron," said Mariya.

"And that's putting it nicely," said another girl.

"Sit, Andrei," I said, first in English and then in Russian. I tried to scare him with my tone, but it didn't work.

"He's lost," said Mariya. "Forget about him."

The classroom door burst open, and Nadezhda came inside screaming. "Andrei Arkadyevich! To your seat now!"

Andrei looked at the floor while she yelled at him. One of the girls in the front row scooted over so that he could sit next to her.

"I apologize for Andrei's behavior," Nadezhda said to me. "His auntie will hear of this."

Andrei stood up again as soon as the door closed. "Fucking cow," he said laughing. I punched him sharply in the shoulder. He looked at me with a cold, unbelieving stare. Before I could apologize he sat down and said, "Sorry, Mr. Aaron. I understand. Really, I'm sorry." No one in the classroom acted as though anything extraordinary had occurred.

Andrei got smacked for mouthing off. What's new?

I told the students to do what they wanted for the rest of class. They assumed I was angry with them, when really I was angry at myself for losing my temper. Thinking back to the beginning of the year, I counted the laws I would have broken if my actions were judged by American teaching standards: drinking at school; drinking with students; hitting a kid. Under normal circumstances I'd have been thrown in jail. But not here.

After the final bell, I intended to walk by the lake to clear my head, but I lost heart and went back to the apartment. I couldn't concentrate long enough to read. Instead I tried to sleep. Twenty minutes into my nap, the phone rang. Dariya's bare feet slapped across the kitchen floor. After a second she called back to me, "Aaron! It's Callie." I swore under my breath. I couldn't imagine what Callie would be calling to complain about. I took my time getting to the phone. I answered, "Yeah?" and waited for her to tear me apart.

"Son?" said a distant, angelic voice.

"Mom!" And then instinctively I asked, "What time is it there?"

It was early morning in Maine. Dad had just gone to work. Mom had been eating breakfast and suddenly felt guilty after realizing she hadn't called me in weeks. We'd always tried to talk once a week, but the rhythm had been disrupted after I'd left for Spain.

"Nothing much to report," she said. "Your dad's plugging along at work. And your brother's taking a class now, a law class—getting ready for the Bar exam."

I didn't share any problems with her. I only said, "Life's been pretty good now that I speak better Russian."

"I'm proud of you," she said. "You already know that. But your father and I don't say it enough."

I told my mother I loved her. In truth, after we hung up, promising to speak the next week, I'd never loved another person more in my life.

Katya poked her head out from the kitchen.

"And how is your Callie holding up in Chismea?"

"That was my mother," I said. "Callie won't be calling here anymore."

Katya waved for me to enter the kitchen, and sat with me for lunch. The borscht was exceptionally red. I pulled a bay leaf off my plate of potatoes and Katya told me it was a sure omen that I'd receive a letter.

The phone rang again.

Katya took the receiver and spoke with a man as though he were an old friend. "Yes, of course, Andrei Nikolayevich. The foreign expert? Yes, yes, he'll be there immediately."

Katya poured my soup back into the pot.

"Get going," she said. "It's something important."

* * *

I met Andrei Nikolayevich downtown at the statue of Lenin. He wore a tailored suit and seemed the type who shaved and washed his hair every day. I didn't know why Riscani's district attorney had summoned me, but I enjoyed that he referred to me on the phone as a *foreign expert*. Andrei Nikolayevich shook my hand and spoke Russian with long and learned words. After talking for a while—after I'd nodded as though I'd understood everything—he asked if I would be willing to help. "Of course," I said without hesitation. Andrei Nikolayevich smiled and placed a hand on my back to lead me into his building. As though in a dream, we pushed past all potential points of resistance, past nodding security guards with machine guns, past laborers in wool suits searching to settle land disputes, into his office past his secretary, to a square inner-office with two flags on his desk split apart in a V—Russia and Moldova. Instead of the leather chair facing his desk, he pushed me around to sit in his chair, at a higher elevation, where he turned a boxy

IBM monitor to face me. The background was black and the electronic script green. On the screen was an official document, in English, in need of editing.

"Please fix all that you can," said Andrei Nikolayevich. "I realize my English is not trustworthy."

The district attorney had studied English in college, back when Soviet professors thought they were training future spies to speak the language of the enemy. After a cursory glance, I saw the document only needed a few touch-ups, not an entire rewriting. I started at the beginning, changing the official government heading of the document to read, *The Republic of Moldova* instead of *Republica Moldova*. Andrei Nikolayevich stood over my shoulder, inspecting my work, nodding his head in agreement with each correction. "You type quickly," he said. He made a joke to his secretary by screaming through the wall and laughing.

I returned my focus to the monitor and finished reading the entire document before I made any further corrections. Halfway through reading I became aware of the pulse in my neck. By the time I reached the end I was breathing heavily and tapping my foot against the floor to release nervous energy. "Mr. Andrei Nikolayevich," I asked in English, "what do you mean by this phrase?" He came around the desk and a special smoky musk filled the air. I coughed. He followed my finger across the screen to the words *unacceptable acts of pleasure*. He screamed through the wall and his secretary appeared, a tiny woman not much taller in appearance now than when she'd been sitting, and they conversed in Russian beyond my capacity for understanding. He explained to her his choice of words. "When sex is forced," she reported. "Forced and not clean." She'd evidently studied English as well.

Andrei Nikolayevich nodded his approval and tapped the screen where I should write those words with my fast typing.

"Rape," I said.

Andrei Nikolayevich threw his hands in the air in relief as though he'd been searching for that word for weeks.

"Yes, yes," he said. "I agree with your word choice."

The document was a formal petition to the Austrian government. It requested the collection of evidence against a smuggling ring. A girl from the Riscani region had accepted an offer to be a chambermaid in a Salzburg hotel. After traveling to Austria, she found herself stripped of her passport and forced to pay off an invented, astronomical debt through prostitution. Andrei Nikolayevich had used bullet points to list the many grievances reported by the girl, including slavery-like conditions, rape, and the repeated injections of narcotics into her veins to maintain a non-combative attitude. The petition requested the assistance of the Austrian authorities in monitoring a Salzburg tavern, the alleged site of the prostitution, as well as a formal police inquiry into an Austrian citizen, the alleged pimp who'd received the girl at the airport. In conclusion, Andrei Nikolayevich's petition summarized the efforts of the Moldovan authorities—the Moldovan man who'd procured the girl an expedited Austrian visa had been arrested—and humbly requested that the Austrians continue with the investigation, as it legally extended into their jurisdiction.

My hands shook from excitement while finishing the corrections. I wanted to do more. Andrei Nikolayevich thanked me profusely, repeated over and over what a great help I'd been.

"Of course," I said. "I will help you at any time."

Andrei Nikolayevich shook my hand and winked at his secretary.

For the first time in Moldova, I felt truly useful. Teaching English to half-focused high schoolers had never given me the same buzz in my fingertips.

Hirjauca

Jesse and I had flipped a coin at the end of Russian language training when it came time to choose our permanent sites. We knew nothing about Moldova's regional topography, population dynamics, local histories, technological limitations. We had two Russian-speaking sites to choose from; he would go to one, and I would go to the other. Now, six months later, the thought of a slight wind, a weak thumb—whatever could affect the spin of a coin—haunted me. Something as small as a hang-nail could have sent me to live in Hirjauca instead of Riscani.

The minibus from the capital drove slowly around deep potholes in the dirt road. The landscape in this corner of Moldova was different than in the north; a surrounding forest of tall pines continued across the border into Transylvania. The air was better here, rumored to have medicinal properties, and people didn't mind opening the bus windows just a crack to allow a breeze inside.

Jesse's directions to his village included a bull and a sanatorium as landmarks. From the bus I spotted the large brown cow enclosed in a pasture and knew the second landmark would be forthcoming. The white-painted sanatorium appeared, a tall brick chimney in the center, and I yelled, "Hirjauca, yes?"

Everyone seated in the bus turned to me.

I pointed out the window. "The sanatorium, yes?"

"Yes, yes," said an old woman dressed in a headscarf. "Are you not well?"

"I'm meeting a friend," I said.

"Is he not well?" asked the woman. "Tuberculosis?"

"I think he is very well," I said. "He's the American in Hirjauca."

"Mr. Jesse!" said the driver into his rear view mirror. "Mr. Jesse, oh yes!"

The driver slowed his bus, but didn't stop, not wishing to lose momentum and traction over the loose gravel.

I walked to the front of the bus and stood over the driver's shoulder.

"You speak Russian," said the driver. "Good. You go there." He pointed to a collection of houses on a hill to our left. "You go to the town hall in the center of those houses," he said. "And Mr. Jesse will be there."

"The town hall," I repeated. Jesse hadn't mentioned a town hall, only a bull and a sanatorium.

"Yes, yes," said the driver. "The town hall. At four in the afternoon it turns into a bar. And at ten in the evening a discotheque."

"Of course," I said. "Thank you."

The driver opened the door. "Yes, it's a tiny village," he said. "Good luck to you." The bus was still moving. "Health and happiness," he said. After I still hadn't exited, he turned his vision away from the road and said, "Now go."

"Where is the stop?"

"I'm not stopping. Too muddy. So just go."

I stepped into the road from the slow-moving bus and kept running so that I wouldn't fall down.

When the bus passed I saw everyone inside had shifted to the windows to see if I'd fallen. The bus struggled away, uphill.

Alone on the side of the road I breathed deeply and didn't cough. The air was clean, yes, the trees vibrant and green, and as I began my walk I felt like this would be a wonderful landscape to hike if there weren't so much mud.

Hirjauca's town hall had transitioned to a bar by the time I met Jesse.

I saw my friend from a distance—his Minnesota Twins cap unmistakably foreign—standing across a barrel table from another man. Jesse's arms moved wildly above his head. This was an argument. The man across from Jesse held a sugar biscuit in mid-air, and I was certain they'd both recently finished a shot of vodka.

When Jesse spotted me approaching, he waved at the man across from him as though to say goodbye. The man came around the barrel and they shook hands. When I got up to their barrel table, the man shook my hand, too.

"One hundred grams for your comrade," said the man to Jesse.

"No, no, no," said Jesse, and then we were walking, the man calling after us, "Just one hundred grams! Fifty! Twenty-five!"

Jesse nodded over his shoulder at the man we'd left behind.

"That guy," said Jesse. "He killed a guy."

"Oh," I said.

"When he was working in Spain he hit a guy at night while driving a car with no headlights."

"I see."

"Yeah, that's why he's back in Moldova. Deported."

"Where do you live?" I asked.

Jesse pointed in the direction of his house; because of mud we weren't walking what seemed the most direct path.

"He speaks some English," said Jesse.

"The killer?"

"Yeah. We'll probably talk to him later at the bar."

As we walked through the mud alleys of Hirjauca, villagers wishing Mr. Jesse a pleasant evening and then speaking about us once past, protecting their voices with cupped hands over their mouths, I compared the surroundings with Riscani. There was no bazaar here, no sports complex, no lake. The sounds of the environment were all natural, nothing mechanical: the wind, boards creaking, horses spitting, the suction of rubber boots pulled with force from muddy footsteps.

"Are there any stores here?" I asked.

"One," said Jesse, and then he pointed.

One of Jesse's students, a boy about twelve years old, came out of the village's only store holding a cigarette pack.

"Ilya!" said Jesse, his voice low and teacherly. "Smoking kills."

The boy laughed.

"Your friend is American," said Ilya. "He teach English?"

"Yes," said Jesse. "He teaches English."

The boy shook my hand.

"Where you teach English?" he asked.

"In Riscani."

"No," said the boy. "Don't know it."

Ilya lit his cigarette and walked away.

"My best student," said Jesse.

* * *

Jesse stuck his hand through a wooden gate and unlatched the door from the inside.

Somewhere nearby, a woman screamed in an unknown language to me—not Russian or Romanian.

"Host Mom might seem angry at first," said Jesse. "She just works really hard."

The yard inside the fence was packed dirt. Past the small house, a baby cow wandered freely through a collection of apple trees. Pigs made noises from their pens adjacent to the house. One chicken raced another around a corner. In the distance, at the edge of the property where the fence ended, I saw the slanted wooden outhouse.

"What the hell!" said a woman to Jesse through the kitchen window. "Is this the friend who speaks Russian? Or is he one of the stupid ones?"

"I speak," I said. "Thank you for having me at your home."

"Take care of him," she instructed Jesse, pointing at me. "Heat the food when you're ready and make the tea. Papa is all set for the night, so don't wake him."

She came outside and walked past us, entering the orchard with an empty wicker basket.

A man with a limp, younger, presumably the woman's son, appeared from the vicinity of the pig noises and shook my hand. He smiled but didn't say anything, and then followed the woman into the orchard with another empty wicker basket.

"Poor guy fell off a horse a couple days ago," said Jesse.

Inside the house, an old man with white hair slept on a cot in the kitchen. An untouched cup of tea, still steaming, waited on a chair within his reach.

"Host Grandpa," Jesse whispered.

We took our shoes off without making noise.

Jesse's room wasn't unlike my own in Riscani. He slept on a converted sofa and kept a library of books on his windowsill. A bottle of Jameson whiskey stood in the corner.

"Do they speak another language?" I asked. "Your host family. It didn't sound like Russian."

"Ukrainian," he said. "A dialect."

I'd learned so much Russian already just from listening to Dariya arguing playfully with Katya; I knew how to bargain now, how to explain why I'd be coming home late, or not coming home at all.

Jesse handed me a remote control and pointed to where I should sit on the sofa.

"You've got a TV?" I asked.

He opened his armoire; instead of hanging clothes there was a flatscreen TV.

"We've got a satellite," he said. "You don't?"

He pointed out the window. From his bedroom I could see to the roof of the kitchen. There, perched atop clay shingles held together by a mixture of mud and cement, was a giant satellite dish with an antenna, pointed upward, extending three feet off the roof.

Jesse pulled the beer we'd bought at the store from his backpack.

"Two hundred channels."

* * *

Paul and Colin arrived the next afternoon.

We just passed the cow, texted Paul. *The driver DOES NOT speak Romanian.*

Mud inched up my pant legs on Jesse's shortcut to the bus stop. We crossed a plank bridge over a stream, and I bent down to touch the water—ice cold—and decided my shoes could stay dirty.

We found Paul and Colin on the side of the road, standing across from a group of women waiting for the bus going in the other direction.

"Are those your friends, Mr. Jesse?" asked one of the women. "Those strange ones?"

When Jesse nodded, yes, the woman screamed, "I told you so!" to the rest of the group. One of the women had a bucket of food to sell, either pickles or cheese, and another a suitcase on rolling wheels caked in mud.

"Look at them," said Jesse to the woman, smiling. "Who else could they be?"

"They don't speak a real language," said the woman. "So we thought they might be missionaries."

Paul and Colin walked across the street and joined in the conversation with the women.

"They thought you were missionaries," I said.

Paul and Colin nodded as though that explained a lingering question for them as well.

"No, ladies," said Paul in Romanian. "We are teachers of English."

One of the women screamed as if she'd been touched by a scorpion, while the others laughed under more control. None bothered to cover their mouths. Knuckles wiped away tears from the corners of eyes.

Jesse wished them all a pleasant day, and we began walking. The noise of their laughter died down as we made progress down the road, then picked up in a sudden burst, audible quite a long distance away.

"They don't hear much Romanian," said Jesse.

"Sure," said Paul. "Standard."

When we entered Hirjauca, Colin looked from his left to his right in a slow arc. I took in the same view: mud alleys, green-painted fences, pedestrians in rubber boots. Jesse watched Colin, waiting for his one-word assessment of the village.

"Bar?" asked Colin

"That's a problem," said Jesse.

"No bar?" asked Paul.

"It's all one building. It's the town hall until five o'clock," said Jesse. "But we can go then and stay until it becomes the discotheque at eight."

"The driver told me different hours," I said.

Jesse waved his hand in the air to dismiss that thought. "Who you going to trust?" he said. "Believe me, I know."

"It's nice here," said Colin. "Peaceful."

Paul snorted. "Well, I can report that Telenesti is still a shithole."

"Yes," said Colin. "Yes it is."

* * *

We took the shortcut from the town hall to Jesse's house, taking turns going over the plank bridge one at a time. It creaked under Colin's weight, but we all made it across.

"Are these the stupid ones?" asked Jesse's host mother when we appeared in front of her house. "Whatever. Take care of them."

Paul and Colin asked us to translate what she'd said.

"Kitchen's this way," said Jesse.

A new sight came to me then—an upright and alert host grandpa. He'd swung his legs over the side of the cot and now pressed his feet into the wooden floorboards as if he would stand at any moment, but never did. Host mother had wrapped his blanket around his shoulders.

Jesse pulled a card table over to his host grandpa, then lit the burner on the stove to heat a cauldron of potatoes. Paul sliced bread while Colin poured tea.

I'm not allowed to touch the stove, I thought. *Katya would slap my hands away like a child's.*

"Where are the plates?" I asked in Russian. "I'll set the table."

Host grandpa turned to me and said, "You are the one who speaks Russian."

I nodded, and said, "*Da, da.*"

"Are these other two the stupid ones?" he asked.

"These are my friends, Grandpa," said Jesse. "Colin and Paul. They speak Romanian."

Host grandpa began mumbling his words; I thought he might be choking.

But soon I realized Paul and Colin were listening intently. The old man was speaking in Romanian.

"Wow," said Paul. "Your host grandpa hasn't spoken Romanian in thirty years."

"I didn't know you spoke Romanian, Grandpa!" said Jesse.

Colin giggled. "Yes. He's asking in highly polite, formal language if we would please pour him a glass of wine from the pitcher that his daughter keeps hidden under the sink."

Colin stood and gingerly opened the cupboard under the sink. He placed a small pitcher of red wine on the table.

"Old man," said Jesse. "Don't tell your daughter."

"No, YOU don't tell my daughter," he said.

We toasted to host grandpa's health and happiness. As we left to walk around the village, host grandpa thanked Paul and Colin for being such gentlemen and asked them to leave the pitcher closer where he could reach it. Jesse returned the pitcher to the cupboard under the sink. Host grandpa cursed in Ukrainian and then wished us a pleasant walk.

* * *

Jesse crossed the plank bridge first. Colin followed and made it halfway before the board snapped; he managed to jump from the plank to the other side without getting wet. Paul and I were left on the other side. The brown water in the stream meandered slowly. The width across where we stood was about six feet. "Don't try it," said Paul. I moved farther down the bank where the width decreased to five feet, took a few steps back and jumped. Both of my feet landed at once on a sun-hardened patch of mud; I'd made it across safely. Paul was relieved to see the jump had been easy. He jumped without stepping back and landed directly in the stream. Colin fell over laughing.

"How's that water feel?" asked Jesse.

I knew how cold that water was.

I extended my hand to pull him out, but Paul brushed it away as he waded to the edge and onto dry land. He'd submerged his left leg below the knee; his right didn't look as bad, as though he'd only stepped in a puddle.

"I'm not letting this ruin my day," he said. "Get me to the bar."

Jesse and Colin walked ahead. Paul stopped to take off his wet socks. He threw them into some bushes. He didn't say anything until we were all standing around a barrel in front of the town hall drinking beer from plastic cups.

"I need a break," he said.

"Don't we all," said Jesse.

"This might seem random," said Paul. "But do you feel like going to Istanbul?"

It took a moment for me to realize Paul had directed his question to me.

"Aaron," said Paul, interrupting my daze. "Let's go to Istanbul."

"Yes," I said without pause. "Of course we will."

That evening at the bar in Hirjauca, we talked about Turkey. Jesse and Colin had spent Christmas there while I was in Barcelona. Over beers they spoke fondly about roaming the old city, drinking real coffee, going to bars in the Russian district and impressing the bouncers with knowledge of what to say when toasting.

"I've been thinking about Turkey for weeks," said Paul. "And now I'm drinking beer on a barrel. It's time to go."

A finger poked Jesse from behind. He turned away from the barrel, aggressive in his movements, perhaps expecting another encounter with a drunk comrade. I looked around for the man Jesse had been speaking with when I first arrived, the guy who'd killed a man in Spain. This was the only bar in the village, I remembered, so he couldn't be far.

"Mr. Jesse," said a girl.

Jesse relaxed his shoulders.

"Yana!" He turned to us. "One of my students."

The girl smiled. In Russian, she said, "I have a question."

"In English," said Jesse. "These men at the table are my friends, and they speak English."

"Okay," said the girl. "Why did your friend lose his socks?"

She pointed at Paul.

We all stood back from the table to look at his wet loafers, his bare ankles, and his dark pant cuffs rolled up several times.

"I fell in the stream," said Paul. "Okay? I fell in the stream."

"I know," said Yana. She held a single black sock in the air. She looked back from the table, across the patio, to where one of her friends hid behind another barrel.

"She has the other one," said Yana.

Paul said, "Keep them."

The little girl Yana screamed in Russian, "They're ours!" and ran off to play with her friend and Paul's socks.

Ozi Buna

"I'm basically fluent in Turkish," said Dima.

Katya and Dariya called him a liar at the same time. Dima smiled into his serving of potatoes. He picked a bay leaf from the center and carefully placed it on the rim of the plate.

"Shush," he said. "You know this, Aaron. Turkish, Gagauzian—basically the same thing."

"They are not," said Dariya.

"Well, we'll see," he said.

"Aaron's going to Turkey," said Katya. "Not you."

"We'll see," said Dima. He winked at me. "We'll see."

Dima pulled a bottle of vodka from under the sink, and we toasted to safe world travels.

* * *

Only two weeks after Paul lost his socks, we arrived in Turkey without an agenda, carrying only small backpacks with a single change of clothes. Spring break would last a week. We knew nothing of Istanbul beyond the Blue Mosque and the general location of a hostel where Jesse and Colin had slept on bunkbeds.

In our first hour Paul and I tracked down the Blue Mosque, removed our shoes, paced around the space inside, took pictures of the beautiful ceiling, and found ourselves deposited on the sidewalk opposite where we'd entered. We put our shoes back on and began walking.

"Great," I said. "What do we do for the next seven days?"

We'd accomplished our only goal for the trip in fifteen minutes.

"I don't feel like I'm in Turkey," said Paul. "I just feel like I've left Moldova."

Over the next few days we appreciated Istanbul for its modernity, not its history. Shopping malls had working escalators. Smiling men with mustaches and white hats swept perfectly clean sidewalks. Cars stopped at crosswalks; the drivers waved hello. All mosques had open doors. The seafood was fresh and safe to eat, not at all radioactive, so we gorged ourselves on fish sandwiches made in front of us on the pier. And coffee never arrived instantly, but took time and patience to create. At dusk one evening, I sipped thick coffee, spitting some of the grinds back into the cup, and realized I'd consumed no other liquid than coffee that day; neither had Paul.

"Callie is quitting," said Paul. "Once the school year ends."

I'd heard the same rumor.

"In retrospect," I said. "I could have been more supportive."

Paul laughed.

"Yeah," he said. "She's got stories."

I waited for Paul to tell me those stories second-hand. But when he didn't speak, instead sipping from his mug and swirling the floating coffee grounds at the bottom, I realized he was waiting to tell me that he was quitting also.

"Do you really feel like you're helping anything?" he finally asked me.

I thought of Andrei Nikolayevich. I thought of the students using my pens to draw pictures of Jean-Claude Van Damme. I thought of the rare occasions when students remembered to use the word *THE*.

"Yes," I said. "Sometimes."

Paul nodded. "I've never once felt that way."

* * *

Back in Riscani, Dima quizzed me on language use in modern Istanbul.

"How did they say *hello*? Was it *merhaba*? They said *merhaba*? Yes! They said *merhaba*! Ha!"

Katya shook her head.

"I told you," said Dima. "Fluent in Turkish."

Dima sat next to me on the couch and looked over each photograph I'd taken of the streets and food and people. "You should wear one of these lady capes!" said Dima to Katya. "Very stylish." Dima was referring to black, full-body dressings that covered the face. Katya came in from the kitchen to investigate this Turkish fashion and slapped Dima in the chest. They both laughed.

The air inside the apartment was finally warm enough so that I didn't shiver when I woke up. I didn't mind shaving in cold water. At school the kids didn't care that I'd been to Turkey nearly as much as that I'd shaved my winter beard. It turned out to be a day of compliments, as girls and women ranging from ten to sixty years told me how handsome I looked with a clean face.

At the end of the day, in the eighth grade class, a girl named Marina told me she needed to leave early to attend a fight; she and another girl were to settle an argument by the lake with timid wrestling and errant punches.

"Don't worry," said Edgar, one of the only boys in the class. "These girls don't know how to fight."

"I'll show you!" said Marina, and she ran over to Edgar and punched him in the shoulder. He didn't react. "You see?" he said, addressing me. Marina called him a dirty name in

Russian and class resumed. Marina left the room without asking twenty minutes before class ended.

"Good luck," said Edgar.

Marina blew him a kiss, and then closed the door.

She returned the next day without any visible cuts or bruises. "Everything is good," she reported. "That *suka* just pulled my hair a little."

"What's a *suka*," I asked.

Marina smiled while others buried their faces to avoid laughing out loud.

"You shouldn't say such things," she said. "Please, Mr. Aaron, let's resume our lesson."

* * *

On a Friday, after school, I skipped lunch and went directly to the bus station.

The minibuses to the capital sat in their normal spots. Beyond those, I found a smaller passenger van marked *Soroca* that would take me east. It was a glorified minivan, meant to carry six or seven passengers. The driver had already squeezed ten bodies inside.

A half hour later, the van pulled to a stop on the side of the road, and the driver pointed me to a collection of houses surrounded by two lakes—in the distance, a five-story apartment block. Colin had mentioned all of these landmarks in the directions to Zgurita. The van sped away and I walked downhill into the lowlands between the lakes, toward the center of the village.

The streets were made of compacted dirt. I stepped off the road twice for horse carts to pass. Tree trunks were painted white at their bottoms. Men holding beer bottles watched me walk by, but no one spoke. They stood in place as though tethered to their alcohol supply. Some children ran across the street in front of me, paying me no attention, down into a field. In a main square I stopped in front of the town hall, and a woman wearing a fur coat approached me with enough speed to make me nervous. I stepped back, thinking she might strike me.

"Foreigner," said the woman in Russian. "Do you understand me?"

"Yes," I said. "I speak Russian."

"Ha!" said the woman. "Thank God one of you speaks a civilized language."

She pointed toward the apartment building on the edge of town. "You've come for the American."

I looked into the distance at that five-story apartment block. On the highest floor a hand-painted banner had been draped out the window. It depicted a yellow smiley face and the phrase *OZI BUNA!!!*

I knew enough Romanian to know *ozi buna* meant *have a nice day.*

"Have a nice day, indeed," said the woman. "He's taunting the Russian community—that's what he's doing!"

"I'm here for Mr. Colin," I said.

"Yes, I know," said the woman. "The tall one. He's probably down in the field throwing hard objects at slow children."

She pointed across the street where the kids had been running.

"By the way," she said. "I'm the mayor. Tell them next time I want a Russian speaker like you."

I walked to the edge of the square and looked down, across the field. Colin was there, a giant among smaller children, teaching them all how to throw and catch a baseball. His church in Virginia had donated a dozen balls and gloves.

The mayor came to stand next to me. "Meester Colin!" she shouted. Seconds later he turned and looked uphill, then waved at me like he was signaling a rescue plane.

"Thank you," I said.

"Thank you, indeed," said the mayor. "Remember to tell them I want a Russian."

* * *

Each squatty house in the center of Zgurita had a green-painted fence that separated the front porch from the main road. You could easily hand something off the street through someone's living room window. But on the outskirts of the village, where the land sloped up away from the lakes, the houses were larger, two and three stories, and spaced out so that you wouldn't run into neighbors unless you walked through muddy fields.

Trailing behind, I stepped where Colin stepped so that I wouldn't sink in mud. In front of a large house with three stories, a Mercedes SUV parked to the side, Colin said, "I lived here." A couple steps from the porch, I strained my neck looking up to the roof; a bronze rooster swiveled with the wind. "You'll see why I moved."

The door opened as Colin reached for the bell.

"Stranger!" said a man extending his arms for a hug. Colin went past the man to greet someone inside. The man on the porch turned to me and said, "And stranger has a friend!" The man wore a thin ski jacket, blue jeans and *Timberland* boots. His eyeglasses had thin gold rims. He cupped my hand in both of his and said in Russian, "Welcome to our home. You must be hungry."

"Aaron," I said. "Pleased to meet you."

"I know who you are," he said. "Oh, yes, the Russian speaker in Riscani, I know. But do you know who I am?"

"I'm sorry, no."

The man pouted his lips and turned to Colin, who stood in the doorway with his shoes off, waving his hand for me to enter. "Mr. Colin isn't a talker," said the man. "I'm Sergei—Mr. Colin's best friend in Moldova."

I began unlacing my shoes and Sergei grabbed my shoulder and said, "No, no, no." He let go of me and pointed around the room. "Hardwood floors," he said. "Stain resistant."

Colin stood next to an older woman who hugged him around the waist, like she was using him for support. Her hair was dyed purple, a color fashionable that spring at Moldovan hair salons.

"Don't be stupid," said the woman. "We're not animals. Take your shoes off."

"But you don't have to," said Sergei. "That's what I'm saying, Mama."

"*That's what I'm saying, Mama,*" mimicked the woman. "Stupidity!"

Colin smiled. "I present to you Lady Svetlana," he said to me.

The woman laughed when she heard *Lady* and slapped Colin on his chest.

"It's my house," said Svetlana. "Enjoy it."

Sergei led me on a tour of the house while Colin chatted with Svetlana.

In the living room there were books behind glass in a large cabinet. When I bent my neck to examine the spines, Sergei steered me away from the bookshelves to look at his television.

"The biggest you've ever seen," he said. "Any channel you can imagine."

Beyond the living room, in a study, a globe opened from the top, exposing several bottles of scotch whisky. "Maybe for later," said Sergei, lifting a bottle by its neck. I couldn't read the label well—Sergei was quick to replace it and close the globe—but I saw 21 written below the distillery name. Before we left he pointed to the walls.

"Real paintings," said Sergei. "No fakes. I know many artists."

The artwork depicted shipbuilding and hunting on horseback with dogs.

I poked my head around a corner while Sergei closed the study. Down a hall, in the kitchen, a woman stirred the contents of a large pot.

"Our servant," said Sergei, catching up to me. "You will enjoy her cooking."

In a formal dining room, gold-plated forks, knives and spoons were positioned on either side of white porcelain plates. Ten people could have sat side by side with plenty of room to stretch. At the end of the table, above the chair of honor, hung an oil painting of a young woman in a floor-length ball gown, a flower in her braided brown hair. The face was younger, the hair undyed, but, yes, there was a likeness in the cheeks and eyes to Svetlana and even to Sergei, standing there at my side.

"We're eating in here?" I asked.

"No, no," said Sergei. "Mr. Colin is a simple man and doesn't feel comfortable in this room." Sergei giggled. "Did you know he turned down the prostitute I bought for his birthday?"

"Sergei!" screamed Svetlana from elsewhere in the house. "Soup!"

Sergei smiled. "Soup," he said. "Let's eat soup."

We found Colin sitting across from Svetlana in a less formal dining room, with a bare wooden table close to the ground and benches for communal sitting.

"No, no," said Colin, as though trying to end an argument.

He slid over on the bench so that I could sit next to him and said, "Tell her in Russian how comfortable I am at my new apartment."

Without hesitation I said, "Colin really loves the simple lifestyle. He's—"

"Enough," said Svetlana. "No dirty Russian talk at my table."

"Aaron only speaks Russian and English, Mama," said Sergei. "What will it be?"

The old woman stared at me, then at her son, then at Colin.

"He's American like you?"

Colin nodded.

"A shame they taught him to speak a dirty language," she said.

"The mayor—" I said.

"The mayor is a hag," said Svetlana. "She's a hag. End of story. You speak Russian? Fine, okay. Enough about hags. Let's eat."

"No," said Colin. "We're not staying."

"Nonsense," said Svetlana. She turned away from the table. "Servant! Immediately bring soup!"

Colin stood, and Sergei shifted over to the door, blocking Colin from his shoes.

"You'll take wine," said Sergei.

Colin nodded, and Sergei stepped into his boots and went outside without tying the laces.

"It was a pleasure," I said.

Svetlana didn't respond.

As we slipped our shoes on Sergei returned with a gallon of red wine in an oversized pickle jar. He presented it to Colin like a trophy.

"Fine," said Svetlana. "Go sleep in filth. Go live like monks."

* * *

Outside, Colin poured the glass jar of wine into a mud puddle.

"You can't be in the Peace Corps and live in a mansion on the hill," he said. He pointed ahead to the banner that said *OZI BUNA!!!* "My new place is better."

"How are they so rich?" I asked.

Colin shrugged his shoulders. "No clue," he said. "I don't want to know."

We were standing in a field. The sun was still up, the figures of women milling around in the next field visible against the sky.

"There's no bathroom inside," said Colin. "So if you have to go, go here."

He pointed to some shrubs at the base of a green picket fence.

"Maybe later," I said.

At the base of the apartment complex, I saw the fifth floor hadn't been completed. Metal rods sprouted from the roof. A worker had abandoned the bricklaying, leaving the rooflines uneven.

Colin pulled a flashlight from his pocket and I followed him toward the entrance.

"A hooker lives on the third floor," he said. "Don't talk to her."

We snaked our way up, around the staircase. Colin's flashlight only illuminated a small patch of the cement steps. A woman opened a door on the third floor and spoke Romanian into the corridor.

"Yup," said Colin. "She lives right below me."

Then, on the fourth floor, the flashlight jumped around the space wildly as Colin fumbled in his pocket for his keys. The light stopped moving and then Colin was inside.

"No need to take your shoes off," he said. "Probably best you don't."

"Fine wooden floors?"

"Ha," said Colin. "No."

The flooring of Colin's apartment was continued from the same slab of concrete as the corridor. Colin turned on a battery-powered lantern to illuminate the entry room. White paint flaked off the cement walls. All the doors between rooms had been removed at the hinges. The kitchen had no sink, no stove, no cupboard. "You can boil eggs here," said Colin, pointing to a hotplate balanced on a card table.

A dozen empty bottles of mineral water formed a pile in the corner of the kitchen.

In his bedroom a sleeping bag lay sprawled over a mattress on the floor.

"Wow," I said.

Colin poured two shots of vodka into tiny glasses.

"It's good, right?" said Colin. "We're supposed to live at the same level of the people where we're working?"

He raised his glass.

My stomach grumbled. I pictured the plate of dumplings with potatoes in the center waiting for me on the table in Riscani. A bowl of borscht. Dima would probably eat my portion.

I swallowed the vodka, shook the last clinging drops to the floor, and inspected the brown smudges on the rim of the glass.

"Even prisoners have a toilet," I said.

"You don't like it?" asked Colin.

"It's perfect," I said, handing him my glass. "Pour me another."

An Invasion

On a Sunday morning, I woke to Katya tapping the frosted glass on my bedroom door.

"Aaron," she said. "We go."

Dariya was by the front door, slipping on rubber boots. Dima came out of the kitchen hefting a plastic tub with a lid. Something heavy sloshed inside.

"We go where?" I asked, putting my shoes on too.

Dima lifted the lid off his plastic bucket. Diced peppers and onions floated in a stew of slimy meat.

"To the woods," said Dariya. "The word in English, I think, is *barbecue*."

"Bar-bee-cue," repeated Dima. "I know this word. I know English."

"Stop it," said Katya, smiling. "*Shashlik*," she said to me. "The real word is *shashlik*."

I'd never walked around the lake in the direction we hiked. Low branches draped over the path, scraping my shins. Small apartment complexes, only two stories tall, formed a line parallel with the shore.

"Romanians," said Dima. "They've got the best view of the lake."

This area, the Romanian district, was drawn in pencil on one of the maps I'd inherited from a previous volunteer. A Californian grandmother had walked this path, scraped her shins on branches, and settled in one of these apartment buildings ten years before.

We entered a clearing with several fire pits where mounds of charcoal marked past barbecues.

"This is good," said Dima. "Aaron, go find a dozen twigs."

Frogs jumped into the lake as I stepped along the waterline in search of sticks for skewering the meat. At first it was just one, then another, and then when I approached a sunny patch of ground, dozens of frogs splashed into the water. I returned quickly to the barbecue pit with several bits of straight wood under my arm.

"Whoa," said Dima. "You're very good at twig gathering."

A fire was going, the flames jumping as high as Dima's waist.

"Where are Dariya and Katya?" I asked.

"Swimming," he said. He patted the ground next to him. "Sit. We'll do the cooking."

Dima pierced a chunk of meat with a twig, placed onions and peppers on top and then added another chunk. When the fire died out, Dima scraped the coals with a long tree branch, and placed a metal grill over the pit. He held his hand over the grill, pulled it away quickly like he'd been stung by a bee, and said, "It's ready."

Ten skewers of shashlik fit on the grill side by side.

"Did you know Cate?" I asked. "She lived around here, in one of the Romanian apartments."

"No, no, no," said Dima. "You're the only American who speaks Russian."

"You never saw one of the other volunteers on the street?"

He shook his head, no, while flipping the skewers one by one.

"What did you think of Bulgaria?" asked Dima. "Was it pretty?"

"I never went to Bulgaria."

"You did," he said. "You passed through on your way to Turkey."

"We flew."

He stared at the sizzling meat. "Istanbul is less than thirty hours by bus."

"That is a long time on a bus," I said.

"No," said Dima. "It's thirty-six hours to Moscow."

Dariya and Katya returned from the lake, their hair wet, their arms pinning towels to their sides under their armpits.

"It's not ready," said Dima.

Dariya pulled a skewer of meat off the grill and plucked a piece of pepper off with her front teeth.

"Delicious," she said.

"Of course," said Dima. "Your Papa can cook."

Katya made a joke about Dima doing all the cooking. I didn't hear every word and didn't laugh at the right time. I just smiled a bit as if I'd understood.

Dariya put the skewer back on the grill. "It's not done," she said. She licked her fingers and said, "It will be so interesting when your friends come to visit."

"Don't worry," said Katya. "I'll do all the cooking."

"Won't that be interesting, Papa?" said Dariya.

"Americans in Riscani," said Dima. "Yes, that would be interesting."

"Next week," said Katya to Dima. "They're coming next week. You forgot, didn't you?"

Dima smiled and pulled a skewer off the grill.

"I didn't forget," he said. "No one tells me anything." He took a bite of meat. Red juice dripped down his chin.

"You forgot!" said Dariya.

"The Americans are invading Riscani and no one tells me!" said Dima.

"Ten days ago," said Katya, laughing. "A week ago! Yesterday!"

"Fine!" said Dima, mashing bloody meat with his teeth. "Bring on the invasion!"

* * *

Colin arrived first.

The vodka drinkers in the stalls outside the bus depot stood motionless as he passed. One man turned to his circle of drinking friends and held his hand high above his head to approximate Colin's height.

"They calling me bad names in Russian?" he asked.

"No," I said. "Just a giant."

Before leaving the bazaar we stopped at Katya's bread stand. She tied a headscarf tightly under her chin

"Does he speak Russian?" she asked.

I shook my head.

She said hello in Romanian and then brushed him away with a laugh, having exhausted her knowledge of that language.

"I'll cook for you all later," she said. And then, waving for me to come closer, to the distance of a whisper, she said, "He's extremely tall." I sensed worry in her voice.

"Very tall," I said, not knowing what response she wanted.

"Okay," said Katya, full volume. "I'll cook for you at home after you finish teaching."

I still had one more class in the afternoon. Colin was going to help instruct my final group of ninth graders. "We're studying the future tense," I said.

Colin didn't respond. He swiveled his head from side to side, taking everything in. "You live in a town," he finally said. "There's actual pavement."

When we arrived at the statue of Lenin, he just mumbled, "Whoa."

Turning into the alleys between the Russian apartments, two boys approached with their hands raised as though warning us of a road block.

"It's Edgar and Pasha," I said. "They should be in school."

"You know them?" asked Colin.

"I'm supposed to teach them in ten minutes."

Edgar carried a two-liter bottle of beer.

"Mr. Aaron," said Edgar. "A present from our class." Edgar presented the beer to us with two hands, softly, like it was a baby. Pasha separated two plastic cups, and held them in the air, one in each hand, waiting for me to pour.

"Thank you for the gift," I said. "Now, Edgar and Pasha, let's go to class."

The boys shook their heads. "There will be no class," said Edgar. "The students have all gone home. They sent us. You are welcome for your present. We go home now too."

"The school director would not like this," I said.

"The school director," said Edgar, and then he flicked his neck with his middle finger. "No problem."

Colin took the bottle and poured an inch of beer into each cup. "*Hai noroc!*" he said, downing the beer and refilling his cup.

Edgar and Pasha looked at the ground, turned purple, then finally laughed.

"I'm sorry," said Pasha, near tears. "Hearing him speak that language is comedy."

"See you in class Monday," I said.

The boys giggled, shook our hands, saluted, and then continued past us toward the center of town.

Colin and I sipped the beer on a bench outside my apartment.

"Your ninth graders are better than mine," said Colin.

The final bell sounded across the street. Shouts from pupils filled the neighborhood and soon Dariya came walking around the corner. "Papa will be upset you started drinking without him."

"Meet Colin," I said.

He extended his hand and she shook it with hesitation after looking at me. "It's what we do in America," I said. "Get used to it."

Colin stood up from the bench and Dariya stepped back, startled as if she'd seen a mouse.

"You're very tall," she said. "See you both soon."

* * *

Colin and I found Jesse and Paul in the alley of vodka bars.

"I could live here," said Paul.

From the bazaar we walked down the main street in the shade of the trees. A policeman waved to us. "You're walking," he said. "Carry on." In front of the town hall, all four of us stood at the base of the Lenin statue. I thought to tell them about Andrei Nikolayevich, but I didn't. I thought someone would ask about the burned building across the street, the ruins, but that didn't even catch their attention. Each of my friends seemed so absorbed in their own thoughts, staring up at Lenin, that I didn't wish to disturb the peace. Nearby a bar door opened, flooding the street with techno music until it swung closed.

At home, Katya opened the door before I could use my key. As I kicked my shoes off, I saw on the kitchen table potatoes and stuffed peppers and salami chunks on tiny slices of bread.

"American invaders!" said Dima. "I surrender. Take me to New York City! Take me to Brighton Beach!"

Jesse laughed and Dima shook his hand first. "You," he said. "You speak Russian very well."

Then Dima shook all the new hands—calling Colin and Paul the mayors of Zgurita and Telenesti—and seated us in the kitchen for an immediate toast with vodka.

"Four Americans in my home," he said, lifting his shot glass. "Seriously, I surrender."

We all drank, even Katya and Dariya. Dima stood over us, watching us eat.

And then, for unknown reasons to me, my host family retired to the bedroom, closing the door. My friends and I went back out into the street, walked around the lake, stopped by the sport complex to watch a pick-up game, drank beer at the bottom of the Lenin statue, and when we returned to the apartment, there were fresh helpings of food on the table, dumplings and cheese-dusted noodles, and a filled bottle of cognac. Again, Dima, Katya and Dariya wished us health and happiness, toasted with us, and then went into the large bedroom and closed the door.

After we finished the bottle, Jesse and Paul slept on the floor in the living room, and Colin made a pallet from the cushions next to my bed.

Later, sometime during the night, Dima and Katya sent Dariya into the hallway to retrieve one of Colin's sneakers; they'd never seen a shoe so large, and Dima wished to inspect it up close.

* * *

A week later, the school year ended.

For a community that loved the ceremony of holidays and festivals, little excitement surrounded the final day of classes. All the pupils in the school stood grouped by homeroom in the courtyard—the first collective gathering since the fire—and a girl from the first grade rang a bell to signify the closing of the year. Dariya and her graduating class of five students received applause from the teachers. The graduates had the same dour expressions as the boy Miroslav had worn on the day he left to work in Russia.

Dariya was the only participant not wearing black; she'd instead chosen a white pantsuit.

At the close of the ceremony a handful of students found me and thanked me for the year. I thanked them in Russian.

"In English!" they commanded, mocking my tone from previous lessons.

One girl stayed behind as the others skipped away.

"I don't have a flower for you," she said.

"It's okay," I said.

"You will return next year?"

"Definitely," I said. "Yes."

"Then yes, it is okay," said the girl. "I will give you a flower next year."

She ran down the hill after her classmates.

The Departed

A year had passed since I'd spoken to my brother. We'd exchanged emails, and he'd sent me updates about his life in law school as well as forwards of articles from CNN and BBC pertaining to Moldova—but I hadn't heard his voice.

When I'd first arrived in Moldova, my whole family had called me after my first week in language training. That morning, a village woman took me to the woods and we drank beer and danced with her friends, and by the time I returned to my house to receive the call from my family, I could barely see straight. The next morning, I vaguely remembered my father laughing through the phone and telling me to go to sleep.

A year later, my brother Justin finally called Riscani. He'd passed the Maine Bar Exam—receiving an award for doing so well—and wanted the family together in Maine to celebrate.

"You need a break," he said. "I know it."

I hesitated, and then gave in.

"I'll get your ticket and plan everything," he said. "We'll do it around the dead spot in your summer."

"So far, the whole summer's a dead spot," I said. "Just don't connect me through Romania."

After I hung up the phone, I felt happy.

My thoughts lingered on that first summer in Moldova, in training, living briefly with that family with the adult daughter who took me into the woods to dance. Then my thoughts passed through my first days in Riscani, walking to the bazaar with Dariya, going to school with a pink tie.

One more year to go.

* * *

One day, early in the summer, I returned to Riscani from the capital with news that Paul had quit and returned to America.

"I predicted this," said Katya. "Telenesti is not paradise."

Dima acted surprised. "I thought Paul would be the next mayor of Telenesti!"

"I'm sorry," said Dariya. "I don't remember who is Paul. Is he the tall one?"

"No, that's Colin."

"Then, no. I don't remember."

"Callie also quit," I said.

Dariya choked on her tea. "Your girlfriend? Really?"

"They come and go," said Dima, dodging a playful swing from Katya.

* * *

That night, Dariya informed me that she and I were going to a restaurant.

"Bring her back at a decent time," said Dima. He didn't move quickly enough to avoid Dariya's punch to his shoulder.

"Change your pants," Dariya told me. "And put on shoes without rounded ends."

She picked out a shirt from my closet and pressed it to my chest.

"Don't wait up," Dariya told her parents.

"Just don't lose him," said Katya, pointing to me.

We walked outside in the darkness by the light of our cell phone screens. Dariya walked quickly despite her high heels. I feared open manholes and, forgetting chivalry, remained a step behind. We walked uphill past the Moldovan lyceum and into a neighborhood with single-room houses. I'd expected a more central location for this restaurant. In my chest I felt the increasing pressure of the strong bass from a discotheque.

"We're almost there," said Dariya. She casually moved closer to me and linked her arm around my elbow. We finally arrived at the source of the techno, a modest house with blacked-out windows.

There wasn't a discotheque inside, but an ongoing birthday party. *Cool*, I thought, *let's sing a song and eat some cake*. But then Dariya went over to the birthday boy and began screaming. We hadn't been invited.

Instead of contributing to the argument, the boy's face froze. Occasionally, he interjected to say, "Will you let me speak? Will you let me talk?" Dariya beat her index finger against his chest and spit out the words she'd rehearsed during the march uphill. Finally, when the argument ended, Dariya walked into the back room of the restaurant. I remained at the doorstep. I recognized one of the guys at the party table from basketball.

"What's up, Mischa?" I moved across the room to shake his hand.

The birthday boy said, "You're Aaron, right?"

Mischa answered the question for me. "Assassin," said Mischa. "Very good three-point man."

"Cool," said the birthday boy in English, and then he pointed in the direction I should follow. "Go to Dariya."

"Happy birthday," I said in English. Everyone laughed. The birthday boy poured me a shot of vodka and we all drank.

In the next room, I found Dariya sitting with her brother Vova and his wife Talia. They'd been waiting for us. Vova shook my hand and yelled to the kitchen for another beer and more French fries. When my beer came Dariya took the first sip. "Who is that?" I finally asked, motioning over my shoulder to the birthday boy. She looked at Vova and Talia and then spoke to me in English, as though in code. "My supposed boyfriend." She paused to eat a single fry. "My ex-boyfriend."

After two more beers and another plate of French fries, it was time to leave. Again Dariya took my arm to parade me in front of the birthday party. As we walked past, the birthday boy pushed a second shot of vodka toward me. Dariya let go of my arm while I toasted with him. "Let's go," she said. The birthday boy saluted me and patted me on the back, called me a good "simple" guy.

Vova and Talia walked ahead. The moon was enough to light the path. Dariya held my arm the whole way home, perhaps to keep me from falling.

Girls Leading Our World

At the end of June, Peace Corps headquarters assigned me a summer posting to serve as a counselor at a self-esteem camp for Moldovan girls at risk of becoming prostitutes. The camp was called GLOW: Girls Leading Our World.

So I traveled south of the capital, to the town Causeni, where I met the camp's other male chaperone, Will, and the camp's director, Veronica.

Will served as a health education volunteer in a village near the Ukrainian border. Everyone there spoke Romanian.

"In the past," Veronica warned, "we've had problems with male counselors."

She waited for us to respond.

"Well," I said. "I think I'm a gentleman."

"Yeah," said Will. "Me, too."

"All well and good," said Veronica. "But seriously, watch it. These girls are direct. In part they're here to learn what's socially acceptable in the real world. So..." She paused to put down a packet of papers so that she could count the *don'ts* on her fingers. "Don't accept their phone numbers. Don't give them your phone numbers. Don't hug. Don't flirt. Don't share water bottles. Don't compliment their clothes, especially when they ask your opinion. No walking alone through the woods. No whispering secrets into your ears. Tell them to step back when they stand too close."

She stopped counting on her fingers.

"Just be careful," she said. "These girls are different"

* * *

The campers arrived at noon.

The girls—all fifteen to eighteen years of age—had been instructed to leave their high heels behind, but no one had thought to ban tiny dresses. Some had traveled long distances, from as far away as Soroca, and wore tight jeans instead of tight dresses. All wore make-up. A girl slowed as she walked by on her way to the registration tent, turning her head, never breaking eye contact with me. She blew a kiss before turning away.

Veronica's warnings no longer appeared harsh.

Will and I circulated, helped with bags, directed girls toward their cabins. "You're the Russian man," said a girl, winking. "You are my counselor." Her name-tag said Natalia. She pretended to naturally lose her balance, and touched my arm for support. She leaned forward and tried to whisper in my ear. I leaned back and she told her secret in a full voice. "We all know about you."

"How old are you?" I asked.

"In my sixteenth year. How old are you?"

"Twenty-five. Very old."

She nodded. I was indeed very old. "A pity," she said. "If you were only a couple years younger we could have some fun."

I found Will. He'd been cornered by a group of Romanian girls. I didn't follow the language of the conversation, but it seemed they were grilling him about his lack of a wife. The girls turned to me. "I only speak Russian," I said in Russian, my palms in the air. The girls turned back to Will. I took him away by the arm. He thanked me for the rescue and we went to a field to play Frisbee while the girls unpacked. But instead of unpacking, the girls followed us and crept closer, closer and closer until we let the brave girls at the head of the encroaching pack try to throw the disc. The first girl wanted Will to demonstrate correct technique by wrapping his body around her and throwing the Frisbee from her hand in the proper manner. "Just throw the damn thing," he said. The disc flew five feet before crashing to the ground. All the girls giggled. "Go unpack," I said, shooing them away.

In my own cabin I read literature from Veronica.

The American State Department monitors international human trafficking and releases a Trafficking in Persons (TIP) report each year, which addresses trafficking on a country-by-country basis. I read these highlights about Moldova:

U.S. Government Reports on Moldova
Trafficking in Persons Report 2007
MOLDOVA (Tier 2 Watch List)

• Moldova is a major source, and to a lesser extent, a transit country for women and girls trafficked for the purpose of commercial sexual exploitation.
• Moldovan women are trafficked to Turkey, Israel, the U.A.E., Ukraine, Russia, Cyprus, Greece, Albania, Romania, Hungary, Slovakia, the Czech Republic, Italy, France, Portugal, and Austria. Girls and young women are trafficked internally from rural areas to Chisinau.
• The Government of Moldova does not fully comply with minimum standards for the elimination of trafficking; however, it is making significant efforts to do so.
• Trafficking corruption at all levels throughout the government continued unchecked during most of the reporting period.
• Moldova's efforts to prevent trafficking remained weak in 2006. The government continued to rely on NGOs and international organizations to provide the majority of public awareness and education campaigns.

These girls of GLOW were approaching the age when they'd get offers, enticements, promises—all too good to be true.

* * *

The twenty Russian campers slept in the same cabin. They came from all over Moldova, from north to south, but several already knew each other, as they'd come to camp from the same orphanage. So already there was a sense of camaraderie when I entered the cabin to meet them. They'd finished unpacking—stuffing their bags under their cots—and were lying on top of the blankets. "Hi, pretty boy," one said.

"Careful," said Natalia, the girl I'd talked to before. "He's too old—twenty five."

"Yes," said the closest girl to me. "Old."

"If only he was a couple years younger," said another girl, talking as if I weren't in front of her.

"Careful," I said in Russian. "I understand everything."

The girls "oooed" and "aaaaghed" at my speaking voice—it was nothing, they claimed, like the harsh Russian voices of other men.

"Just remember," I explained. "You're all just girls. Don't pretend to be anything else. Act like yourself. Do what you want, but not what you think others think you should do. Don't pretend to know what others think. Be yourself." My extemporaneous pep talk didn't translate well into Russian. The words I wanted to tell them were clear in my head, but I couldn't get them out in English or Russian. I thought about translating the TIP report for them. "Just have fun," I concluded. "And don't flirt with me."

A girl raised her hand. "Will you be with us the whole time?"

"I will be, yes."

The girl smiled. "Very, very good," she said in English.

I followed the girls to their classes and was asked to stand in the corridor while other Peace Corps volunteers taught them about dental health, résumé writing, study skills and applying to universities. These volunteers were women, and the girls clearly respected them, listening intently. I knocked on the door to enter, wanting to join in, but the eyes of the presenters asked *please* and I continued waiting in the hallway. A Moldovan woman translated the volunteers' words into Russian. Through the walls I could hear the girls then begin contributing to conversation more now that the male presence had disappeared; they responded to questions, furthered ideas, shared life stories. I felt at once happy and useless.

Outside the classroom, sitting on the floor, I flipped through a book about baseball while a female doctor instructed the girls in reproductive health and condoms. I listened through the thin walls as the girls brainstormed ideal futures—abroad and, more difficult to imagine, in Moldova. Many understood that being doctors and lawyers and secretaries would make them happy. They just didn't know how to get there.

During a formal presentation I was allowed to reenter and sat to the side as the female director of an NGO called Winrock presented a PowerPoint diagramming the steps involved in human trafficking. I watched the girls' faces. Some cried single tears and some mouthed the words, "No way."

Women were having an impact on these girls' futures, I could see it, and I could only feel impotent in my purpose as a male observer. Sitting there on the folding chair, listening, I extended this feeling to my entire existence as a volunteer in Moldova.

Was I helping? Was I even capable of helping? Or was I just meant to be an observable model of how others in the world acted? Had the value of my work, then, exhausted itself after my first day in country?

Later, finally called into direct action, I was the fictitious attacker in the self-defense workshop, and the victim during the first-aid course. The girls took turns kicking and reviving me with chest compressions.

I filled water bottles.

I gathered firewood.

I killed insects that wandered into the cabins.

When the classes finished each evening, the girls played Frisbee with Will and me, danced to music on the camp boom box, and melted chocolates near the campfire. They didn't flirt.

On the last day, the girls received photocopied "yearbooks" to commemorate their time in camp. I signed each copy. At first I refused to sign my email in Natalia's yearbook. I thought she was flirting. "Part of the networking and résumé workshop," she insisted. "We need contacts."

"Do you have email?" I asked.

"No," she admitted. "But I expect to any day now. Email helps to get a job, yes?"

Eventually I relented and signed my email address into every book.

After the girls had packed their bags, cleaned their cabin, cried their goodbye tears, received their supportive hugs from their new sisters and high-fives from me, they found their places on the bus, and the counselors could finally celebrate.

The girls had completed *before-camp* and *after-camp* surveys on topics such as reproductive health, trafficking, condom effectiveness and education. Before the camp, most of the girls hadn't believed in the effectiveness of condoms;

now the majority did. Most hadn't known the domestic dangers of human traffickers; now the majority was aware. The girls all had new toothbrushes and toothpaste and knew how frequently to use each. The girls all had a list of counselor emails, should they one day get internet in their villages. In short, there were long-term and short-term reasons to celebrate.

The spirits of the group were extremely high, but I couldn't help from qualifying the success in my mind because I'd contributed so little. *Only a hundred girls in the entire camp*, I thought. *Not so many.*

Once back in Chisinau, Will and I chose to take our celebration to McDonald's. We each finished two Big Macs without speaking, and then in short time we were stacking empty beer cups on the table. We toasted to the success of GLOW camp and would have stayed in the courtyard of McDonald's all afternoon, unluckily stacking cups, had a strange couple not taken up the table next to us.

A man had purchased a young girl a milkshake. The girl wore a short skirt, high heels, and a black bra under a see-through red fishnet blouse. We'd chastised our campers for wearing this wardrobe on the first day of camp. The man wasn't Moldovan; Will and I were certain. He wore atypically rounded loafers. His khaki pants were loose. His dress shirt wasn't tucked in. His hair went down past his ears, and he hadn't shaved that morning.

Will noticed the couple first and motioned for me to turn around and look, but then said, "Don't be obvious."

"What," I said. "The Italian and the hooker?"

"No," said Will. "They're speaking Romanian." Will listened intently. He spoke English to me, keeping his voice at a normal conversational volume. "She's not a hooker," he said. "Not yet. But he wants her to be."

"What's he saying?"

183

Will paraphrased: "If you don't like it, if you want to come home, you can return freely whenever you like. Think about this seriously. Don't make your decision quickly with worry."

Perhaps the don't-be-a-hooker camp we'd just completed overly influenced us. To Will and me, this was clearly human trafficking.

"Your business is dirty!" said Will in Romanian. "You are dirty, Sir!"

The man turned toward our table and swore under his breath. Will repeated his statement, again calling him *Sir*.

"Tell the girl not to prostitute herself," I whispered to Will. I think that's what he said next; the girl's face lost blood and she said, "No, no," and then something else I didn't understand. I heard the word *bine,* which I knew meant "fine."

"Did you tell her?" I asked Will.

"This is totally a traffic deal," he said.

The foreign man got up and walked away, ignoring the girl's request for him to stay.

"Let us buy you a soda," said Will.

"I'm leaving," she said. "You leave, too."

We were again alone, the only patrons sitting at the tables outside McDonald's.

Will and I stood on shaky legs and shook hands before parting, confident we'd accomplished something heroic.

Adalet

Back in Riscani, Dariya had received life-changing news.

"I go to college in Balti," she informed me.

She'd won a scholarship and could now continue her studies in the fall at the economics university. She extended her hand to me to receive a congratulatory handshake in the American style. "Come here," I said, and we hugged. Dariya was just then leaving the apartment when I entered. She went off to celebrate with her friends. In the kitchen, I found Katya stirring a pot of soup. "Such as sweet girl," she said. "So hard-working." She mimicked the real tears she'd cry when Dariya went off to college. I found Dima on the couch in the living room; he wasn't as happy as I'd thought he'd be. "You came back," he said sleepily, sitting up. He wasn't wearing a shirt. "Let's have a drink and play cards."

We toasted Dariya with wine and played *durak*.

Dima didn't care to hear much about camp. He wanted to know about Paul back in America. Had I talked to him? Had he started law school?

"The president of Telenesti," mused Dima. "And what about Colin and Jesse?"

"On vacation," I said.

"Rome? Athens? Sofia?"

"Closer," I said. "They're spending a week in Odessa."

"I lived in Odessa!" said Dima. "You didn't know this? I studied art at the university."

"Art? Like, painting?"

"Yes. Engineering, too, but mostly I enjoyed the painting classes." He spoke loudly through the wall so that Katya would hear in the kitchen. "I was a great painter before the Red Army."

"Oh yes," said Katya. "You were better than K-------------!" She mocked him with the long name of a famous Russian painter I'd never heard of.

Dima laughed. He couldn't get the Americans in Odessa off his mind. A few moments later he said, "They probably won't leave the beach. It's beautiful there. Some like Kiev, but I'm an Odessa type." He paused. "I used to go to the sea every year. Now I work and work every day."

"Poor baby," said Katya from the kitchen.

"You're going to meet them on the beach in Odessa?" said Dima. "You'll love it there."

"No!" shouted Katya. "His next trip is to home, to see his brother the lawyer and parents!"

"People never tell me anything!" Dima smiled. "Goodbye, Moldova!"

* * *

The overnight bus trip from Chisinau to Kiev normally took twelve hours if nothing went wrong; but usually something broke down. The driver pointed to my seatmate and me. "The border guards always have questions for the foreigners," he said. By foreigner he meant: not Moldovan, not Ukrainian. The man sitting next to me barely spoke Russian and had only partly understood the driver's explanation.

"Just tell him what I tell you at the border," said the driver to me, as though I could then translate into this stranger's language. I knew not where this seatmate came from, only that men from his homeland kissed each other goodbye on the cheeks at bus stations.

We began the trek northward at 9 p.m., just after the sun went down in Chisinau. My seatmate reached down to the bag between his feet and produced a bottle of carbonated water. He offered me the first sip. I declined, but said "thank you." He extended his hand to me and said, "Adalet," pointing to his chest with his free hand. "Aaron," I said, tapping my own chest.

Adalet was the type of nervous traveler who checks his passport every twenty minutes. I saw the cover and had to process the Cyrillic letters in my mind. It took me a few seconds to decipher: Adalet was from... Azerbaijan. He was Azerbaijani. I didn't know the capital of that country, so I asked him. We spoke in slow Russian.

"From Baku I," said Adalet. "Capital, yes. You New York? You Michigan?"

"Maine," I said. "I'm from Maine."

He shook his head. No, he didn't know Maine.

"Work in Moldova?" he asked, pointing at me.

"I'm a volunteer," I said. "No pay."

"Work in Moldova *with* pay," he said, again tapping his chest. "No other reason for be in Moldova."

I thought back to Nadezhda asking about the jobs available in Alabama. Now I'd come across a man who'd immigrated to Moldova for work. What kind of job did he have? Adalet didn't have a clean answer when I asked about his work. He tapped his passport with his finger and said, "Problem at the border I?"

The engine block began smoking around midnight. We stopped for a breakdown an hour later, still in Moldova. During this lull I helped Adalet fill out his entry and exit immigration cards. "When the border guard asks," I said, "don't tell him you're going to Kiev. No. Say you're going to 'Borispol.' That's the name of the airport. You'll sound more official." It was a trick an older volunteer had told me; the border guards would care less about you if you were leaving their country immediately.

The driver used a hammer to fix the mechanical problem and we were back on the bumpy road, still an hour away from the border. Adalet checked his passport. We traded passports for fun, I assumed to look at the stamps. Adalet turned to my back pages and passed his fingers over the markings from Romania, Spain and Turkey. I opened Adalet's passport and found the final pages blank. His passport showed no signs of use. I didn't know how he'd arrived in Moldova, but it certainly hadn't been through normal channels. Indeed, I also envisioned problems at the border.

The bus passed through the Moldovan checkpoint in under ten minutes. The border agent took all the passports into his cubicle, stamped the exit pages, and returned them to the driver. We drove through the no man's land and watched the driver hand the stack of passports to the Ukrainian agent. "Two foreigners," reported the driver. The agent was dressed in military uniform. He nodded before disappearing into his cubicle with the passports. Twenty minutes later, the agent stepped onto the bus and handed the stack of passports—minus two—back to the driver. "Let me see the other one first," said the agent. He pointed to Adalet.

Through the window I saw Adalet tense up under questioning and repeat the word "Borispol" a few times. After a few minutes he got back on the bus with a smile. He winked at me. "Now the American!" shouted the agent from his cubicle.

I gingerly approached the agent's workspace. "You speak Russian?" he asked. I nodded. "Good," he said. "There's a problem. I've found mistakes in your passport that demand explanation."

He pointed to the exit stamp I'd just received on the Moldovan side of the border. "You have an exit stamp right here," he said pointing, "but you have no entry point. Show me how you entered Moldova."

Everyone on the bus watched through the windows as I flipped through my passport, wondering after how many minutes the agent would simply detain the American and instruct the bus to continue on. I couldn't find an entry stamp with the proper date. The Moldovans at the airport hadn't stamped me back into the country when I returned from Turkey.

How had Adelet made it through with a clean passport?

"This isn't my problem," I told the agent, handing him back my passport.

"It *is* your problem," he said. "Very much."

"This is a problem of the Moldovan agents. You can't blame me for a Moldovan's mistake. They probably ran out of ink. They probably sold the ink pads or played with them or God knows what."

The Ukrainian agent giggled at my disparaging remarks about Moldovans.

"Okay," he said. "Your transit papers indicate you are reporting to Borispol. Let me see your airplane ticket."

I broke off eye contact with the agent. "I can't," I said.

The agent regained his sharp edges. "You must."

"My ticket is electronic. It will be printed when I arrive at the airport."

This explanation must have sounded like nonsense. The bus driver honked and held his hands up, seeking the agent's permission to leave me behind. "You're not making this easy," the agent told me.

"I tell the truth."

The agent nodded. "Are you a spy?"

"What?"

"Are you an American spy?"

"No."

"I believe you," said the agent, stamping my passport. "Get back on the bus."

We'd spent a half an hour at the checkpoint and the driver said, "Not as bad as I thought," when I stepped into the bus and returned to my seat.

Soon we stopped at an all-night convenience store. Adalet purchased a Ukrainian beer and tore the cap off with his side teeth. I drank a pineapple juice box with a straw.

"Ukraine," Adalet said smiling.

Back on the bus I fell asleep.

Adalet elbowed me awake when the bus began its crawl through the industrial outskirts of Kiev. We arrived at a dirty bus station. Adalet shook my hand. He would not take my directions to Borispol. He said *"udachee"* and began walking on a random course away from the station, into Ukraine at large, I imagined, perhaps in search of other paying work.

* * *

My brother Justin picked me up in Boston. We ate at the Burger King at a rest stop off the highway, and then we drove as far as Portland. I slept on his couch. He lived alone in a space larger than the entire apartment in Riscani. In the morning my brother and I argued because I didn't want to bathe; I'd showered at headquarters before getting on the bus to Kiev, and I felt taking a shower so soon after would be wasteful. In Augusta, my mom and dad hugged and kissed me. The dog continued barking until she recalled my smells. After an hour, it felt like I'd never left; nothing had changed in the year I'd been gone. I didn't call my friends because I knew nothing had changed with them, either. Moldova felt like a dream I'd awoken from. At dinner my dad and brother drank beer; I drank soda. The next day I went driving on my own and got pulled over for speeding. I smiled at the thought of bribing the officer. "Know why I pulled you over?" I nodded and received a verbal warning. I drank quarts of Dunkin' Donuts coffee and stayed up watching the Red Sox. After awhile it felt unnatural understanding all the words on the TV, so I flipped to the Quebec channel and listened to them speak French. I didn't speak French, and as I listened I had no desire to learn. I read each night before sleeping. Four nights. I didn't snap out of the dream feeling until my mom and dad hugged me again, before I left, and said, "Only one more year."

My life would feel like this again in a year. Perhaps by then I wouldn't feel lost. By then I would have accomplished something. By then I would have a foundation for the rest of my life.

Three Countries in One Place

I returned to Moldova through Romania.

From the airport, I walked past the unlicensed taxi drivers in the parking lot as though relying on muscle memory. In a licensed taxi, I spoke softly, using the two or three words in Romanian I'd know would get me to the train station. I remembered the roads. It was warmer now since the last time I'd been in Bucharest with Callie. The city looked cleaner without its coat of gray snow.

At the station, I ate lunch at McDonald's with a chatty Canadian who asked if I liked wine—*because she had a bottle.* She would have shared a cabin with me on the train if she'd been going to Chisinau and not Sofia, toward tourism. I instead bunked in a cabin with a young Moldovan woman seeking refuge from Russian men on the train who assumed she was a prostitute. Before falling asleep, she asked why I spoke Russian and not Romanian. In the morning, the girl refreshed her make-up. "Thank you for staying on your side of the cabin," she said, offering me a stick of mint gum. We'd arrived in Moldova. A minibus raced alongside the train on its way into Chisinau; I remembered this scene, but in my memory there was snow.

* * *

At home in Riscani, I found Dima and Vova sitting on the couch in their underwear. Dima thought it was Katya coming through the door and shouted, "I was just on my way!" When he saw it was me he said, "*Slavabogo*—thank God," and shook my hand. It was a hundred degrees in the apartment. Vova was trying to get Dima to agree to something. "No, no, no," he said. "You know my day. Back to work." He put on his wool pants with his cotton shirt, shook our hands, and left.

Vova spoke around me, shouting to Dariya in the next room. "Dariya!"

She shouted through the walls. "What, Vova!"

Vova increased his volume. "Let's go swim!"

A second passed without sound.

"Okay!" said Dariya.

A moment later the glass door to my room swung open, and Dariya came out in her bikini.

"Aaron," she said. "You came back."

"I know," said Vova. "I didn't think he would either."

Dariya nodded her approval. "Let's go swim."

Vova called his wife Talia and soon the four of us were driving northward in the bread truck.

After half an hour of driving, we parked at the edge of a campground adjacent to a lake. Here, only a few plastic bottles floated in the water, and hardly any rubbish collected on the shoreline.

"Over there," said Vova to me, pointing with both his index fingers. "That is where the borders of Romania and Ukraine meet." He connected his pointing fingers. "From this spot we can see three countries."

I knew he was wrong. I'd seen a map of Moldova and knew we'd have to drive another two hours from Riscani to see the point he referred to.

"Geography is interesting," I said.

"You're wrong," said Dariya. "We're not anywhere near the border."

"Smart college girl," said Vova, waving away his sister, and he took his wife's hand. The couple went off into the woods for privacy, a blanket tucked under Talia's arm. I followed Dariya into the lake, getting in up to my neck, but careful not to swallow any water. I pointed to the distant shoreline and said, "Romania?"

Dariya shook her head. "Vova doesn't know what he's talking about."

We floated until the sun went down and I began to shiver. I'd expected Dariya to have a million questions about America, but her mind was elsewhere. In a week she'd move to Balti for college. My shivering produced ripples in the water. I watched a dozen tiny waves lap against Dariya's face as she floated on her back. Finally, she returned to the moment. "Are you cold?" she asked me. My teeth were chattering.

"I feel great," I said. "Swimming is great."

"Let's get out anyway," she said. "Vova and Talia must be finished by now."

As we walked uphill from the lake Dariya called out her brother's name.

An Arrival

Katya locked herself in the kitchen while Dariya gathered her belongings. Dima watched his daughter like a vulture, periodically asking why she'd need that much make-up for classes, or why she wasn't bringing more sweaters. "I'll be back Saturday, Papa. For now be quiet!" Dima put his hands up in surrender. "Okay, miss college student. You know best." During the week Dariya was to stay with a family friend in Balti while she attended classes. She'd be home on the weekends. Sobs originating from the kitchen filled the apartment. "Stop crying, Mama!" said Dariya.

"I'm not," said Katya with a whimper.

Outside Vova honked the bread truck's horn. We ignored his impatient shouting from three stories below. Dariya hugged Dima, let him kiss her cheek, walked into the kitchen and came out crying a moment later. "Bye, Aaron," she said, putting on her shoes. "See you next week." She left. Dima didn't feel like talking or playing cards. He turned on the news and didn't take his attention away for the rest of the night. Katya finally came out of the kitchen and pointed to a plate of cabbage and a cup of tea. She locked herself in the bedroom while I ate.

Alone at the table, I was excited about the future. I liked the idea of Dariya attending college. Her plans for study were vague—business, communications—but I was convinced that only something good could come from those studies. I hoped all of my pupils would go to college. But closer, more immediate to my mindset, a new volunteer was coming to live in Riscani.

* * *

I found Michael staring up at the Lenin statue. He was tall and red-haired and had a firm handshake. He pointed to the monument and said, "So it's Russian here."

I nodded. "Very."

"I learned Romanian," he said. "Think I'll get by?"

I nodded. "You're not the first to speak Romanian here."

Michael held up a stack up papers—hand drawn maps and site reports from previous volunteers.

"I hope so," he said. "We'll see."

I gave him the brief tour of Riscani: my apartment block, the Russian School and Moldovan Lyceum, the sport complex, the church, the lake and the lake bar. I pointed in the direction of the bazaar.

"I've seen the bazaar," said Michael. "And the vodka bars."

I sensed reservation in his tone.

"I'm sure *someone* there speaks Romanian," I said.

We returned to my apartment to eat and avoid the midday sun. Another American in the apartment shocked Katya out of her sadness. She buzzed around him like a bee and shooed us into the living room to watch TV while she cooked more food and set another place at the table. We went to my room instead, and we read over the site reports from Riscani's past volunteers. "Doesn't look great," he said.

"No, no," I said. "The mayor's not that bad. And, no, I don't think it's a ghost town. No way."

He leafed through the papers before stopping at the report from a California woman named Cate: she'd lived in Riscani for nearly two years before leaving the Peace Corps early to be with her newly born grandson. She'd also been an Agro-forestry volunteer, like Michael, had spoken Romanian while working with local farmers, and had neutral, if not pleasant, things to say about the Riscani community.

"Look," said Michael. "She lived alone."

Now we had an address, a possible apartment for Michael.

In the kitchen, we showed Katya the street name and she rolled her eyes.

"It's the Romanian district, right?" I said. "The apartments along the lake."

She waved in the air as though to communicate great distance. "So far," she said. "So far across."

"Where we ate shashlik?" I said.

Katya nodded.

"Don't get lost looking for it," she said. "I wish Dariya were here to take you."

* * *

Michael and I crossed the dam on the lake, continuing to the path leading to the barbecue pits. Chickens and geese roamed in the yards in front of the squatty apartment buildings. Past the barbecue pits, now off the path, we walked a mile along a road that ran parallel to the lakeshore. After ten minutes, we came upon more Romanian style apartment blocks—built horizontally instead of vertically, never rising above a second story. We found the address of the apartment the California woman had once occupied and stood in front, working up the nerve to knock on a neighbor's door. The building appeared to be empty. We walked inside the apartment block, shook off the feeling of trespass, stepped up to a door and knocked. A large woman answered and demanded to know our business. She spoke in Romanian, so I pointed to Michael and stepped back. Michael said "excuse us," placed his hand over his heart, and the woman calmed and listened. His Romanian impressed me; he inquired about the apartment, and if the woman had known the American, Cate.

"You must mean *Catia*," said the woman. "Of course I knew her. She lived right there." The woman pointed across the hall. "She baked cakes."

Michael asked again about the apartment.

"Take it," said the woman. "We'll be neighbors."

Michael asked about rent.

"How should I know? I'm not the owner."

Michael asked about the landlord.

"Yeah," said the woman. "Leave that to me." She went inside and called someone who spoke loudly through the receiver; from the corridor I could hear an agitated female voice on the other end of the phone. The two spoke in Romanian. The woman before us explained that another American had come for the apartment—another volunteer, not a missionary. The conversation ended cordially. The woman replaced the receiver on its wall mount and said, "There, there. We'll be neighbors."

This landlord would meet him in a week to discuss rent and give him keys.

"I also bake cakes," said Michael. He promised one to his future neighbor. "That will be good," she said. "You'll live right there." She pointed.

Michael left Riscani with his mission accomplished. We walked past the empty bazaar to get to the bus station. It then dawned on Michael he'd have to be at this bazaar every day to get food.

"Do you always eat so well?" he asked me. "If so, I'll drop by all the time."

My mind jumped to Katya, no doubt in the kitchen that very moment controlling her grief by killing something for dinner. "Um...no," I said.

"I like to cook," said Michael. "Riscani seems like a good place to live."

We shook hands and made plans to meet again when he returned from the capital.

I walked back to the apartment. Katya was sleeping. In the kitchen on the table was a platter of salted white beans surrounded by a dozen chopped tomatoes and cucumbers. An entire chicken had been torn apart, boiled, and placed with love into a decorative pattern on the plate next to my cup of tea.

Teachers' Day

The night before school began my mother called from Maine to wish me luck and say she loved me. "Remember," she said, "it might not seem like it, but everything you do influences eternity." I went to sleep happy and ready for work.

The first week at school passed without any major incidents. There weren't any fires or drunk students or kids challenging me to fights. As they had the year before, the students hesitated to participate—even the pupils who'd been in my classes the year before. I might have felt stress if I were a new volunteer. In retrospect, my comfort level with craziness was the only difference between the beginnings of the first and second school years. This time nothing fazed me, not even when a boy went after his classmate with a belt.

Several parents and guardians had requested the school keep their sons and daughters under my tutelage. Natashka's class—the class that had started the trash fire—were now sixth graders. Two boys I knew from basketball, Vova and Alexander, were now in my ninth grade class. And the rambunctious pupils belonging to Lyudmila Petrovna's homeroom, a different class of sixth graders, also remained with me.

The group of ninth graders from the previous year had moved on; there weren't enough left to justify a space in my schedule. Edgar and the other boys who'd preferred drinking to English lessons had "graduated" to the work force or technical school to learn tractor mechanics. Nadezhda had absorbed the remaining girls into her own tenth grade class. In exchange she'd given me a new group of fifth graders—all girls. They listened to me, they conjugated, they played nice, they thanked me when class ended, never asked about grades and surrounded me in an awkward group hug when the bell rang.

The final class on my schedule, a village class, would prove to be my greatest challenge during this second year.

After watching me teach for a year, the school director had decided I was tough enough to handle a village class. A third class of sixth graders came into my room and began throwing playful punches while they waited for the bell to ring. I screamed for them to respect the classroom and they grew silent; this was the only time all year they'd respond to my yelling. They arrived in Riscani each morning on a bus from Novi Balan, a nearby village without a school. Their clothes were plainer than the town kids, with muted colors. Most had brown finger nails. The boys shaved their heads to keep dirt away, and the girls appeared to eat no more than once a day. Two of the boys called themselves gypsies, Artem and Maxim, of the Roma ethnicity. I soon learned that because of these two boys, Nadezhda had talked the school director into passing this class on to me.

"All right," I said. "Let's learn English."

"As soon as you kick Artem and Maxim into the hallway," said one of the girls. "Then we'll begin."

The class laughed.

Maxim calmly nodded his head to Artem, pushed his chair out, stood up, took off his belt and lunged after the girl. Two Russian boys promptly tackled him. The girl smacked Maxim over the head while the two boys held him down.

"Okay," I said. "I guess that's enough."

I pulled the two boys off Maxim and got everyone back to their seats. The kids watched me silently, waiting for me to dispense punishment. Instead of yelling at Maxim, I directed my anger toward the girl. "Listen, little missy," I said. "In

English class I'm the only one allowed to hit people!" The class laughed. I tapped the girl on her forehead with her own text book.

I switched into English.

"Who wants to talk first?"

The room remained silent.

"What is your name?" I asked a girl.

Silence.

"Who speaks English?" I asked. "Any words at all."

Continued silence. Artem took out a cell, which I confiscated immediately.

"Give it!" he yelled in Russian.

"Ask me in English!" I said.

Artem laughed. The class laughed. This was a sixth grade class, so they'd studied English for three years.

I pointed at a girl, indicating it was her turn to speak.

"Not a word," she said. "We usually draw in English class."

"I know a word," interrupted Maxim. "Motherfucker." The class laughed.

"Who has a textbook?" I asked. "Raise your hands."

Only one girl in the class of fifteen raised her hand.

"Only you?" I said.

"Yes, Mr. Aaron. Don't you remember hitting me over the head with it?"

* * *

The pupils I'd instructed the previous year took a few days to recall what they'd forgotten over summer. The angelic class of fifth grade girls was able to follow everything the textbook threw at them. The village class had to restart at the beginning—hellos, goodbyes and colors—but was making slow, daily progress. My work seemed like a real job; I wasn't babysitting.

Colin and Jesse were off to rocky starts. One day Colin texted during a class to share that one of his students had glued and taped his exam to the desk so that it couldn't be collected; the school's director had subsequently dragged the boy off school grounds by the ear. Jesse was happy if a day passed without a child lighting a cigarette in class.

My setback was Teachers' Day.

From the previous year's celebration, I recalled group circle-dancing and cognac toasts to Soviet tradition. This year the school director upgraded me to the men's table; I wouldn't be sheltered. The men of the school had talked amongst themselves and decided I was a good, simple person; I spoke Russian well and deserved to toast with them like a real man. I sat between the two men I'd bested at table tennis: Andrei Vasilyavich—the *Patron*—and Sergei Stepanovich. Then a familiar figure walked into the gymnasium; Ivan Vasilyavich, the old-man basketball trainer, now shuffled toward the table carrying three bottles of vodka. "Call me Vanya," said Ivan Vasilyavich. We toasted to being men and sitting at our own table. During this celebration I wasn't called up to circle dance or forced to listen to students' teacher-inspired poetry; I, like the other men, merely had to drink.

Students passing through the gymnasium waved to me and smiled. "Enjoy yourself, Mr. Aaron! This is your day!"

When the men's table ran out of vodka and cognac, Ivan Vasilyavich sent Sasha the basketball player to the corner store with fifty lei for more booze. We ate tiny sandwiches until Sasha returned, and then the next toast honored America.

After we drained another bottle of vodka Sergei Stepanovich asked how much I'd be making as a teacher in

America. "The same job as you have here," he clarified. "How much?" Everyone at the table moved closer to hear my answer. I was too drunk to censor myself. "Forty thousand dollars," I said. The table erupted in cheers. When the women in the gym looked toward the drunken men, Andrei Vasilyavich announced the sum of money I'd sacrificed just to live and work in Riscani. Everyone in the gymnasium toasted my sacrifice. "You're not a bad guy," said another male teacher I'd never met, patting me on the back. He handed me a chicken leg off his plate. "Eat," he said. "Never drink without eating."

I don't remember if I ate the chicken leg.

* * *

I returned to consciousness just after 3 a.m.

Again I found myself in my bed in my clothes. After passing my tongue over my teeth, I tasted vomit. Nothing bad was in my room, so I must have gotten sick at school. The realization quickly arrived that I'd have to teach my Friday classes only a few hours later.

When the sun came up, I changed into a shirt without wrinkles. I didn't change my pants or socks. My hair moved at the command of my fingers into acceptable position. I didn't feel a reason to shave. My head didn't bother me much, so I must have vomited a great deal; I was sure to hear every bit of detail once I arrived at school.

All my books and teaching materials were still in my classroom from the day before, so I arrived at school empty-handed with my head down.

The school director met me at the door.

We rarely spoke, the director and I, but now of course we had something to talk about. "I'm sorry," I said. He shushed me quiet; pupils were watching and he didn't want them eavesdropping. He shooed them away and offered to walk me to class.

"Let me begin," said the director, "by saying how pleased I was to see you enjoy yourself yesterday."

I didn't understand his elevated tone. The director was happy.

"We've had Americans before," he continued. "In Riscani, yes, one or two, and I wasn't impressed. Maybe because they were women—maybe—but you've clearly connected here and I'm glad to see it. Keep up the good work."

"Okay," I said.

He left me at my classroom door. As the students walked in they also expressed their happiness that I'd enjoyed a pleasant Teachers' Day. "You were so happy!" said Natashka. Word of my *happiness* had traveled around town, in fact; those in town who knew me confirmed to strangers that I was indeed the nice, *simple* man I sounded like—an American, finally, who fit in.

Between classes Sergei Stepanovich winked at me in the hallway and Andrei Vasilyavich snuck up behind to slap me on the back. "You *really* enjoyed yourself!" he beamed. "*Maladits*, Mr. Aaron! Well done!"

By all accounts, the school was proud of me.

My beloved fifth grade girls asked if it was true, had I gotten drunk at the Teachers' Day celebration?

"It's true," I said. "I'm sorry."

"For what?"

"Teacher's shouldn't drink," I explained. "Certainly not at school."

The girls shrugged their shoulders. The class's chosen spokesperson, a girl named Olia, explained in Russian why I shouldn't apologize. "You respected those who honored you."

"By getting drunk?"

"Yes," Olia told me. The others agreed. These girls were twelve years old. At the end of class, they saw I was sad and gave me a group hug when the bell rang.

During my final break of the day I sat with Nadezhda in the faculty lounge watching the Russian Victory Network on TV.

"Does your head hurt?" she asked.

She too expressed her pleasure and surprise that I'd enjoyed myself so greatly. I repeated what the fifth grade girls had tried to explain. Nadezhda attempted to tie their threads of logic into a cleaner knot:

"You fit in now, I think. You must feel so, yes? Before you were apart, and now you are together. By celebrating...by accepting honor, in general, you honor those who honor you. By sharing honor you validate the honor. Does that make sense?"

"No," I said. "No sense at all."

"Russian tradition," she said. "You don't have to understand everything."

After school, Katya asked if my head hurt. Dima came home later and called me "comrade" in jest: a "working" man of the people, he said. I made plans that evening to leave Riscani for the weekend. I didn't want any more congratulations. I texted Will and invited myself to his village. Ten minutes later he texted back: *Come tonight, not tomorrow. Dying of boredom.*

I threw a change of clothes into my pack and told Katya and Dima I'd return in a couple days.

The Road to Corjeuti

Will's village, Corjeuti, was 60 km away from Riscani. The trip should have taken a couple hours on a minibus; but this day the voyage would turn into an epic six-hour trek involving buses, hitchhiking and trudging through dusty villages.

At the Riscani station the minibus northward was full. All the seats were taken and standing passengers were spilling out the front door. The driver recognized me as the American and promised to find me a seat. He squirmed his way inside the bus and pushed everyone back until there was space for me to sit on the dashboard, facing away from oncoming traffic, my spine contoured snuggly against the windshield. A few villagers got out when the bus made its first stop, and then I was able to face forward. An hour later we arrived at a city called Edinet, the transit point for those continuing northwest, toward the Ukrainian city Chernovtsy—a city of origin for many of the black market goods sold in Moldova. I waited in Edinet two hours without a bus going by. I kicked a rock around the empty street, trying to score it into a puddle twenty yards away. Finally a bus arrived. It was the bus Will had said I needed, but as it was two hours late the driver had changed the route; he wasn't going through Corjeuti like he normally would. The driver was angry and yelling into his cell phone. I interrupted him to ask about alternative options to Will's village. "How should I know?" he said. "Hitchhike."

A lady passenger on the bus screamed at the driver to act kindly. "Can't you see he's not one of ours?" she said, pointing to me. "He needs help."

The driver looked me over and asked where I'd come from.

"Fine," he said. "We'll find you a ride in Briceni." He waved me onto the bus. I texted Will and received the following reply: *From Briceni you'll have to hitch or walk. But I guess that beats sleeping at the station in Edinet.*

Twenty minutes later, the bus pulled into a field. The driver killed the engine, so I knew this wasn't a scheduled stop. "Let's settle this now," said the driver. "*This*" referred to me. The lady who'd convinced the driver to help me thought the bus should go back to the original route and drive through Corjeuti—"in the name of showing our guest Moldovan hospitality"—which would add another half hour onto the current trip to Briceni.

The twenty passengers interrogated me.

What is the nature of your business in Corjeuti? How will you get to the house of this American "health" teacher if you don't know where he lives? What will you do when your cell phone runs out of battery and only Romanians live within shouting distance? Who will rescue you then?

"Enough!" said a Russian businessman wearing a tracksuit. "Here's what we'll do." He explained that the detour was unacceptable, as he had pressing business in Briceni; however, he'd be willing to drive the American to Corjeuti himself in his cousin's car, providing I would pay for the gas.

"Liar!" said the lady passenger trying to protect me. "No one believes you!"

The businessman called her a bad word in Russian and everyone laughed. The matter was settled.

Thirty minutes later, just before Briceni, the lady passenger got off the bus in her village, but not before handing me a slip of paper with her phone number. "Call me if anyone tries to screw you," she said, pointing to the businessman. I thanked her.

Once she departed, the driver called back to the businessman. "Does your cousin really have a car?" The businessman brushed the silly thought away with a limp wave of his hand. "Let the American hitch," he said.

"It's fine," I said.

"You speak Russian?" said the businessman. "Well, it's nothing personal."

Everyone remaining on the bus wished me well when we reached Briceni. The driver pulled over at the best spot for me to hitch, entrusting my care to a middle-aged woman with a bucket of cheese. The driver asked her to assist me in hitchhiking. She responded, "And why is he incapable of securing his own ride?"

"He's American," said the driver. "But you can talk to him. He speaks Russian."

The cheese lady sneered, but told the driver she'd help me. The driver shook my hand and returned to his bus.

The cheese lady and I stood for ten minutes without talking. She was primarily a Romanian speaker. I texted Will. He responded, *Not good. You're 30k and three villages away. But it's a straight road. You can't get lost. Have fun walking.*

I rationalized that any car passing by this hitching post would eventually find me on the straight road through the three villages to Corjeuti, so I began thinking of words to pleasantly excuse myself from this cheese lady and begin walking. Just then a rusted Lada stopped in front of us. The cheese lady stuck her face into the opened passenger window to speak with the driver and immediately pulled her head away. She touched her nose. "You sit in front," she said to me. A wave of mixed alcohol smells engulfed me when I opened the door—vodka and cognac and beer. I asked how long it would take to reach Corjeuti and the driver responded with spit bubbles. In back, the cheese lady crossed herself twice. She sat next to an unrestrained toddler who played with the driver's hair over the headrest. For the first time in Moldova, I used the seatbelt. The road leading into the villages was empty of other automobiles, so the drunk driver dodged imaginary ones. We swerved casually from one side of the road to the other, like a boat drifting with the current. I turned around and saw the cheese lady had grabbed the toddler and hugged the boy close to her chest for protection. A small truck appeared from the opposite direction. Our driver reacted by jerking the wheel toward the correct side of the road. The right tires of the car skidded over the gravel shoulder, a dust cloud erupting behind us. "Drive normal!" said the woman in the back, clutching the child. I pressed my palm against the dashboard, pounded my feet into the floorboards. *Grab the wheel,* I thought.

The car spun out into a cornfield.

Everything was quiet. The engine was off, and the only sound was the rustling of the cornstalks against the body of the car. It's seemed wrong to speak, like I'd disrupt the peacefulness of our new surroundings.

The driver burped.

"I'm fine," I finally said in English. "Are you fine?" I said in Russian over my shoulder.

The cheese lady swore at the driver in Romanian. She buckled the child into the back seat, and got out of the car and crossed herself several times. I followed her on foot. The driver inched his car back to the road, cornstalks falling off his hood, and took off in the direction of Briceni.

"The fool doesn't even know where he's going," said the cheese lady.

From the cornfield, we walked to the cheese lady's village. Her name was Maria. She didn't understand the pronunciation of my name, so I asked that she call me Anton. She allowed me to carry her bucket of cheese. We entered her village after a few minutes of walking and she promised to find me a car-owner in her village who would take me farther toward Corjeuti. As we walked through the village, doors and windows opened and the villagers asked Maria, "Who's got your cheese?"

"He's an American," she answered. "I'm helping him get a ride. He speaks Russian! Says his name is Anton!" This last bit of information consistently made the villagers giggle.

After Maria had flaunted her association with an American to a number of her village peers, she stopped a man driving a Mercedes and told him to drive me to the village limits. The man hesitated and only accepted once Maria offered him cheese. The man in the Mercedes never tried to converse with me. He dropped me at the village limit and nodded when I thanked him.

I stood at the village limit for twenty minutes before a delivery truck stopped for me. The driver apologized he couldn't take me farther than the second village on the way to Corjeuti; he had deliveries to finish. He laughed at me. "You speak Russian," he said. "You're not from America." He ate a candy bar and threw the wrapper out the window. At the limit of the second village he shook my hand and wished me a pleasant onward journey. He refused money and drove back into the village to continue his deliveries.

I texted Will. He responded, *Good work. Only fifteen more kilometers. Let me know when you see the lake.*

The landscape opened into an expanse of fields. The lowering sun cast golden light over tall grass and wheat. The lake appeared on my left, an expanse of rippling gray water. I texted Will. *Only five kilometers more to walk.* A car driven by teenagers stopped and offered me a ride to Corjeuti. I waved them along. The walk had turned meditative and I wished to continue on foot. The sky color changed quickly, and soon I was walking through darkness. I stepped off the road and hid among trees when cars passed, illuminating the path forward with their headlights. From the roadside I saw a pedestrian's figure far ahead on the straight road. It disappeared when the carlights passed by. It was Will. Ten minutes later we met on the road. The moon offered faint light.

"Bad day?" asked Will.

"I feel good now," I said.

Will flagged down the next passing set of headlights. We sat in the back seat of a Lada filled with lumpy bags of apples. The man wouldn't accept money, and insisted we each take two apples.

* * *

Will lived with a Baptist woman in a split house; he occupied the smaller half with the kitchen and guest rooms, while she remained in the main house. He only saw her when she cooked.

"It gets a bit lonely," said Will. "Glad you made the trek."

That morning at school, talking with my fifth grade girls, felt like the events of several days in the past.

Will opened two fresh beers, and we toasted America.

I spent the next two days at Will's place. We cooked potatoes with peppers and drank beer, but never got drunk. Corjeuti was a clean rural village that seemed removed from the world. I felt recharged and ready to teach again. The ride back to Riscani only took ninety minutes. At a gas station the bus began rolling downhill while the driver was out talking to the guy pumping gas, so I jumped forward and pulled the emergency break. The other passengers applauded me and the driver patted me on the back. "Okay, okay," he said. "You don't have to pay full fare."

Hram

Riscani's town birthday, a day festival called *hram*, fell on a Tuesday.

Only a handful of students had come to school; none of the kids higher than sixth grade or any of the village classes showed up that day. I was thankful that my older kids had taken the day off. They would have certainly arrived to class intoxicated. Instead, they wandered the streets with cans of beer, toasting anyone they recognized.

My fifth grade girls asked if I'd be celebrating in the town center. I assured them I wouldn't be drunk.

"Why not?" asked Olia. "It is *hram*."

"Do you realize that drinking so much can damage your health?"

"You are not little," the class explained. "You can drink without problems."

After school, I called my friends. I wouldn't be going out into the *hram* without backup. Michael was in the capital, so he couldn't help. With such short notice, Colin was the only one who could make it there in time. He was in Riscani an hour after I called, ready to take on the best the Russians could offer.

Colin was in the apartment for ten minutes before I realized he'd arrived. Dima had met him at the door and taken him to the kitchen for a shot of vodka in honor of Riscani. I walked into the kitchen and found Dima talking to Colin in broken Romanian. Dima pushed out a chair for me, explaining that he and Colin had started while I finished my nap. "Dude," said Colin, his cheeks flushed. "I really like your father."

Dima poured three more shots of vodka. We drank. Then Dima reached down to the cabinet below the sink and produced five different bottles: apple garilka, Moldovan samagon, cognac, high-class vodka, and red wine. We took a shot from each bottle. Then Dima took a bottle of cold beer from the ice box and we drank that. Colin had been a bartender in Virginia before joining the Peace Corps. Now he offered his professional commentary: "Dude, we just drank ten shots of alcohol in twenty minutes."

"Go enjoy yourselves in the street," said Dima. "It's a party."

"Should we wait?" I asked Colin.

"I can walk. Can you?"

I stood to test my legs. After ten seconds I still hadn't fallen over.

"All good," I said.

Dima hugged us. We put on our shoes and hit the street.

Colin was already something of a celebrity in Riscani. The town folk who'd met him on his first visit recalled meeting the tallest man in the world. Those who hadn't seen him carried in their minds an image akin to Big Foot.

From my front door we followed the techno music to its source at the Lenin statue. A crowd of a thousand cheered when we arrived. People hugged me and shook Colin's hand, took pictures of us with their cell phones. In Russian, Colin said, "Good evening, Riscani," and the crowd lost it. Students appeared holding beers for us to drink. I refused and told Colin not to accept anything from a minor—even former students like Edgar. Soon enough adults gave us drinks. The Riscanians gyrated to the techno music in disorganized, Russian-head-bobbing, non-circle dancing. Dariya appeared, only the second time I'd seen her since she went off to college. She'd dyed her hair black and wore even tighter clothes than she'd worn in high school. She kissed me on the cheek without her previous childhood awkwardness, whispered she'd see us back at the apartment, and then disappeared into the crowd.

A couple of my fifth grade girls came to give me a hug and meet Colin. I shook their parents' hands and toasted with them. Everyone I'd ever met in Riscani filtered through the center over the next few hours. Each offered Colin and me shots from unlabeled bottles. More people approached Colin and soon he was throwing up in the bushes down the hill from the monument. The party died around 2 a.m. Dariya walked home with us.

"College is tough," I said. Colin agreed.

"I like it now," said Dariya. "I feel important."

"That makes me happy," I said.

"I love Riscani," said Colin.

"That makes me happy," said Dariya.

* * *

Soon after *hram*, a well-known student from the Moldovan lyceum passed away from illness. My ninth graders had played with him as kids and weren't in the mood to study, so I let class out early. With a handful of sunflower seeds, I walked down the main street. Live music carried through the air, trumpets and drums. I said hello to Katya at the bazaar and ate one of her sugar rolls. Outside the bazaar, I stepped into a tractor-trailer that had been converted into a shooting range, and I paid five lei to shoot twenty bee-bees at paper targets. I only hit one. Back on the main street, I decided to have a beer. As I walked toward the lake, the live music grew louder. The drumming vibrated my stomach. Then the funeral procession for the dead boy turned a corner into my view. Pedestrians stopped walking and removed their hats; I did the same. The casket was carried on the back of a flat-bed truck. His body was open to the air and slightly blue. Some type of jelly made his face look shiny. The priest walked directly behind; he made eye contact with me and smiled, placed his hand over his heart and bowed his head. I mirrored him, placing my hand on my heart and bowing my head. Several of my students were in the procession following the casket and the priest. They waved to me. Everyone looked sad, but no one cried. I continued on to the lake. The sounds of the trumpets and drums diminished until I only heard them in memory. At the bar they only had liters in the fridge, so that's what I drank.

* * *

A car beeped at me, so I stepped from the street onto the unswept sidewalk. The car pulled over just up the road. The man driving got out and walked directly toward me, and my instinct said I must fight this man. I tensed my hands, but then I recognized the portly elegance of his movements and the threat disappeared, though something kept me from remembering his name. The man swayed as he approached, not able to advance in a perfect line, but he wasn't drunk.

"Aaron!" said the man, his hand outstretched.

A light went off in my head. "Andrei Nikolayevich!" An entire winter had passed since I'd helped to translate his petition to the Austrian government about sex trafficking. Images and feelings returned to me: of walking past farmers before entering an office, of sitting before a black-screened computer, of reducing terrible thoughts to single words.

"The Austrians finally wrote back!" said Andrei Nikolayevich.

I smiled.

"Do you speak German? No? But the official letter is in German! I thought you might know German. But do not worry, I'm sure the letter is rubbish. I'm not getting my hopes up. But you and I—you and I—we—you and I—we should go fishing!"

I smelled vodka on his breath. He was in street clothes, not his lawyer suit. I apologized that I couldn't provide a German translation. He waved his hand in the air and returned the conversation to fishing. Even while tipsy, he still used large words. He wanted to go fishing and talk about the Soviet Union and what he'd learned about America in the Russian schools.

"I'll find a German speaker in the capital," I said.

Andrei Nikolayevich brushed that thought away. He thanked me anyway. "But we'll go fishing," he said. "We'll talk about—" and the only words I understood of what he said next were the ones that sounded the same in English and Russian, like *communism* and *democracy*. I nodded my head as though I agreed with everything.

We shook hands and went our separate tipsy ways.

At home, I collapsed into my bed, but didn't sleep. Although my head buzzed from alcohol, not without pleasure, my mood soured as I thought about the many girls who'd left Riscani, about Austria, about translating, and about the use of language. In the capital, several weeks back, I'd entered a bookstore. In bed now, I remembered the entranceway marked with nothing more than the single word—*book*—as though the store sold raw materials in the same way butchers sold meat. The shopkeeper wasn't interested in learning why my accent in Russian sounded strange. With a cigarette he pointed to his selection of foreign texts. The pages of the books in this store smelled more of smoke than the sweet notes of aged American paperbacks. I didn't hold any books up close to my face for inspection because I felt no connections. But now I remembered the further disappointment that washed over me when I discovered that dictionaries dominated this foreign book selection. I'd been looking for novels, so I left immediately. And now, in memory, I was certain that bookstore contained a Russian-German dictionary. And this felt important to me. With that book it would be possible for me to accomplish something heroic.

I woke sometime later in my clothes and left the apartment, walking in the dark with the dull outline of the Lenin statue as a landmark, until I arrived at the bus station. When no bus arrived I hitchhiked, offering to pay extra for gas if we reached the capital before dawn.

"Are you drunk?" asked the driver. "Your accent is funny."

I assured him I wasn't. I wanted to reach the capital. I wasn't running from police.

"I don't care," he said.

"I want to buy a book," I offered.

"I don't care," he repeated. "It's best if you sleep. Your accent is funny and I don't wish to talk."

In the capital, I found the storefront quickly, but hadn't considered the possibility that Russian booksellers didn't operate on the same sun-schedules as farmers. Hours later I returned and passed by the same smelly storekeeper I'd seen before without speaking. There were no dictionaries on the shelf. The raw materials of the day were a collection of nonconsecutive X-men comics, several Bibles in various languages and an English translation of *War and Peace*, which I took home with me.

On the slow bus ride back to Riscani, I wasn't too upset about my failed dictionary mission; accomplishing nothing had come to feel normal. Since arriving in Riscani, I'd experienced the personal shock of uselessness on repeat.

Everyone experienced futility, and the only social requirement was to keep functioning. The only failure would be in not trying to help, in denying the biological impulse to move toward action.

For a moment, I was inside the mind of Andrei Nikolayevich and I felt heroic.

Still on the bus, passing through the sunflower fields belonging to other villages going northward toward Ukraine, I decided I would call on Andrei Nikolayevich instead of going home. If I showed up at his office, he would probably take me fishing.

* * *

As we drove by Balti, I received a text from Michael, *At the bazaar...help!*

When I arrived, I made eye contact with Katya from a distance and she pointed excitedly in the direction where Michael had gotten lost. A few minutes later I found him with a duffle bag wandering from vendor to vendor trying to find anyone who spoke Romanian. To his credit, he'd managed to get vegetables and all the food he wanted on his own. He opened the duffle and showed me kilos of peppers, onions and garlic. He needed me because he'd found his white whale: a black market coffee maker. The vendor only spoke Russian. Michael took me to the vendor, and the woman said, "Greetings, Mr. Aaron." I didn't know who she was until she asked about her nephew's progress in class. I told her that nowadays little Victor only rarely started fires. She laughed. I pointed to the coffee maker. "It's really no good," she said. "It's from someplace crazy like Germany and doesn't make instant coffee. You have to put beans or some nonsense into a metal filter, which you then have to clean and, in short, it's just a big headache." The woman pointed at Michael. "He's

American too?" I nodded. The woman laughed. "He was here earlier and I told him to go to hell. I thought he was Romanian!" She laughed and touched Michael's arm for forgiveness. "Only one hundred lei," she said. "It's yours."

* * *

I finally got to see inside Michael's apartment when a few friends from his group came to Riscani for a house-warming party. Michael even invited Colin so that I wouldn't be among strangers. Inside the apartment Michael had a small kitchen with a gas stove and a fridge, a bathroom with a flushing toilet, a small bedroom with a collection of the landlord's Russian books, a living room with rugs on both the walls and the floor, and a balcony for smoking.

Michael's friends were all good guys; they came from Kansas, Illinois, Maryland and Florida. All of them wrote grants for community or agriculture groups, and could take time off to visit Michael whenever they wanted. Colin and I didn't have trouble fitting in. We all drank beer while Michael turned a care package from home into dinner. He made lasagna with spicy pepper flakes and mashed potatoes covered in Ranch dressing. We all slept on the floor in sleeping bags and in the morning ate pancakes with real syrup. We brewed a pound of Dunkin' Donuts coffee and finished every drop.

Colin and I only spent the one night. Without a strict work schedule, Michael's friends were able to stay a few days. "You're lucky," Colin told me.

By the lake, Colin stopped to look over the gray water and said, "Only nine more months to go. A lot can happen in nine months."

"A lot can happen in nine months," I agreed.

It took twenty minutes to walk from the Romanian district to the Russian apartment blocks. Upstairs, Dima was sipping borscht at the kitchen table. He stood when Colin and I entered, and went straight for the bottle of vodka under the kitchen sink.

Tuberculosis

I read *War and Peace* into the evening and finally put the book aside to rest my eyes after Pierre became a mason. It was midnight and I decided then I might as well stay up for the night. My bag was already packed. The first bus out of Riscani would leave in four hours. If I couldn't sleep now, I could sleep on the bus.

I'd been called to the capital against my will; each volunteer was required to pass a yearly physical, and my visit with the PC doctor was a few months overdue. I didn't mind seeing doctors, in general, but an epidemic of tuberculosis was passing through Moldova and several volunteers had already been exposed. I'd been inoculated against it, so even if I'd been exposed I wouldn't contract it, but anyone exposed had to take a tuberculosis blocker for nine months, and patients on this liver-damaging medication couldn't drink alcohol.

Life in Moldova without drinking seemed unthinkable. I couldn't remember a time with Jesse when we didn't have beers in hand. Most of my memories with Colin involved shots and someone slapping me on the back. I imagined the look of disillusionment on Dima's face when I told him I could no longer drink with him at the kitchen table, and the disgust on the faces of the other teachers when I refused to celebrate with them. Without drinking my friendships in Moldova would dissolve.

On Vasia's bus, I sat in the back against the heater and fell asleep instantly. The bus swerved around the rotary outside of Balti and I knew we'd been traveling for an hour. I went back to sleep. I opened my eyes again in the half-light of early morning to inspect the passing fields; they were interlaced with ponds, so I knew we were in the stretch of farmland between Balti and the town of Orhei—another hour completed. The road was bumpy in this stretch and if I kept my eyes closed it was only to avoid eye contact with other passengers. I couldn't sleep. I was nervous again.

In the doctor's office at headquarters, I breezed through a battery of tests that would have terrified me once upon a time. I didn't have any sex diseases, my heart was fine, my lungs expanded properly; everything, according to the doctor, was in tip-top shape. He warned me of pain and then punctured my forearm to inject a serum under the skin. The doctor was from Romania and was another with Dracula's accent. "Come back in three days," he said. He'd check the TB test then. "And don't drink alcohol. That will invalidate the results." I exhaled deeply and shook his hand. Jesse was outside in the waiting room flipping through a *Sports Illustrated* from the previous summer.

"Want to get a beer after this?" It was a logical question, even for ten in the morning. I shook my head and showed him the puffed up bubble of skin on my forearm. "Shit," he said. "Me too. We can't drink?"

"Three days."

Jesse started laughing. "What the hell are we going to do in Chisinau for three days?"

We found an abandoned DVD of *The Departed* in the lounge and watched that on a loop for twelve hours. We checked our email, claimed books from the library and watched *The Departed* again and again. I took three showers on three consecutive days for the first time in Moldova. Jesse and I had claimed the lounge for the weekend and others understood not to bother us. By now, Jesse and I were two of Moldova's veterans. Other groups had come and gone, and now no one in country had been there longer than us. Jesse spread himself horizontally over the three-person couch and I sat sideways on the loveseat. If anyone else wanted to watch *The Departed* they had to sit on the floor. I inspected the puffy blotch on my arm every ten seconds. I measured it with a protractor I'd found discarded in the library. Jesse was certain he'd been exposed to tuberculosis. I recalled all the dirty little hands I'd shaken, all the uncovered sneezes, all the wool-clad women coughing into the air on the bus and robbing my breath. As others in the lounge went out to McDonald's for beer, Jesse and I brainstormed ways to survive Moldova without drinking. We wouldn't quit. Thus far, our training village, Ivancea, was the only training group that hadn't lost a volunteer to quitting or health concerns. It was a point of pride that we finish out the twenty-seven months.

"Egypt," said Jesse. "Let's go to Egypt. They don't drink. And geographically, we'll never be closer in our lives."

As a boy, I'd always dreamed of visiting Cairo. I saw no downside to Jesse's proposition. In fact, this seemed the best idea Jesse had ever had. While I investigated ticket prices online, Jesse called Colin and tried to strong-arm him into coming along. Colin balked. He didn't like the price, the idea of a New Year's without liquor.

"It's only if we get tuberculosis," said Jesse into the phone.

When I returned from the computer room, Jesse was watching Martin Sheen get thrown off a building. I didn't say anything until after the character hit the pavement, when blood sprays in Leonardo DiCaprio's face.

"I found a good flight to Egypt," I said.

We'd travel two days before Christmas—through Romania, unfortunately—and return two days after New

Year's. It would cost the rest of our Peace Corps travel money, but I thought it was worth it.

"Well," said Jesse. "It's a good idea. If I go, though, I'll come back for New Year's in Chisinau."

That idea seemed silly to me.

"Well, do whatever. Christmas through New Year's for me."

Something in my tone took Jesse's attention away from *The Departed* and put it fully onto me.

"What's that paper?" he asked, nodding at the computer printout in my hand. I passed him the sheet of paper, my ticket conformation and itinerary.

"You already bought a ticket!"

I nodded.

Twenty minutes had passed since Jesse first mentioned the idea and it still sounded brilliant. For once in three days my mind was filled with thoughts other than tuberculosis.

"Are you drunk?" he asked.

I shrugged my shoulders. Jesse called Colin, who still didn't wish to go, though he dubbed my ticket purchase impulsive, yet badass. Colin's approval sent Jesse over the top. He went to the computer room. I heard him say, "Fuck it," and a minute later he returned to the lounge with his own ticket.

"Christmas in Egypt," he said.

On the third day, we both cleared the tuberculosis test. With beer we celebrated our clean health and our trip to Egypt just two months away.

* * *

On the bus ride home, to Riscani, a woman asked to sit next to me. She'd first spoken in Romanian, asking for the seat,

225

and then, rather than switch to Russian after hearing my response, she spoke to me in English.

"I think you are American," she said. Her accent wasn't bad. "And I'll guess you live in Riscani," she said. "And work for the Peace Corps."

"Do I know you?" I assumed that we'd met while I was drunk at hram. "Where did we meet?"

The woman shook her head. "Elvira," she said. "Now I'll explain."

Six years in the past, she'd been a student of a volunteer named Wallace at the Romanian lyceum in Riscani. I recognized the name Wallace from the Riscani site reports. She claimed just the sight of me had triggered those memories.

"He wasn't a happy guy," I said.

"No," Elvira agreed. "He wasn't."

Wallace had been in Riscani during 9/11. For the next month, he didn't go to work, preferring to stay in his apartment. He felt the town wasn't sympathetic to his pain—especially the communist mayor—and was appalled when some community members expressed joy that America had been attacked. Elvira didn't remember how Wallace's time in Riscani came to an end. He was seen walking around town for several days before he disappeared, buying vegetables, inspecting the lake, but never returning to work at the school.

Elvira also remembered hearing that a female volunteer was sent to work with the Russians and had only lasted a month. "The Russians are not good people," said Elvira. She complimented my Russian while at the same time expressing her shock that the Russians had been given another volunteer.

"Honesty," she said. "You surprise me by lasting this long in Riscani."

"Honestly," I said.

Elvira nodded. "A teacher."

From the bus station, Elvira walked me through the center of town.

"You seem happy," she said.

"Yes."

"I'm glad to see the Russians haven't intimidated you."

We parted at the Lenin statue. "The prostitute hotel," said Elvira, pointing to the ruins across the street. "I thought it was an asylum," I said. Elvira giggled. "Perhaps some Russians call it that." She wished me a pleasant day. I never saw her again.

At home, Dima insisted that we toast my good health and lack of diseases. We drank vodka and ate pickles. In his questioning way of conversing, Dima asked where I'd been in life and then answered himself: to Ukraine, Turkey, Romania and Spain. I thought to add more countries to the list, my travels before coming to Moldova, but thought better of it. At this kitchen table, in this moment, my life before the Peace Corps didn't exist.

We toasted to travels. "Russia," said Dima. "Russia is next for you."

I expressed a hypothetical desire to visit Egypt.

"Egypt, too, would be nice," said Dima. "You've said that before, and I agree."

We munched on pickles without speaking for several minutes. Dima lost himself in thought. A minute later he snapped back to reality and poured two more shots. "I think about it sometimes like a joke," Dima explained. "Moldova should take the army back to Germany and invade. And the second we see another army, we throw up our arms. 'We surrender! Take us to your cities for work!'" Dima laughed but said he might be serious. Surrendering to Germany would be a smart move for Moldova's president.

We toasted to Germany.

A Gun Story

One day after school, Michael called to complain about the Russians. He'd awoken me from a nap to complain that the Russians held a local monopoly on important cooking supplies like peppers and mayonnaise. He'd just received a care package from home and promised me lasagna if I came over to watch a movie.

Down the street I entered a store and accepted the collected greetings of all the women who knew my name. They called me Mr. Aaron, as though they were students. The shopkeepers of Riscani knew me as a finicky buyer. I'd ask unanswerable questions about the ingredients of chicken-flavored potato chips, or which part of Ukraine a particular beer was brewed in. When I bought eggs, they gave me the best, knowing I'd reject any with visible cracks. After a year had passed, they thought they knew me well. When I presented the shopkeeper with Michael's list of needs it was the shopkeeper's turn to ask questions. What would I do with twenty eggs? Why did I want plain mayonnaise, when the essence-of-garlic mayonnaise was clearly superior? And why was I taking two extra bottles of the Ukrainian beer? Was it an American holiday?

All the grocery stores in Riscani offered vodka shots for three lei; usually the shots came with a free cookie. Before I left with my bag of groceries, a man who'd stumbled off the street insisted I drink with him.

"He's a respected teacher," said the shopkeeper. "And shouldn't be bothered."

"I know who he is," said the man. "It won't be his first drink!" He laughed.

The shopkeeper gave me a look that conveyed a warning; if I accepted his offer she'd think less of me. So, I then successfully declined my first drink in Moldova. When the man expressed his surprise and contempt the shopkeeper shouted him down.

"You see!" she said. "He's a good teacher to those kids!"

The man held his shot glass up to me in tribute and toasted alone to education.

As I crossed by the lake, the wind froze my exposed hands and my grip tightened on the grocery bag handles.

Michael's front door was unlocked when I arrived. When I knocked I could hear him yell from the bedroom for me to come inside. He hadn't emerged from his apartment in several days, not since he'd convinced the landlord to let him hook up the internet. The landlord thought plugging anything into the phone jack would start a fire. A guy from Moldtelecom, the local monopoly, finally came over and, with a simple landline hookup, turned Michael into a hermit. His boss at the farming NGO in Riscani was on extended holiday—possibly working abroad—and so now Michael's workday consisted of waking up naturally in the late morning and surfing the internet for grant opportunities. When he finished looking for grants he went for a jog or cooked lasagna or played his guitar while the computer downloaded pirated movies off Romanian servers.

I put the groceries in the kitchen. Onions and garlic quickly permeated the fibers of my clothing like cigarette smoke would in a bar. A pot simmered on the stove. I found Michael in his room under the covers with the computer on his lap. He hadn't shaved for a while and soon he'd have a full beard.

"A good week," he said, meaning he'd procured several new films. "Thanks for dealing with the Russians."

We ate chicken-flavored chips and popcorn and lasagna and drank Ukrainian beer while we watched Kevin Costner's *Robin Hood*. Then we watched episodes of *The Office*—new shows that had only come out in America the week before. It felt like I was at a friend's house back home, eating, drinking beer, relaxing. I didn't think about going to school the next day and the day after that, and almost forgot to leave. Michael told me to stay the night, even offered to help me make a fort out of the couch cushions in the next room. His heater worked perfectly and I'd be comfortable without a blanket. I thought of the cold I'd feel the next morning when I woke up for school. Soon I'd have to begin wrapping myself in my sleeping bag to stay warm at night under the covers.

My shoes were in sight across the hall. Michael saw me look to them and knew I'd decided to leave. He wished me well and I walked home in the dark. I buried my hands in my pockets and was thankful I had nothing to carry.

* * *

It was cold in the morning and once I finally got out of bed my movements were quick. I shaved in cold water. My clean face felt every bit of wind as I crossed the street quickly, only pausing to relax once I entered my classroom. The jolt of cold left me and sleepiness returned. At my desk, I sat and rubbed my eyes. In the corner of the room one of the eighth graders, Vladimir, was threatening to spray a girl with a black water pistol. They sold these types of realistic looking toy guns in the local bazaar. *The water in that gun must be cold*, I thought. I didn't feel like yelling at him. I wasn't going to intervene in a water fight; I'd only get sprayed myself. If Vladimir sprayed the girl, she and her friends would hit him over the head with closed fists and then normalcy would return once the bell rang. I assumed that's what would happen. Vladimir pointed the pistol at different girls—as though saying, "who will it be?"—and popped his lips to imitate the sound of gunfire. I put my head down for a minute of sleep before the bell rang, ignoring everyone.

A student tapped me on the shoulder. "Vlad's got a gun," said the girl.

"I see this," I said. "I hope he doesn't shoot me."

A familiar sound then echoed through the room. I recalled the noise from many police films; the cop says, "Don't make me shoot you," then cocks the gun, the metallic grating meant to intimidate before he waits a second, then shoots. That metallic cocking sound was the noise I recognized. "Damn it," I muttered. "I might have to address this."

I prepared my loud teaching voice by coughing to clear my throat.

"VLADIMIR!" I screamed.

Others in the class cringed and shuddered at the volume of my voice, but the boy knew why I'd yelled and hugged the pistol against his chest to protect it.

"Give it to me," I said.

Vladimir instead ran to the back of the room. He tried to open the window and jump out, but the windows had been painted shut long ago. "I will not give!" he said, not threatening, but pleading. He spoke English, perhaps hoping I would reward his effort. "I will not give!"

He hugged the gun instead of pointing it.

I held my hand out. He shook his head. A boy punched him in the stomach, and the others screamed at him in Russian that was too personal and too fast for me to understand. Vladimir handed me the gun backwards, for safety, as though it were a pair of scissors. My hand dropped down from the weight of the pistol. I was no expert on guns. I wanted to see if there were any bullets inside, but I struggled to remove the bottom piece. "Allow me, Mr. Aaron," said the boy who'd punched Vladimir in the stomach. He took the gun, pressed a button, coolly caught the clip in his free hand, and passed me both pieces.

"Thank God," I said. "No bullets."

"Don't forget to check the chamber," suggested one of the girls.

The boy who'd disassembled the gun checked the chamber and shook his head.

"I'm not stupid," said Vladimir. He dug into his right pocket and produced a single bullet. He pointed from the bullet in his palm to the pistol in my hands. "I'd never mix the two at school."

At this moment, I went back to the Peace Corps cultural training. Don't overact to what you perceive to be crazy. You'll lose respect if they think you don't appreciate their culture. Was this one of those moments? The students didn't appear scared. Apparently, I was the only one in the room with an elevated heart rate. Perhaps this was normal. I was in this country to teach English, not disarm the populace. I didn't know what to do next. Vladimir provided me with a succinct version of what would happen if I confiscated the gun: at home that night his father would beat him, the next day he'd come to school to learn he'd been expelled, and then at home that night his father would beat him to death. The other students agreed. The only possible result would be a series of beatings and expulsion. A friend from another class had borrowed the gun, claimed Vladimir, and was just now returning it. He'd never bring it to school again.

"Why did your friend borrow the gun?" I asked.

"To shoot stray dogs," said Vladimir. "Nothing bad."

I imagined one of the village policemen laughing at me, asking if I'd been frightened by the little boy with the gun.

The bell rang for class to begin.

Keep order, I thought.

The Peace Corps trainer's voice echoed, *Don't overreact!*

"Fine," I said. "Put the gun in your backpack."

Vladimir thanked me. The class agreed that I'd been fair. As a reward they decided to participate in the day's lesson.

I was fully awake now, and a little jumpy. We got through some new vocabulary and no one even objected to the confusing pronunciations of cough and tough. After twenty minutes the students then began to fade. I turned my back to write a sentence on the board. When I spun around, I saw a boy playing a game on his cell phone. The other students watched as I crept up on the boy with silent steps, and they cheered when I snatched it from him before he could react. "Give it!" he pleaded. I placed the cell phone on my desk and lectured him on actions and consequences. Since the first day I'd warned them of cell phone use. I'd learned the words for *crime* and *punishment* long ago, overhearing a fellow teacher as he hit a boy over the head for touching a girl's butt. I said those words now.

"For the love of God," the boy said. "Vladimir got to keep his gun!"

Everyone laughed. I felt stupid.

"Touché," I said, but none of the children knew what that meant.

After class, I entered the school director's office and asked what to do in the hypothetical event of a gun in the classroom. "It's not a very good thing, no, but nobody has bullets," he said. "So I wouldn't worry about guns." He opened his desk drawer and pulled out two tiny glasses and a bottle for us to drink. He opened a bag of chips for us to share also. We spoke about my classes and then about how much money teachers earned in America. I wasn't able to leave the office for another twenty minutes, not until we'd finished his half bottle of vodka. I was tipsy, but warm. The wind outside didn't bother me. Vladimir was waiting for me in the road between the school and my square block of apartments. "The bullet?" he asked. I took off my glove and dug into my pocket. The little piece of metal was warm from my body heat. I passed it into his small hand.

"Good teacher," he said, and took off running toward a pack of street dogs.

First Snow

All of my students, young to old, village to city-folk, shut down their brains at the first sign of snowflakes. The girls frolicked in snow banks and the boys pelted each other with icy snowballs. On my way to school, Artem, one of my village students, threw a snowball in my general direction and was immediately tackled by a scrum of town boys, which ignited a fifty-kid brawl between the Roma students and the Russians. All the fighting happened in snow, so nobody got terribly injured. Soon the tornado-like mass of fighting boys progressed down the street and out of view.

Only the girls were left to study. I shrugged my shoulders and waved my girls inside. In the classroom, the girls held their hands under their armpits until their blue fingertips disappeared. Then we wrote small essays.

That night at home in my chair, correcting those essays while I waited for supper, I knew I'd lost the kids for the winter season. Even the brightest girls who'd shined earlier in the year could now barely string together two sentences.

At dinner, I measured the amount of food on the plate against my hunger and knew I'd be going to sleep unsatisfied. The Moldovan economy was following the global trend downward and, subsequently, the food prices were heading up. Each day milk and rice cost more and more. The price of meat skyrocketed. To Katya's dismay, only the price of bread remained constant; she explained it as the final indicator of poverty, during Soviet times it was understood that the government was strong as long as the people could afford bread.

Dima never complained after he came home from work to find a small meal, hardly any protein available, so neither could I. After finishing my bread topped with salted cheese, I returned to my room to look at more student essays.

A sampling of the students' verse (reflecting on the theme of family):

- Friendship of family is very powerful sense, if it,
  yes, true, without dirty hypocrisy spots.
- Tight cherry is best type family.
- I like brother. And cat also.

Jesse and Colin weren't faring any better in their roles as second year volunteers. Instead of unresponsive children and the occasional firearm, Jesse had to contend with a new school director who didn't trust Americans. The director told Jesse to stop confiscating cell phones from students during class, as he claimed it infringed upon their sovereign rights. Mr. Jesse also shouldn't yell at them, claimed the director, because a foreigner didn't have the right to scream at a Moldovan. And Mr. Jesse should certainly buy the school a set of computers, as that type of money shouldn't be difficult for an American to come by.

Colin slipped in frozen mud on his way to school. The effects of his concussion lasted a month.

As I read my students' essays on the night of the first snowfall, my stomach grumbled. I myself was cold and hungry and couldn't imagine what the empty stomach of a growing child felt like. As a boy I'd never been without food. Not once. I'd never been this cold either.

Dima knocked on my door and entered. He saw my pile of papers and picked up the discarded essays to inspect, tracing with his finger the lines of my red pen.

"Reading Tolstoy?" he said.

"Hardly."

Dima laughed. He nodded over his shoulder, back toward the kitchen. "It's cold," he said. "Have a drink with me."

We drank vodka and followed each small shot with bites off a stale bread loaf. After a few moments the emptiness in my stomach departed. I felt a pleasant lightness in my head that grew each time I smiled. Dima and I talked about the bad economy and the price of bread. We talked about the Great Depression in America and then argued about whether there was a president between Hoover and Roosevelt. Dima claimed there certainly was, and I insisted the opposite. We turned to books and Dima retold me all he knew of Jack London. I told Dima about the boy who'd brought a pistol to class and then we talked about why Canada had no gun crime. I felt happy. I'd sleep well without thinking of my stomach. I hadn't consumed so much vodka that I couldn't work in the morning. In fact, I'd consumed the perfect amount. As had Dima, evidently; he poured two final shots and then capped the bottle and put it away under the sink. We toasted the first snow, tore at the hardened bread loaf like wolves, and then went to sleep.

* * *

Dima would have continued his daily routine through the winter indefinitely, without complaint, had his strength not finally left him. He wasn't eating enough to last through fourteen-hour work days. After school, I'd find him asleep on the couch where he'd passed out, only having intended a brief nap after lunch before returning to work. He'd awaken at the sound of my soup spoon scraping the bottom of the bowl, ask the time, and then put on his boots and return to the bakery across town.

Katya called a friend in Malinovscoe who agreed to barter bread for a pig, provided Dima and Vova came to Malinovscoe and slaughtered the animal themselves. It was a fat pig that was sure to fight back. Dima wanted to bring me for the extra set of hands, but Katya refused to let me do such brutish work; I hadn't grown up killing pigs and would only hurt myself. So I didn't know about the pig development until Dima woke me up mid-morning on a Saturday. He was panting slightly. His pant cuffs were covered in blood.

"Come help me," he said.

"You've killed something," I said.

I put on my boots and helped carry buckets of pig flesh from the bread truck up the three flights of stairs and into our apartment, making sure not to let blood touch anywhere it shouldn't. Afterward Dima and Vova stripped down to their underwear, deposited their bloody clothes in the bathtub, and collapsed onto the couch to watch TV.

"He was big," said Vova. "A hundred fifty kilos. He fought back."

Dima pumped his fist and nodded. "We'll eat well."

Katya locked herself into the kitchen for the next few hours. Soon the apartment smelled like a butcher shop, and then like a barbecue shack. My mouth began watering. Katya called me into the kitchen and handed me a fork with a small piece of meat. "Try this." It melted on my tongue. It held a bizarre aftertaste that I wasn't prepared for, slightly metallic and salty, but the reality of fresh meat warmed my body.

"Delicious," I said.

"Oh, good," said Katya. "No one else likes the liver. That will be your part of the pig this winter."

She pointed to a bucket in the corner overflowing with the gigantic purple pig liver. *That's all mine*, I thought. *I'll have meat every day.*

"I'm grateful to you," I told Katya.

She smiled. "You're a simple man."

* * *

Igor, one of my ninth grade pupils, hadn't been to class since the second snow had fallen a week earlier. With only another week before the winter recess, I hadn't expected to see him until after Christmas—possibly until spring. He came to class this day because he wanted to drink with me. It was his birthday. He was already drunk.

I looked at my watch: 10 a.m.

Igor was so drunk that he wasn't offended by my refusal to drink with him. He folded his arms on his desk and went to sleep. The other pupils looked at me and flicked their necks—the hand signal cue that someone had had too much.

"No kidding," I said, as if I hadn't been able to smell his wine-flavored body odor. "He's obviously drunk."

His lips were purple and I thought he'd stopped breathing, but upon closer inspection it was merely the stain of wine. The boy periodically licked his lips.

After class, I went to the market. On Main Street, a familiar Mercedes drove past honking and I assumed it was one of the priest's sons taking a joy ride. The car was parked outside the market when I arrived. As I entered, the priest himself greeted me. I'd never seen him without his black wardrobe, that frock-dress and the gold cross medallion. But today he wore a blue tracksuit. "Mr. Aaron!" he said. Despite a mutual recognition in the streets when he went by in a funeral procession or in his Mercedes, the priest and I had never spoken beyond his blessing at Orthodox Christmas.

The market ladies stopped working and soon everyone in the store watched our conversation.

"Again," he said. "I really like your beard." He extended his hand for me to shake. He looked at the bottle of wine I held in my hands and calmly took it from me to inspect the label. "Moldovan," he said, then placed the bottle on the counter among the other items he was purchasing.

"You are kind," I said.

He nodded

"What do you know about state Oregon?" he asked.

"Forests," I said. "And ocean."

"Is it pretty?" he asked.

"Yes," I said. "I think it is."

He blessed me, again, and handed me the bottle of Moldovan wine.

That night, I presented Dima with wine. "Blessed by the priest," I said.

I would leave the next morning for Egypt and miss his fiftieth birthday. He held the bottle close to his chest like a baby and thanked me. He insisted I go to bed early, as I'd need my strength for the trip.

"We'll drink this when you return," he said, placing the bottle under the sink.

I packed two changes of clothes into my backpack and decided that's all I would bring.

Egypt and Jordan

When I arrived in Chisinau, Jesse informed me that another volunteer named Sadie had joined our trip. Jesse knew her well, better than me at least, and promised me she'd be a fun addition. She was from New Jersey, a health volunteer somewhere in the south of Moldova, and promised not to get in the way. "Unless you go to a strip club," she said. "Then I'll get in the way."

I pulled Jesse aside.

"This isn't okay," I said.

"We were looking for a third person," said Jesse. "Weren't we? This way the rooms will be cheaper."

"I was thinking Colin," I said. "Or Will."

"Colin is still concussed and Will is AWOL. In Romania again, I think."

I wasn't mad, just annoyed. "Just so you know," I told Jesse. "I'm never sleeping outside because you and your new girlfriend want the room to yourself."

Jesse put his palms in the air, swore Sadie wasn't his girlfriend, would never be, and if he found the two of us sinking to death in quicksand, with only time to rescue one, he would certainly save me and let Sadie perish.

I was satisfied.

"But one more wrinkle..." said Jesse.

He was coming back for New Year's. I'd be on my own for three days.

"I knew that," I said.

"Sadie's going to stay with you in Egypt, if that's cool."

"Did she already buy the ticket?"

Jesse nodded.

"You owe me a beer," I said.

At McDonald's I drank and felt wonderful. Soon we'd be on a train to Romania, not my favorite place in the world, but soon after that we'd be on a plane to Egypt. In twenty-four hours we'd be in Cairo.

Jesse only wanted to see the pyramids. After that, nothing else we did mattered to him. I was excited to take the ferry across the Red Sea, find a way into Jordan and see the lost city, Petra. Sadie wanted to sleep in the desert—specifically the White Desert west of Cairo. After going over all the possible routes and itineraries we realized Sadie and I would be alone for that trip to the desert. We looked at each other awkwardly.

"Hope we still like each other by then," she said.

Jesse and I had stacked a few plastic cups before I realized that Sadie wasn't drinking.

"Let me buy you a beer," I offered, slightly drunk. "We'll toast to new friendship."

She smiled. "I don't drink."

Silence consumed the table. Sadie was kind not to interrupt while I glared Jesse down. "Well," he said, standing up and pushing in his chair. "Let's not miss that train to Romania."

* * *

The pyramid complex was abandoned on Christmas Day. No other visitors stumbled into the backgrounds of our photographs. A camel-riding police officer asked our business and offered to let us ride his steed, Mickey Mouse, for twenty bucks.

We lost each other in a crowd outside a mosque. Someone understood my look of panic and must have shouted, "Help the foreigners get back together!" Everyone on the sidewalk paused and pointed us through the maze of people until we reunited.

On our third visit to a kushari restaurant we discovered the waiter had taken the menus and doubled the prices of everything we'd ordered the previous day. Magic marker came off on our fingers when we rubbed the laminated paper. I thought I might include this moment if I ever became a travel blogger.

We climbed Mt. Sinai at dawn.

We crossed the Red Sea on a ferry.

We smoked shisha at a tea shop after a day hiking through Petra.

This wasn't a bad final adventure.

On Jesse's last day with us, we woke up in Wadi Musa, in Jordan. If Jesse was to catch his flight back to Romania, we needed to cross the Sinai Peninsula and reach Cairo by nightfall. A car-owner from the village drove us to Aqaba, where the ferry docked. We survived the stampede of passengers getting onto the boat, found a place to sit, and emerged at the Nuweiba port in Egypt in the afternoon. Every bus in sight went to Cairo; the bus we chose broke down a few hours later. While we waited, we ate chicken and salad at a truck stop within walking distance; no one spoke English and we ordered by pointing at the food on other people's plates. We got back on the fixed bus, crossed under the Suez Canal, and made it to the outskirts of Cairo by 9 p.m., an hour before Jesse's flight.

Sadie and I were alone.

She had won me over immediately by traveling light and laughing at the right times; I hadn't hoped for more. Before she had joined the trip, my plans once Jesse left had been to wander the streets of Cairo for three days. But now I, too, was excited about the desert. Camping like nomads sounded fun.

But now something was wrong with Sadie. After we said our goodbyes and put Jesse in a taxi for the airport, she swiveled her head from side to side as though looking for an escape.

"Everything okay?" I asked.

"Sure."

"You want to go find a room for the night?"

"Sure."

We found our way to the hostel where we'd spent Christmas night. Sadie locked herself in the shared bathroom for a half hour. I'd taken off my shoes, unrolled my sleeping bag over my twin bed, and was tucked in for the night when she returned.

"Um, I have to go get something," she said. It was midnight. When I moved to get out of my sleeping bag and retrieve my boots she said, "No! Don't. Stay. I'd rather go alone." All the color had drained from her face, from embarrassment rather than sickness; she still seemed strong and energetic.

"Alone?" I said.

She nodded.

"You want to go alone, into Cairo, at midnight? No. I'm going with you."

She looked like she might cry.

"Look," I said. "I know what you need. Let's go get them and not make a big thing of it."

She exhaled and the color returned to her face.

We both laughed. I think that was the moment Sadie started to like me.

I'd never been in a city less likely to sell tampons at midnight. All the stores catered to men. "We can get you a full-body black dress," I joked. "Wouldn't you like a nice full-body black dress?" She didn't think I was funny. Jesse would have laughed.

As we walked down the dark Cairo streets, Sadie and I were the shadowy characters. People crossed the road to stay away from us. Amazingly, we located an all-night pharmacy within minutes. A young boy sat behind the counter, the fluorescent lights illuminating the wispy hairs below his nose that were years away from growing into a mustache. He looked scared. Sadie pointed to a box under the glass counter that seemed to have a picture of what she wanted. The writing was in Arabic, so she couldn't be sure. She asked to see the box, pointed to it, repeated her request, and still the boy didn't move. Finally, the boy looked at me, as though asking permission to serve my companion. I nodded and he took the small cardboard box into his hands and wiped off the layer of dust with his shirtsleeve.

"All set?" I asked.

"Um, I guess so."

I paid the boy, who nodded profusely and wished me a pleasant evening, I think, in Arabic.

Sadie and I went back to the room. She took my arm as we walked.

* * *

The next morning, we woke early to begin our trek west into the Sahara. I was driving a hundred miles per hour and didn't know it because the speedometer was in kilometers and the wide landscape masked any sense of forward progress. The road turned sharply and the tires skidded over the sandy road surface. I nearly crashed the 4x4 into a sand dune before swerving back onto the road.

In the White Desert, where towers of calcium deposits that resemble mushroom cloud explosions cover the landscape, white chalk stuck to our clothes. At night, our guide Mohammed made our camp, started a fire and cooked us chicken that he'd brought along. He didn't speak much English, but didn't have to. He knew how to make a camp and cook food and position the 4x4 so that wind wouldn't extinguish his fire. We slept over the sand, under four wool blankets apiece. The temperature hovered around the freezing point. Mohammed buried himself completely under the blankets, but Sadie and I kept our heads poked out to look at the stars.

In the morning, when I went off to pee, Mohammed asked Sadie if we were married. That day we retraced the long road back to Cairo and arrived in time to experience New Year's.

It was a letdown. No one even counted.

Andrei Nikolayevich

I'd only been away from Riscani for two weeks, but it seemed like more when I returned. The apartment was once again filled to capacity: in my absence Vova and his wife had moved back in; Dariya, on break from college, was using my room; in the living room Dima and Katya sat with Andrei Nikolayevich. I'd phoned from the capital to announce my arrival and since then everyone had been waiting for me. The men stood and shook my hands, careful to avoid superstition and not shake through the threshold. When I took off my boots, desert sand fell to the floor. I apologized; Dima clapped in amusement. "He brought back the Sahara!" I kissed Katya, Talia and Dariya on the cheeks. Dariya had lost ten pounds and had kept her black hair. She looked frail. "Beautiful," I said, knowing she'd want a compliment.

"You see," said Dariya to Dima, concluding a previous argument. "I've got American style."

Vova and Talia closed themselves inside the bedroom. Dariya went to my room to collect her things. Katya went to the kitchen, telling me she'd bring food momentarily. The group had decided to greet me warmly at the door as a family, and then leave me alone in the living room with Dima and Andrei Nikolayevich and a bottle of vodka. Although everyone was glad to see me back, this plan was meant to benefit Andrei Nikolayevich; a few days previously his brother had passed away from a heart attack. He'd spent the last three days grieving and receiving the well-wishes of the entire town, one citizen at a time. The family feared Andrei Nikolayevich would soon drown in sorrow. But if he could talk with me, he could enter an outside world, if only momentarily. I was the only man in town who hadn't known the district attorney's brother. So for this reason, Andrei Nikolayevich, above all others, had awaited my return.

We drank a first, somber toast to his departed brother, and afterward Andrei Nikolayevich asked me to drop the formality and call him Andrei. He wanted to hear about Egypt, about things I might have seen that were in the Bible, about the men, their business, the women, their clothes, the landscapes and transportation and food and language. I told him about the trek eastward, away from Cairo, and Andrei interrupted to say, "Like Exodus!"

"Indeed," I continued. "Like the part where Moses goes east and climbs the mountain."

"You climbed Sinai."

I nodded.

"How formidable," said Andrei.

I shook my head. "Not really. A woman from Russia climbed alongside us. She wasn't very tired at the top. And she'd climbed the whole mountain in high-heels."

We toasted to formidable Russian women.

Using simple words, I retraced our route over land and sea to Jordan and back again to Cairo, leaving Jesse at the taxi stand and heading into the desert to camp. "Just like one of those...!" said Dima, his last word trailing off. Andrei laughed. I didn't understand what Dima had said, but I thought it might be a slight against people from Afghanistan. We then toasted the desert-sleepers Dima had slighted.

Katya brought in plates of food once she heard laughter. Until then I'd forgotten about the pig kill and my winter supply of liver. I gobbled up the meat and slouched back into the couch.

After we'd finished eating, we placed the plates in a pile by the door and toasted to my safe return. "Any surprises along the way?" asked Dima.

"Actually, yes," I admitted. "I met a girl."

Dima and Andrei giggled respectfully. Then Andrei said something quickly to Dima and they both began cackling. I wanted to laugh with them at full strength, but I hadn't understood the joke. I waited for Dima to calm down and recover his voice. "Did she have a full-body black dress?" he questioned, nearly breathless. "Or the kind where you could see her face?"

The image of Sadie wearing a black, head-to-toe dress made me laugh. When it wasn't funny anymore, I continued giggling politely, as Dima and Andrei weren't finished. They seemed to be enjoying it.

"Actually," I said finally. "She's Jewish."

Andrei and Dima quickly reached the stage of laugher where they emitted no sound, only gasps of air. They smacked their thighs with open palms. They mouthed the words to each other in soundless shouting. "She's Jew-ish! She's Jew-ish!"

For the first time in days, Andrei Nikolayevich cried because he wanted to.

Dima refilled the glasses for a final shot. All three of us coughed.

"Well done, guys," Dima said, holding Andrei in a half-hug.

"Sleep," I said. "I go."

"Go, go," said Andrei. "And listen how well you speak Russian!"

Dima and Andrei saluted me.

As I left the room Dima began talking about Germany in a quiet voice, as though he knew people nearby were trying to sleep. Andrei responded with vigor—*yes, yes, I know, exactly*—and I imagined Dima would tell Andrei about my father stationed there with the U. S. Army, about him listening to radio conversations in different languages, about that cosmic coincidence of Dima being stationed on the opposite side of Checkpoint Charlie with the Red Army. Deep into the night I listened to Dima and Andrei's muddled voices through the walls. *I know what they're talking about*, I thought. *They're talking about how things used to be when they were both in the Red Army.*

And then I fell asleep.

Work and Travel

Natashka put her pen down. I sat up in my chair, thinking she might ask me a question about the essay topic. Instead, she held her cigarette lighter to the frayed end of her pant cuff and accidentally lit her jeans on fire. The fabric was more plastic than denim, so the burning was more smoke than fire. She screamed and shook her leg in the air and finally extinguished the flames. The room now smelled like burnt hair. Strangely, I was the only one who seemed to notice. A boy said, "Nice job, Natashka," and then returned to his work. A couple of kids waved the smoke away from their faces as if someone had passed gas. I asked Natashka if she was okay. "Oh sure, Mr. Aaron," she said. "Just wanted to burn away the frays." She sat down and returned to her essay.

In the next class, a boy, sixteen years old, asked to leave the room. He wanted to smoke. I told him not to smoke, smoking was bad, but if he was going to smoke he had to do it after class. He asked every five minutes and grew angrier at each rejection. He finally stood up and came to the front of the class. We stood eye-to-eye, two feet apart. "Don't Vitaly!" pleaded a girl. The boy bit down on his cheek and then spit a gob of blood at my feet. Through bloody teeth he said calmly, "I seem to be bleeding, Mr. Aaron. May I please visit the nurse?" I finally excused him. He chose to smoke in the courtyard that was visible from my classroom. He waved to me through the windows.

"Does this school even have a nurse?" I asked.

The children shook their heads. "Not today, Mr. Aaron."

I watched Vitaly smoking in the courtyard. *He's not wearing a hat*, I thought. *Spring is almost here.*

During the last class of this day, my village pupils, I had to confiscate Artem's belt after he tried to attack a classmate.

"My pants will fall!" he pleaded.

"How many times have I told you?" I said. "Your belt isn't a weapon."

Artem sat down at his desk, crossed his arms, and pouted. "I'm not working," he said. I sized him up. He was ten years old and probably weighed sixty pounds.

I can lift him, I thought.

I walked over and pulled Artem out from under the desk. "I'm not working," he insisted. I picked him up, chair and all, and carried him outside and deposited him in the hallway. The other pupils clapped. "The classroom is for workers," I said. Artem responded predictably to this Russian insult. "I'm a worker!" he insisted. "I'm a strong worker!" I shut the door. Artem wandered the school for twenty minutes before returning. He opened the door quietly, carried in his chair and began writing the words from the blackboard onto a piece of paper. I walked over to inspect his work. "You see?" he said, showing me his writing. "I'm a strong worker."

At home, I tripped over a tiny pair of shoes near the door. Vova's wife Talia was the only one with such tiny feet. Once again, she'd stayed home from work.

Since Vova and his wife had moved back into the apartment in January, I'd spent more time with Talia than anyone else in the family. Katya was able to stay at the bazaar longer, knowing Talia could feed me and that I wouldn't starve.

Talia was a delicate, blond, twenty-three-year-old woman with pencil-thin legs and a soft voice. She always smiled when I made mistakes in Russian, but would never correct me like Katya or Dariya. Talia's father was Russian and her mother Romanian. She'd grown up in Riscani, had met Vova at one of the discotheques, had gotten married the year before I arrived, and now worked downtown in one of the shops. Recently, however, for the past several weeks, she'd been at home every day when I returned from school. Usually, she was still wrapped in wool pajamas, her eyes blood shot from vomiting. Sometimes she'd stay in bed all day, never emerging from the bedroom, and I'd have to sneak into the kitchen and heat my own food. According to *Where There is No Doctor*, Talia's symptoms indicated malaria.

I walked past Talia's shoes at the door and found her in the kitchen cooking enough lunch for thirty people. She smiled broadly as I entered. Potatoes and pork rice sizzled on the stove while Talia attacked and pitted a pile of green peppers; she'd eventually stuff them with the pork rice. On the table was my lunch: red borscht, two sugar rolls, and noodles topped with the salted cheese I liked.

"Are we expecting guests?" I asked.

Talia smiled. She knew me well enough to understand when I was joking.

"I feel good today, and just felt like cooking."

Our conversations never went very far. This one had been nice.

I began eating my soup. Talia waited for my judgment of her borscht. It was very important that I enjoy it, as though I might inform Katya that her daughter-in-law's cooking skills were substandard. "Delicious," I said. Talia exhaled deeply and then returned to her pepper operation. She indeed looked healthy. Her hips had widened slightly since January and I thought this was a good thing; she was eating normally and it appeared she might be past her sickness.

After I finished my borscht, Talia took my bowl away, cleaned it, and filled it again with borscht.

"It was lovely," I said. "But please no more."

"It's for me," she said smiling. I felt dumb. All the other bowls in the apartment were in use for Talia's cooking frenzy.

"I finally feel good," she said. "It's just so hot in here."

I nodded.

The mornings were still cold, but the afternoons were warming up. I went to school fully bundled, but when I walked home, I carried my coat.

"You're wearing two wool sweaters," I said.

Talia smiled. "I felt a chill earlier."

In my head I catalogued that symptom to later cross-check with *Where There is No Doctor*.

"Now I feel silly," said Talia. She stood and unwrapped the outer parka. Then she took the lining of the inner sweater from her waist, pulling it over her head. Her belly came into view as she struggled to get the tight collar over her head and soon she began laughing inside the sweater trap.

I stopped eating. I was, in fact, paralyzed. The white skin on her belly was stretched taught. Her shape was bulbous. As Talia shifted from side to side, trying to free herself, her stomach swung from center to profile. The sweater finally snapped off her head like an elastic band. Talia continued laughing. She tucked her white t-shirt back over her belly, into her pajama pants. Her face was bright pink from the exertion.

"There," she said, fanning her face with her palm. "Much better."

I'd never seen such a pregnant belly. *Eight months along?* I wondered. *Nine?*

I'd seen this woman every day for three months and hadn't known she was pregnant. *So not malaria,* I thought.

"Baby," I said, pointing to Katya's belly. "When?"

Talia smiled. She cupped her belly with her palms and said, "Tomorrow, I think."

* * *

Dariya returned to Riscani on the weekend. I was still sleeping when she entered the apartment.

"Wake up, please, Aaron," she said. "I need your help to go to America."

She spoke in English and whispered in case Dima, who was lurking in the bathroom, understood any cognates. She still had her black hair.

She handed me a stack of papers and I thought she might be passing me a set of quickie-marriage certificates to sign. Instead, I soon realized the documents were an application to work and study in America. She'd found a program through her college in Balti and needed me to proofread her essays. She was competing against applicants from all the former Soviet republics. If she won a place she'd study at a community college and work a minimum-wage job.

"You sure about this?" I asked. "I didn't know you wanted to visit America."

"*Work* in America," she corrected.

"Work where?" interrupted Dima, entering and sitting in the free chair. "America? I knew it!"

Dariya frowned. "Quiet, Papa."

"What? My baby wants to leave us for America?" He grabbed her cheek and pinched it. She brushed him away. "What? All will be good! Dariya will work! She'll live with Aaron and live in happiness!"

"Don't make fun of her!" yelled Katya from the kitchen.

"What? We're family. Of course Aaron will help his little sister."

Dariya punched Dima in the shoulder. "Quiet, Papa!"

"What?" he asked. "Of course he'll help you."

I leafed through the pages. Dariya's English had greatly improved during her year at the college. The first essay outlined what experiences in America she could use to help Moldova as a future leader, provided she came back. The second essay commented on her unique heritage, and what her family meant to her, and how she could never live in America forever, knowing that her home and family awaited in Moldova. The third essay concerned her definition of leadership; she used Vladimir Putin as the only example.

"Bad idea," said Dima.

"Quiet, Papa."

"I know things," said Dima. "I watch the news every night. Americans don't like Putin... he's ex-KGB... aren't I correct, Aaron?"

"Um..." I answered. "He's... strong, I guess."

"There," said Dariya. "See, Papa. And anyway, it's my essay."

I typed the essays on my laptop and put them on a flash drive Dariya could take to a printer in Balti. She'd know the results of the contest in six weeks.

"My baby's going to America," said Dima.

After thanking me, Dariya put her shoes back on. She explained to Katya that she didn't have time to eat or take tea, that the application was due back in Balti that afternoon. She kissed Dima on the cheek and left.

"Goodbye, Moldova," said Dima.

Later that night, Dima called me into the kitchen to toast Russia's new president, Medvedev. We drank the first shot of vodka and then switched to apple *garilka*.

"You will help Dariya, yes?" asked Dima. "When she wins her contest and goes to America?"

I nodded. "Of course," I said.

"Of course," Dima repeated. "She's like a sister." He poured two more shots of *garilka* and pulled a small notebook from his pocket. "Something to show you," he said, putting it within my reach on the table. I picked it up and turned it over. A passport. It took me a second to decipher the Cyrillic writing—slightly different than Russian—which said *Republic of Bulgaria*. I found a recent, unsmiling photo of Dima on the first page.

"I, too, think of travel," he said. "Don't tell anyone."

The Famous Sadie

At night I could sleep without blankets. In the mornings I didn't see my breath in the bathroom and I could walk across the street to school without a coat, only needing to cross my arms for a bit of warmth.

Nadezhda took this break in the weather as an opportunity to have me sub more classes. In fact she took consecutive weeks off, so I had double the course load for the weeks leading into the summer.

I was a month away from finishing my two years in Riscani.

The productivity of my upper level classes had been spiraling downward since a boy had brought a bottle of vodka to celebrate the Russian holiday called *Man Day*. The students grew angry when I refused a second shot of fifty-proof vodka, so they went and retrieved Andrei Vasilyavich, the *Patron*, who slugged me on the back and said, "Let's drink like men—cause that's what we are!" After this second shot the kids in this ninth form class gave me their present—a four-inch retractable hunting knife. Andrei Vasilyavich inspected the knife, poking his fingertip with the point, and declared, "This is a good gift."

My lower level students, specifically the village class, had been in a frenzy since one of the Roma girls at the school, a fifteen-year-old, had been sold into a marriage contract with a man from a neighboring town. "How old is the groom?" I asked. The students paused. "About your age," they said. They knew I was twenty-six. They explained the affair in terms of debts and dowries and contracts and such, and nobody seemed overly shocked. During our discussion of the Roma bride, one of the boys looked out the window and noticed an airplane flying overhead, northward, probably toward Moscow. He screamed, "Airplane!" and all the children rushed over to put their noses on the glass windows to inspect the jet stream.

Later, in one of the classes I subbed for Nadezhda, it came to their attention that I'd never competed in a legitimate fistfight. "How is this possible?" asked a concerned girl.

"For the most part, I was a good, quiet kid," I explained.

"Absolutely not," responded the girl. "Fighting has nothing to do with being good." She looked around to see if her peers agreed. "Fighting happens to everyone," she continued. "And you don't know all you can know about life until it's over."

At night, I ate a croissant with apple jam. It was after ten and Dima still hadn't returned home. I felt like playing cards and asking Dima what he thought about the Roma marriage and fighting. "Is Papa still working?" I asked Katya.

"He's gone for the weekend," said Katya. It was Thursday. "On a bus over to Bulgaria. Maybe looking for the right place to work." I hadn't realized that Dima was already thinking of work in Bulgaria. He'd shown me his newly obtained passport only the week before. "He said he'd be home on Sunday," said Katya. "But that probably means Monday."

* * *

That weekend, I began the trek into the capital at 4 a.m. This day, I carried my largest duffel filled with supplies I no longer needed and was returning to headquarters: my medical kit, my teaching manuals, my space heater, my water filter, and also the thick clothes I was planning to donate to the newer volunteers who still had winters ahead.

At the bus station, I had to fight with a woman for space in the back storage compartment of the minibus. "Where are you selling your things?" she asked me. "I know a man in the central bazaar."

I slept on the journey to the capital.

After depositing the supplies in the basement at headquarters, I received my end-of-service physical exam. The new doctor from Romania, Ion, said I had "weak giardia," an intestinal parasite I probably got from well-water. But he wasn't overly concerned. He asked if my stool was green, and when I shook my head, he waved his hand in the air and said, "Didn't think so." My blood work was perfect, my joints were all in working order, my sight hadn't deteriorated from malnutrition and I was still as tall as the day I'd arrived two years before. Doctor Ion finally signed off on my health. "I don't think you'll bring any problems back to the States."

Upstairs in the lounge, I didn't recognize any faces. These new volunteers belonged to the new groups that had only been in the country a few months. The newest ones were still in training. Napping volunteers occupied all the couch spaces, and those who weren't sleeping were on the computers, still sending updates home whenever they could, worried they'd miss out on life in America if they stopped writing. I couldn't remember the last time I'd emailed home. I'd spoken to my parents a few days before. Everything had sounded fine. We'd spoken nonchalantly about my coming home in a few weeks, as though I was returning to Maine from somewhere close by like New Hampshire.

One of the volunteers poked my shoulder. "We've run out of towels," she said. "I want to take a shower."

"What do you want me to do about it?" I said.

"Oh my God!" she said, cupping her hands over her mouth. "I'm so sorry. I thought you worked here!"

The girl had thought I was Moldovan because she'd heard me swear in Russian about the state of the communal sink, filled with unwashed mugs.

"Aaron!" said a familiar voice. It was Sadie. We'd seen a lot of each other during the past few weekends. She had also been called in to get her exit physical. She came close to me, brushing her chest against my arm, and whispered into my ear, "Let's get a hotel room."

"I suppose," I said, smiling. "But did you get your blood work back? I don't want to catch anything before I leave. Not so close to the end."

She punched my shoulder. "Very funny." The new volunteers were fighting over my winter clothes as we left.

* * *

Sadie stood back and didn't say anything while I talked to the Zarea receptionist in Russian.

"You want a room?" said the man. "For how many hours?"

"If possible, the entire night," I said.

The man laughed. "Your woman is skinny," he said, pointing to Sadie. "I don't think she's up for it all night." He smiled, exposing brown smoker's teeth.

"It's not like that," I said.

"Sex?" he said. "Love-making, yes?"

I hesitated.

"I apologize," he said. "Good for you. Okay, a room for all night." He brushed his palms in the air when I tried to pay. "Pay in the morning," he said. "Have a good night." We shook hands. "Don't break her in half."

Sadie and I walked to the elevator. "He seemed pleasant," she said. "Russians are generally so rude."

We shared the elevator with a young man and a prostitute. She was a slender woman with blonde hair pulled back in a ponytail. I assumed the two were together. Nobody spoke or made eye contact as the elevator moved. The young man looked at the ceiling and the prostitute looked at the ground. Our floor arrived, and when we squeezed past the couple Sadie said, "Excuse me," in Romanian, and the prostitute smiled and sneered.

The Zarea had always been empty on my previous stays. On this day, this hour, it was fully occupied. A woman stepped out of the communal bathroom and, after briefly catching my eyes, she continued back to her room with her focus down on the ground. She closed the door quickly so that I couldn't see inside. Involuntary mental pictures came from the sounds filtering through the walls: rattling bedframes shifting millimeters at a time over bare floors; thumping; moans muffled with pillows; a hand smacking skin; male voices saying yes-yes-yes, da-da-da, and giving directions, commands.

Inside our room, with the door sealed shut, we still suffered the noises. I turned on the television to a music station. The outside sounds disappeared. I kissed Sadie on the eyebrow. She turned away from me and put sheets on the bed. We lay down, and once I realized for certain we'd only be sleeping, I turned off the lights and went to sleep. Time passed. I slept. Sadie turned off the TV and the noises returned. I woke up. The absence of light focused all my hearing on the noises from the adjacent rooms.

Sadie's head had been on my shoulder for awhile and I'd lost sensation in my arm. "Come to Riscani," I said. "It won't be private, but it'll be okay." She said *okay* in a weak voice. I think she'd been crying while I'd slept.

"We'll leave first thing in the morning. Now give me back my arm—it's all pins and needles."

She said, "No, it's mine."

* * *

In the morning we rode the bus to Riscani. Vasia, the driver, forced a man to give up his seat so that the American could sit next to his female "colleague." I hadn't slept much the previous night, so I fell asleep more or less instantly. Sadie stayed awake, stimulated by the unfamiliar landscape of the road northward.

I awoke in the Balti bus station after Sadie jabbed me in the ribs. Then I got nervous: when we arrived in Riscani only Katya would be home; I felt like a teenager who'd done something wrong, inviting my girlfriend to stay the night without permission. The final stretch of road to Riscani passed quickly. I pointed out the vodka bars, the asylum and the Lenin statue, and then we were home, ringing the doorbell.

Katya answered the door, welcomed me home, and then took a step back when she saw Sadie.

"My apologies, Katya," I said. "This is my friend Sadie."

Katya giggled. "The famous Sadie?" she asked.

I nodded.

Katya waved us in, and I knew all was well when we went into the kitchen and Katya served three bowls of soup.

"I'm glad you're home," Katya told me. "I've been so lonely."

I could tell. She'd cooked enough food for ten people.

So we sat and ate. Katya wasn't in the mood to toast the new guest. She'd been cooking food all day and didn't feel like drinking, and was relieved when she learned Sadie didn't drink. Regardless of this information, thinking I'd be sad without a shot, Katya poured me a portion of cognac.

Then Katya started saying things I didn't understand. To my amazement, Sadie answered. It was a conversation in Romanian.

"Katya," I interrupted. "How well you speak Romanian."

"Only a little," she said, and then poured me another cognac so she could speak with Sadie without interruption.

I don't know what they talked about. They giggled. A few minutes later, when I'd taken another cognac and was slightly buzzed, Katya told me to wait while she changed the sheets on my bed.

"I won't let Sadie sleep with you on dirty sheets," Katya told me in Russian. "We aren't savages here."

I hugged Katya. She said she was glad Sadie had come, and hopefully Dima would return from Bulgaria the next day. Katya imagined how disappointed Dima would be if he missed meeting the famous Sadie.

* * *

Sadie accompanied me to school the next morning. I hadn't had time to plan my classes for the day, so I decided that each class would interview Sadie about life as an American woman. The eighth graders were ambivalent about her presence. A couple of the boys were hungover. The girls in the class asked what type of music she liked—if Sadie could recite Pussycat Doll lyrics—and then lost interest. The village class had long-since decided they'd finished learning for the year; they decided to ignore her, assuming conversation with another American would be more work. My beloved class of fifth grade girls, however, treated Sadie like a goddess.

What color lipstick do you wear? What size dress do you take? Do men in America drink too much? Why are there no discotheques in America, and what is the alternative? What do American girls do for fun? What do they do for fun without boys? Do American little brothers make big messes? What is your favorite color of sport-water? What do you do to make your hair curly? What is a good age to begin kissing?

Each girl screamed a different question in Russian.

"Ladies!" I screamed back. "Miss Sadie doesn't speak Russian. This is English class. Miss Sadie speaks English."

Nastia, the star pupil, then asked a direct question using perfect English.

"Why is Miss Sadie wearing your clothes, Mr. Aaron?"

Sadie blushed.

Nastia translated into Russian for the other girls. Everyone nodded, wanting to know my answer. That morning Sadie had taken a t-shirt from my bureau and also my fleece jacket.

"Yes," said another girl. "We've all seen you in town wearing these clothes."

"Friends in America share clothes," I said in Russian.

"In Moldova, only lovers," said Nastia.

The girls laughed at me. When the bell rang all the girls hugged Sadie before leaving class.

Before I walked Sadie to the bus station, we sat at the lake bar. One of the barmaids peeked outside. She didn't care we were using the bench without drinking. She knew I'd be back.

"We need to talk," said Sadie.

I cringed. We'd only been together a couple months, but it seemed a year of understanding had passed between us. Sadie was going to medical school in New Jersey. She had a plan once she left Moldova in a month; I still had nothing. Sadie wanted to know about our future; I imagined she wanted to know if I'd follow her to New Jersey.

Everything is ending so fast, I thought.

Before I could respond, a boy came charging toward us. I was glad when he interrupted the conversation that would have taken place. "Mr. Aaron!" said the boy. "I've bought you a beer!" The boy wasn't one of my students, but I knew his face. He'd always nodded to me in the corridor, too timid to speak, only now talkative because he was drunk. I thanked him, took a sip from the beer and handed it back. He was pleased. "To the bus stop," I told him in Russian. "This one needs to find her bus." I shook his hand. He extended the beer can, offering to let me finish it while I walked across town to the bus stop.

Sadie was happy to leave Riscani. We both felt uncomfortable. She'd tried to begin a conversation about our future, and I was pretending the most profound conversation of the day had been about sharing clothes. "It's something to think about," I finally said. "We'll talk during the conference next week." She let me kiss her cheek before she got on the bus.

Our Close-of-Service (COS) conference would be held the next weekend.

On the walk home, I realized I'd eventually have to explain myself. Everyone at the COS conference would ask about my plans for the future. But I had none that stretched beyond the next day: tomorrow I'd wake up, go to work, drink a shot with my lunch and try to get rest for work the next day. I then remembered the dream sensation I'd felt when I'd gone back to Maine the previous summer, the dream feeling when Moldova hadn't seemed real.

On the walk home, I bought a can of beer. As I walked past the police station I waved to a detective on the porch. He was a man I recognized from Vasia's bus. I held the can of beer up in mock-toast and nodded my head. The detective returned my gesture, toasting with his cigarette. *You can't drink on the streets in America*, I thought, sipping the beer. I walked back to the lake bar and bought another beer. As I got buzzed, I watched the lake water crash into the shore and I played with the memories of those four days from the previous summer in America.

COS

After reading *War and Peace* off and on for a year, I'd finished all but ten pages when Dima returned from his expedition to Bulgaria. It was Wednesday. He called out my name after looking at the shoes in the doorway and realizing I was the only one home. "I'm home, Aaron," he said. "In Riscani!" I replaced my bookmark in *War and Peace* and went to greet him in the kitchen.

"Here's a thing about Bulgaria," began Dima. "It's still more government than business." He tore into a stale loaf of bread and poured two shots of vodka. "Sofia is a nice city. There are mountains nearby, which I like greatly. You can see them. You'd see them every morning you walked to work. But the city itself is not good. Dirty. The streets are dirty. And the women!" He raised his glass. "You wouldn't believe, Aaron!"

"Pretty?" I asked.

"Absolutely not!"

I laughed and we toasted to Riscani and local women.

"You wouldn't believe them, Aaron. The women smoke and swear in public. Just horrible. And they do both while sipping coffee on the street corners."

Nothing Dima saw in Bulgaria convinced him that he should leave the family in Riscani to work there. The more he described his ideal workplace, the more it seemed to me that the nature of the work Dima sought mattered little; the environment where he would live was far more important. He wanted clean streets, fresh air, people to stop and chat up while he strolled across town to his job.

"There is some tragedy to this situation," said Dima. "Romania has the best jobs." He didn't explain the tragedy of the situation because he knew I disliked Romania as much as he did. He'd stopped in Black Sea towns as he passed through Romania on the return trip and decided to stay an extra day. He wandered through one of these towns until he found a group of Moldovan men doing construction work. "There's work," they explained. "Always work. But you have to take orders in Romanian." Dima waved his hands in surrender, wished the men well, and took the next bus back to Moldova.

"But the whole trip wasn't a waste," he explained. "I put in the paperwork to get passports for Vova and Dariya."

We toasted to future opportunity.

"I must sleep," said Dima. He'd only taken two shots and felt the need to explain. "I'm excited to return for work in the morning. I must rest."

Back in my room, I was slightly buzzed and I didn't understand the final pages of *War and Peace*. While trying to fall asleep, I imagined Dima working across the border in Romania, taking orders in a language he hated. I knew Dima wouldn't take those orders. He wouldn't go to Romania and he wouldn't go to Bulgaria because the women there drank coffee on the street corners.

* * *

The COS conference convened on a spring weekend at a campground that wealthy Russians used as vacation property. The Peace Corps staff had reserved us several cabins that overlooked the river separating Moldova and Ukraine. For the first time in two years, the entire group of remaining volunteers was in the same place at the same time. Our original class had dwindled from thirty-seven to twenty-two. The meetings were brief and confusing. Our boss, the

Country Director, described how we should avoid areas like shopping malls and rock concerts when we returned to America; large groups of people would probably unnerve us. He read updates from the previous volunteers who had quit or been evacuated; Callie was teaching English in Turkey and Paul was completing his first year of law school in Cincinnati. They were happy. We listened less to their advice for readjustment, and more to where these people lived. America was a big place. Jesse would live in Minnesota, Colin in Virginia, Will in North Carolina. And Sadie would be in New Jersey. I wouldn't be anywhere near those places. The medical officer asked that those of us who'd contracted ailments continue our medications when we returned home. Jesse—in direct relation to his refusal to ever seek medical treatment—was awarded recognition as the group's healthiest volunteer over the two-year period. The safety officer asked that we not celebrate our final days in country with binge drinking; our final benefit package would be delayed if we were arrested and deported from the country at the last minute.

The lecture portion of the conference now concluded, the necessary advice for readjustment into American life dispensed, the Country Director congratulated us and excused us to our exit language interviews.

* * *

The Country Director's secretary was the only one in the office who spoke Russian well enough to test Jesse and me. I waited outside as Jesse spoke with her for ten minutes. He came outside smiling and said, "Piece of cake." The secretary had given him an *advanced* mark.

Inside the cabin, I found the secretary sitting on the bed, her feet not touching the floor. She pointed to a chair in the corner and asked me to sit. She asked me to spell my name and then we began. We talked about transportation using verbs of motion, of food preparation, of my likes and dislikes and specific events in the past and future. It took five minutes to finish her checklist of language proficiency.

"So," said the secretary. "We have some time to kill. What shall we talk about?"

I shrugged my shoulders and said, "It's all the same to me."

The secretary giggled. "Your accent is good. Your body language is good, also. Very Russian, it seems to me."

I nodded, brushing aside the compliment.

"You live with Russians, I must guess. Is this true?"

I nodded.

"Tell me about them."

"Not much to tell. Very good people. They treat me well."

"Do you respect them?"

"Of course."

"What do you mean by, 'Of course?'"

We sat in silence for a moment as the secretary allowed me to compose my thoughts. My mind returned to my imagining Dima working across the border in Romania, taking orders in a language he hated. *And in Bulgaria the women drank coffee on the street corners*, I thought. *Dima would never be happy anywhere else.*

"I spend most of my time in family with the father, Dima. He's a baker and enjoys working, perhaps not the amount that he must, but the work itself."

I paused to see if the secretary understood me. She nodded encouragement and waved her hand in a rolling circle to keep me going.

"Like this there is happiness, which I respect. In Riscani, where we live, the streets are clean and pleasant; there is always someone to stop and chat with along the way on these roads. The purpose of life is open and understood, I think. Every day, life has a simple and direct purpose. Walk to work, don't hurt anyone along the way, and get back home at night for a drink and a sleep."

The secretary nodded and then dismissed me from the cabin. She scored me *advanced* as well.

* * *

We drank beer on the river's dirty-sand beach. Jesse, Colin, Will and I made plans to see each other in Washington, D.C. in a few months. It seemed a logical middle point to where we'd all be living. None of us had plans for jobs. I imagined I'd be at home with my parents in Maine until I got on my feet, or perhaps with my brother, sleeping on his couch, while I looked for a job in Portland.

To change the subject, I decided to restart an argument Jesse and I had begun the previous summer.

"My God, Jesse. I still can't believe you didn't like *Tortilla Flat*."

Colin and Will went for more beer when they realized it was a Steinbeck argument between former literary students.

"Just a bunch of drunks," said Jesse. "No sympathy, no motivation." Jesse shrugged. "*East of Eden* was okay."

Sadie walked down the beach to fetch me. "We need to talk," she said, again, this time with more immediacy.

Jesse cringed on my behalf.

As Sadie and I walked to a more secluded place on the beach, I thought of a way to explain my feelings. If only we'd had more time. Did I think our happiness would continue in America if we stayed together? Perhaps. Probably. Well, most definitely. This wasn't like the fling I'd had with Callie. This was closer to love—but without enough time to know for sure. Would I be happy living in New Jersey? Probably not, but who knew?

I was ready to tell Sadie.

Sadie abruptly stopped and said, "Listen."

I said, "Okay."

"I'm leaving Moldova early so I can get ready for med school. I'm leaving in a couple days. We're done, you and me." I didn't say anything and I think she felt guilty for sounding curt. "This was fun, but I think we have to be done," she said, trying to sound soft. "Don't you?"

I nodded. We didn't touch.

Colin and Will were back on the beach when I returned. Jesse was working on a fresh two-liter bottle of Ukrainian beer. No one said anything when I sat down. They all understood what had happened. "Everything okay?" Will finally asked. I nodded. I must have looked sad. I was sad.

"It guess it was okay," Jesse told me.

"Yeah, dude," Colin said to me. "You and Sadie had a good little run."

"No," said Jesse. "*Tortilla Flat.*"

Tradition

Back in Riscani, the in-swing of the apartment door met with the resistance of several pairs of shoes. I brushed the footwear aside with the door and realized there were ten people in the apartment. Instead of Dima, it was Andrei Nikolayevich who greeted me. "Come, Aaron," he said, motioning me into the living room. Various guests occupied every possible free space, on the stools from the kitchen, on the sofa chairs, a few on the floor. I recognized the wife of Andrei Nikolayevich sitting next to Katya. Dima was slumped over on the couch, his arm around a man I'd never met. "Aaron!" said Dima. "A celebration!" These people had been celebrating for a long time, perhaps all day. Several empty bottles were collected in a cluster in the corner of the room.

I accepted a shot glass from Andrei Nikolayevich. Everyone watched as I raised my glass. "And to what are we toasting?" I asked.

"To Danil!" answered everyone.

I nodded and chugged my shot, realizing it was double-strength *garilka* once it reached my stomach.

"Delicious!" I said. "And who is this Danil?"

"A baby boy!" said Katya. "Our new grandson!"

My mind went to Talia, pregnant no more, and then to Vova, now a father. To the delight of the room I held out my glass, in search of another shot, and again toasted Danil.

After the energy level of the room returned to normal, the group returned to the conversation topic they'd been probing before I'd interrupted: how to diminutize Danil. It was an unfamiliar name to the Russian ear and suggested no nickname.

"Danny," I said.

"It's a common name in the world, Vova assures us," said Katya. "Tell them, Aaron. It's a common name in America."

"Yes," I said. "Daniel. Nickname, Danny."

"Danilka," said Dima. "We'll have to call him Danilka."

I excused myself from the celebration. Dima would have protested my departure if he hadn't been so happily drunk. Inside my room, I found Dariya resting in my bed. She'd earlier toasted too much and was now sleeping it off. She stirred when I entered and offered to get up. "No," I said. "Keep sleeping." She replaced her head on my pillow and I left the room.

The guests weren't going to leave that night (the celebration wouldn't end until the next morning), so I decided to slip out of the apartment and walk towards Michael's side of town. As soon as I touched my shoes, Katya appeared from the living room, asking where I planned to go.

"Not a bad idea to stay at Michael's," she said, flicking the side of her neck with the drunk signal and pointing toward the living room. "First let me make you some food."

I said *no thank you* and hugged her.

"Vova's a father now," I said.

"Go," she said. "Before I start crying."

Michael's lights were off when I walked up to his apartment block. I made my way through the dark interior corridor and, thankfully, heard movement inside the apartment when I rang the buzzer. He'd been watching a movie on his computer and said he would be happy to restart the film once we went to the store for beer. His refrigerator was empty. At the nearby market, Michael greeted the clerk behind the counter in Romanian, a man he clearly knew well, perhaps who he saw every day. The man refused to sell us beer. Instead he pulled a bottle of cognac out from under the counter and we drank shots. He told us to take a bag of chips off the shelf as a chaser. We thanked him, and he thanked us in return and asked us to stay for another minute to drink another shot with his friends, who were to arrive shortly. His friends didn't believe he knew an American, and he wished to introduce them to Michael. The store clerk grew more excited when he learned I was the American who'd been living in the Russian district for the past two years. He shook my hand. "I've heard some interesting things," he told me.

The clerk's friends arrived and soon we were taking bottles off the liquor shelf. The clerk shooed away a patron who cursed him for not giving her service. The clerk locked the market's front door. We went to the back room with a bottle of vodka and chocolate bars. At one point, Michael ran back to his apartment to get his guitar. While he was gone we all spoke in Russian about jobs in America and salaries and such, and how I'd be finished with my service in ten days. We toasted to my return to America.

When Michael returned, the conversation resumed in Romanian and we sang songs in that language. Next, we piled into a Lada—the clerk, his two friends, Michael and me—and then we were at the clerk's home in the Romanian quarter where his wife served us pizza with mayonnaise instead of tomato sauce. We drank and ate and sang. After, we all got back into the Lada and the clerk used the road like a ski course, swerving from side to side, observing the grass on either side in the darkness as imaginary bumpers, until he thought Michael and I were in walking distance of home. We shook the hands of the clerk and his friends.

"You're both normal," said the clerk. "So pleasantly normal."

I could barely walk. Inside the apartment, I took the cushions off Michael's two sofa chairs, threw them on the ground, and passed out on top. Michael finished watching his movie.

* * *

Most students had stopped attending school for the year. Only the little ones remained in classes. Finally, after weeks of begging, I took my fifth grade class of girls on a picnic to the lake.

"Take them," said their homeroom teacher. "Maybe they'll listen better outside."

I led the group of ten girls down the hill from the school. When I entered the store to buy supplies, the women behind the counter greeted me warmly and asked how many bottles of beer I'd like.

"Only apple juice today," I said. The clerk then realized the group of girls who'd followed me inside were students, not curious admirers, and they began quizzing the girls on the English translations of the items in the store. The girls became very girl-like and youthful as they shouted: "Apple juice! Cookies! Onions! Eggs!" One girl pointed to the cooler and said, "Beer!" The women laughed and gave each girl a biscuit. I bought a carton of juice and a large bag of chips.

We settled into a spot in the sun next to the lake. The girls spread out the blankets they'd brought with them to school, and we drank apple juice and ate potato chips and spoke like adults.

"Sadie is very pretty," said a girl. The others agreed. "You should get married."

"I won't get married," I said. "I'm too young."

The girls scoffed.

"We've talked about this," I said. "America is different. I'm young in America."

"I'll live in America, too," said another girl. "In California."

"I'll take Great Britain," said another.

The girls took turns claiming the English-speaking world. I suggested Australia and New Zealand to the final two girls who'd felt they'd lost out in the lottery. The girls then asked me to list all the countries I'd ever visited.

The next few minutes turned into a scavenger hunt for wild mushrooms.

"Stop touching those!" I screamed. "Poison!"

"Don't be naïve, Mr. Aaron," they said. "Just a few dozen more."

The girls quickly collected their weight in giant, orange, slimy mushrooms. They promised not to eat any bits until knowledgeable grandmothers inspected them.

We followed a path through the woods back into town. I led. In the marshy portion just before the bar, I spotted a shifty-looking older gentleman and stopped the group. He was fishing with a style of pole and net I'd never seen, clearly hadn't bathed in days and appeared to be homeless. "We should walk around," I suggested. Then one of the girls let out a small, happy shriek and jumped into the man's outstretched arms. I cringed. *So dirty*, I thought. "Grandfather!" said the girl. "We've found mushrooms!" His attention was on me, not the mushrooms. His granddaughter introduced me as the English teacher. He smiled and came over to shake my hand, his suspicions relieved.

"An English teacher," the old man repeated. "I used to speak German back when I lived in Kazakhstan."

I shook the man's hand a final time and he wished us well as we walked toward the center of town. The girls, thinking I'd get lost, had agreed amongst themselves to walk me to the Lenin statue before they went on their separate ways.

Dima was walking across the street as we approached the statue. He was returning to the apartment for lunch, I suspected, and we'd caught him at just the right moment. My students again acted like little girls as he asked them to say things in English. They wanted to know who he was; they objected to my explanation.

"He's Papa," I said.

"Not true," said one of the girls. "Your papa lives in America."

They seemed satisfied when I explained Dima was my Moldovan father.

The girls hugged me one by one and then scurried off to their separate corners of Riscani.

* * *

Instead of going back to the apartment, Dima led me in a different direction. Vova and Talia were now living in their own place, and it was there we would see the new parents and little Danilka.

Not far from where we lived, we came up to a different Russian apartment block and went inside. Vova had taken residence with his new family on the second floor. There was a small kitchen, a bathroom, and a living room that turned into a bedroom at night when you folded the couch down. It was folded down now. I came into this living room and greeted all of the people circling the bed. Vova, Dariya and Katya. Dima quickly introduced me to Talia's parents, who were also there. Talia was on the bed, lying sideways next to a naked, doughy, baby boy. Little Danilka.

I congratulated everyone in the room. Vova shook my hand and then he and I drank a shot of vodka. At that moment he seemed tired and, in my estimation, more of a man.

We all stayed in the tiny apartment for the rest of the afternoon, watching as Talia attended to every belch and squeal of little Danilka.

At night, back in our apartment, Katya heated borscht and then left to go sleep. Dariya put the cushions from the sofa onto the floor and fell asleep in front of the television in the living room.

Dima and I were alone in the kitchen. He pulled the bottle of vodka out from under the sink.

"Let me just say thank you," he said. "It's been a pleasure having you in our home. Thank you." He filled the glasses. We drank. "Tomorrow I must leave to visit my parents in Gagauzia. My father is ill and I must attend his affairs."

He poured another shot.

"So this is it," he said. "I'll be gone for two weeks. I'll be gone when you leave. This is it."

I nodded so that he knew I understood.

Everything so fast.

We drank our final shot together. Dima stood and extended his hand for the strongest handshake I will ever endure. He hugged me. He put his hand on my shoulder as we walked out of the kitchen and then he disappeared into the living room, closing the door behind him. In my room I cried. I believe Dima did as well.

* * *

No students attended my classes on the final day of school. I reported for work in the morning, and then Nadezhda came into my classroom during the first period and said I was free to leave. She made no mention of this being my last day at the school, only that she would see me at the last bell celebration on the other side of the weekend. I informed her I would be leaving Riscani just after the last bell ceremony.

"I think you have not always been happy here," she said. "But you stayed, so perhaps I didn't understand everything."

I left the school and walked downhill, toward shouting I heard coming from the stadium. A semi-professional soccer match was underway, with teams from Balti and Izvornas competing. I'd never heard of the town called Izvornas. I stayed until the goalie for the Balti team hit his head on one of the goal posts. He was on the ground for a while and for a time I thought he was dead. Two of his teammates dragged his limp body to the bench and soon he was able to sit up on his own without support.

At home, Katya had red borscht waiting for me. Without Dima in the house, there was too much soup left over. Katya and Dariya and I sat at the table trying to finish it. For the first time in my presence, Katya went under the sink to retrieve a bottle for herself. She poured glasses of red wine.

"To Aaron," she said. "For his safe trip home."

"You're not leaving until Monday!" said Dariya. I nodded. It was Friday. "Good," she said, clutching her chest. "I was worried. I can't take so many departures."

We drank the wine in sips.

Dariya asked her mother if there was any word yet of Dima reaching Germany. Katya shook her head.

"Excuse me," I interrupted. "Germany?"

Katya nodded. "For work," she explained.

"What about Gagauzia?" I said. "His parents."

"Oh, yes," explained Katya. "He had to say goodbye to them, too." Katya turned to Dariya to finish her thought. "Papa will call as soon as he gets settled and with a cell phone. He doesn't know the town yet, won't know until he arrives, but he didn't seem worried. He says construction work is everywhere. And he only left a few days ago. The bus takes a long time. A week, I think."

My thoughts turned to Dima riding a bus from the south of Moldova all the way to Germany, clutching his European Union passport from Bulgaria the entire way. I didn't know why he hadn't told me of his plans; I couldn't understand a reason except shame. This seemed strange because I felt no pity for Dima. Germany was better than Romania; Dima had liked Germany, once upon a time, and now Germany offered a chance at enjoying life while he worked.

"Departures," lamented Katya. "Vova with a new family. Dima on his way to Germany. Dariya at college. And Aaron, little Aaron, going away until God-knows-when."

Dariya told a Russian joke about a lonely old woman.

Katya smiled. "Don't joke," she said, swatting at Dariya. "It's not a joke if it's real."

* * *

A child playing with a bell across the street woke me. I drank the cold tea Katya had left for me on the table alongside a bowl of noodles with salted cheese sprinkled on top.

Several hundred people gathered in the courtyard of the school for the graduation ceremony. It was also my last day in town. In the back I found a shady area under a tree. The students were arranged in classes, from first up through the graduating seniors. Several students caught my eye and waved. Others left their groups to give me flowers.

One of the boys I'd dismissed from class on the day of the fire approached me holding a plastic bottle filled with red wine. "From my parents," he said. I shifted all the flowers, a dozen or so, into my left arm so that I could shake his hand. I thanked him three times, but he didn't go away.

"You must drink some of the wine," he said.

I promised I would.

"In front of me," he said. "Tradition."

I pretended not to know Russian.

He scrunched his face and muttered, "Russian tradition," in a soft voice, unsure of the pronunciation in English.

I unscrewed the cap and tasted the wine in a big gulp. Saliva pooled under my tongue, but I'd tasted worse liquor on school property, and I was able to stomach another sip to prove I could handle the boy's house wine.

He was happy. It was the first time I'd seen him smile, and I thought he might confess to setting the trash fire. He stood there waiting for me to say something else, and I thought he would definitely confess. But then I realized he was waiting for me to dismiss him as though I were a commanding officer. I waved my hand and the boy took off running down the hill.

I stood alone under the tree.

Before the boy reached the bottom of the hill, I began walking also. I was thankful other students didn't notice my departure. If I hurried, I could catch the bus to the capital. I walked past the Lenin statue for the final time. In the alley leading to the bus depot I took a shot of vodka for strength and wished health and happiness to all the people I loved in Riscani. At the depot I took my place next to the bus driver, Vasia, a man I'd known the entire two years. We shook hands. He asked why I'd bought so many flowers. The bus engine didn't turn over, not at first, and I sensed delay. Perhaps Vasia would have to call the mechanic, who would come with a large hammer, or perhaps I'd be told to go home, go back to rest, until the evening bus departed. Katya wouldn't be surprised to see me. Things broke—it happens—and there would be red soup while I waited. I smiled. Then the bus engine turned over on the third try. Vasia said something that made the others laugh, but I hadn't heard it. The bus rolled away and I left Riscani by motorized conveyance, on a one-way trajectory, with no immediate plans to return.

Acknowledgments

I'm forever indebted to my parents, Richard and Mary, for their love and support. My brother, Justin, has always been an inspiration; he, too, served in the Peace Corps (Guinea, 1998-2000).

To the citizens of Riscani, and to the members of Group M18—I thank you. Abigail, Alexis, Aliona, Anastasia, Andrea, Andrei, Andy, Angela, Anna, Ben, Bridgette, Brigitte, Charles, Chris, Crystal, Dan, Drew, Elena, Elizabeth, Emily, Geoff, Heidi, Jacob, Jessica, Kellee, Kelly, Liz, Lynne, Mary, Matt, Natalia, Natasha, Nina, Patrick, Peter, Rebecca, Rene, Renell, Ryan, Sarah, Sophia, Tanya, Tatiana, Tima, Trifon, Vladimir, and Vladislav—you forever have my respect and love.

Excerpts from this book first appeared in the following journals: *1966: A Journal of Creative Nonfiction*, *Drunk Monkeys*, *Eunoia Review*, *Gravel Magazine*, *Hippocampus Magazine*, *Luna Luna Magazine*, *Pure Slush*, and *Vol. 1 Brooklyn*.

I'm grateful to those editors who sacrifice time and sanity to support writers—especially Matt Potter.

And to Sarah and Ophelia—I love you both.

About the Author

A. A. Weiss continues to work as a modern language teacher after having lived in Ecuador, Mexico and Moldova. His essays and short stories have appeared in several literary journals, and he was a recipient of the BRIO Award in Nonfiction from the Bronx Council on the Arts. He lives outside Washington, D.C. with his wife and daughter.

Also from EVERYTIME PRESS and TRUTH SERUM PRESS

https://www.everytimepress.com/everytime-press-catalogue

- *All Roads Lead from Massilia* by Philip Kobylarz
  978-1-925536-27-0 (paperback) 978-1-925536-28-7 (eBook)
- *It's About the Dog* by Guilie Castillo Oriard
  978-1-925536-19-5 (paperback) 978-1-925536-20-1 (eBook)
- *The In-Betweens* by Davon Loeb
  978-1-925536-56-0 (paperback) 978-1-925536-57-7 (eBook)

- *all you need is … a whiteboard, a marker and this book*
  by Matt Potter
  978-1-925536-27-0 (Book 1) 78-1-925536-28-7 (Book 2)
- *Kiss Kiss* by Paul Beckman
  978-1-925536-21-8 (paperback) 978-1-925536-22-5 (eBook)

www.ingramcontent.com/pod-product-compliance
Lightning Source LLC
Chambersburg PA
CBHW031136160426
43193CB00008B/156